GLENCOE

Grammar &
Composition
HANDBOOK

Mc Graw Hill **Education**

Bothell, WA • Chicago, IL • Columbus, OH • New York, NY

Education

Send all inquiries to:
McGraw-Hill Education
8787 Orion Place
Columbus, OH 43240

ISBN: 978-0-07-662448-5
MHID: 0-07-662448-X

Printed in the United States of America.

2 3 4 5 6 7 8 9 QTN 15 14 13 12

The McGraw-Hill Companies

Table of Contents at a Glance

Table of Contents

Chapter 14 Sentence Combining

Chapter 15 Spelling and Vocabulary

Part One

Ready Reference

The **Ready Reference** consists of three parts. The **Glossary of Terms** is a list of language arts terms with definitions and examples. Page references show you where to find more information about the terms elsewhere in the book. The **Usage Glossary** lists words that are easily confused or often used incorrectly and explains how to use the words correctly. The third part is **Abbreviations**, which consists of lists of many commonly used abbreviations.

By day and night
I sing this song:
"All right's all right,
Alright's all wrong."

— Willard R. Espy,
Say It My Way

continued

continued

continued

continued

Regardless
[not irregardless]

neither . . . nor   either . . . or

correlative conjunction

both . . . and

not only . . . but also

this

demonstrative adjective

that

these

Tues.

RSVP

abbreviations

AVE   CST

B.C.

abbreviation An abbreviation is a shortened form of a word or phrase. Many abbreviations are followed by periods (pages 276–278).

EXAMPLES Mrs., Tues., Dec., NBA, ft., St., RI

abstract noun An abstract noun names an idea, a quality, or a feeling that can't be seen or touched (page 82).

EXAMPLE Her **bravery** and **courage** filled us with **admiration.**

action verb An action verb is a verb that expresses action. An action verb may consist of more than one word (pages 97–98).

EXAMPLES The director **shouts** at the members of the cast.

The lights **are flashing** above the stage.

The play **has begun.**

active voice A verb is in the active voice when the subject performs the action of the verb (pages 111–112).

EXAMPLE Thornton Wilder **composed** that play.

adjective An adjective is a word that describes, or modifies, a noun or a pronoun (pages 144–152, 164–165).

HOW ADJECTIVES MODIFY NOUNS

WHAT KIND?	We studied **ancient** history.
HOW MANY?	I read **four** chapters.
WHICH ONE?	**That** invention changed history.

adjective clause An adjective clause is a subordinate clause that modifies, or describes, a noun or a pronoun in the main clause of a complex sentence (pages 195, 197).

EXAMPLE The Aqua-Lung, **which divers strap on,** holds oxygen.

adjective phrase An adjective phrase is a prepositional phrase or a participial phrase that modifies, or describes, a noun or a pronoun (pages 178, 206–207).

EXAMPLES The servers **at the new restaurant** are courteous.
[prepositional phrase modifying *servers*]

The musician **seated at the piano** is Erik. [participial phrase modifying *musician*]

adverb An adverb is a word that modifies a verb, an adjective, or another adverb (pages 158–167, 179–180).

	WHAT ADVERBS MODIFY
VERBS	People *handle* old violins **carefully.**
ADJECTIVES	**Very** *old* violins are valuable.
ADVERBS	Orchestras **almost** *always* include violins.

WAYS ADVERBS MODIFY VERBS	
ADVERBS TELL	EXAMPLES
HOW	grandly, easily, completely, neatly, gratefully, sadly
WHEN	soon, now, immediately, often, never, usually, early
WHERE	here, there, everywhere, inside, downstairs, above

adverb clause An adverb clause is a subordinate clause that often modifies the verb in the main clause of a complex sentence. It tells *how, when, where, why,* or *under what conditions* the action occurs (pages 198–199).

EXAMPLE **After we won the meet,** we shook hands with our opponents.

An adverb clause can also modify an adjective or an adverb.

EXAMPLES Carson is younger **than I am.** [The adverb clause *than I am* modifies the adjective *younger.*]

Sherry walks faster **than her brother runs.** [The adverb clause *than her brother runs* modifies the adverb *faster.*]

adverb phrase An adverb phrase is a prepositional phrase that modifies a verb, an adjective, or another adverb (page 178).

ADVERB PHRASES

MODIFIES A VERB — The servers *dress* like movie characters.

MODIFIES AN ADJECTIVE — The restaurant is *popular* with young people.

MODIFIES AN ADVERB — The restaurant opens *early* in the morning.

agreement Agreement is the match between grammatical forms. A verb must agree with its subject. A pronoun must agree with its antecedent (pages 73, 132–133, 181, 216–224).

EXAMPLES Both **ducks** and **swans swim** in this lake. [subject-verb agreement]

Jerry and his **brother** visited **their** grandparents. [pronoun-antecedent agreement]

antecedent An antecedent is the word a pronoun refers to. The word *antecedent* means "going before" (pages 128–130).

EXAMPLE **Max** likes to read books. **He** particularly likes novels. [*He* refers to *Max*. *Max* is the antecedent of *He*.]

apostrophe An apostrophe (') is a punctuation mark used in possessive nouns, possessive indefinite pronouns, and contractions. In contractions an apostrophe shows that one or more letters have been left out (pages 273–274).

EXAMPLES Shefali's friends don't always understand her.

Cameron's asking for everyone's help.

appositive An appositive is a noun that is placed next to another noun to identify it or add information about it (pages 89–90).

EXAMPLE James Madison's wife, **Dolley,** was a famous first lady.

appositive phrase An appositive phrase is a group of words that includes an appositive and other words that modify the appositive (pages 89–90).

EXAMPLE   Madison, **our fourth president,** held many other offices.

article The words *a, an,* and *the* make up a special group of adjectives called articles. *A* and *an* are called **indefinite articles** because they refer to one of a general group of people, places, things, or ideas. *A* is used before words beginning with a consonant sound. *An* is used before words beginning with a vowel sound (page 147).

EXAMPLES **a** union   **a** picture   **an** hour   **an** easel

The is called the **definite article** because it identifies specific people, places, things, or ideas (page 147).

auxiliary verb *See helping verb.*

B

base form A base form is the simplest form of a word. *Small* is a base form; other forms of *small* are *smaller* and *smallest. Be* is a base form; other forms of *be* are *am, is, are, was, were, being,* and *been* (pages 104, 113–116, 149–151, 163).

C

clause A clause is a group of words that has a subject and a verb (pages 192–201). *See also adjective clause, adverb clause, main clause, noun clause, and subordinate clause.*

closing A closing is a way to end a letter. It begins with a capital letter and is followed by a comma (page 249).

EXAMPLES
Yours truly,   Sincerely,   With love,   Your friend,

collective noun A collective noun names a group of people, animals, or things. It may be singular or plural, depending on the meaning of the sentence (pages 85, 220–221).

EXAMPLES The **team** shares the field with its opponent.

The **team** share their jokes with one another.

colon A colon (:) is a punctuation mark. It's used to introduce a list and to separate the hour and the minutes when you write the time of day. It's also used after the salutation of a business letter (page 269).

EXAMPLES Please buy these fruits: apples, bananas, grapes, peaches.

It's now exactly 2:43 P.M.

Dear Editor:

comma A comma (,) is a punctuation mark that's used to separate items or to set them off from the rest of a sentence (pages 262–267).

EXAMPLES Shoes, socks, hats, and gloves lay in the bottom of the closet.

Tessa's great-grandmother, who is ninety, loves to travel.

common noun A common noun names any person, place, thing, or idea. Common nouns can be either concrete or abstract (pages 81–82).

EXAMPLE **Children** learn **handwriting** in **school.**

comparative form The comparative form of an adjective compares one person or thing with another. The comparative form of an adverb compares one action with another (pages 149–152, 162–163).

EXAMPLES Is Venezuela **larger** than Peru? **[adjective]**

The pianist arrived **earlier** than the violinist. **[adverb]**

complete predicate *See predicate.*

complete subject *See subject.*

complex sentence A complex sentence has one main clause and one or more subordinate clauses (pages 193–194).

EXAMPLE   Since Mariah moved to Springfield, she has made many new friends. [*She has made many new friends* **is a main clause.** *Since Mariah moved to Springfield* **is a subordinate clause.**]

compound-complex sentence A compound-complex sentence has two or more main clauses and one or more subordinate clauses (page 194).

EXAMPLE   Ahmal has never scored a goal, but he plays soccer because he loves the game. [**The two main clauses are** *Ahmal has never scored a goal* **and** *he plays soccer. Because he loves the game* **is a subordinate clause.**]

compound noun A compound noun is a noun made of two or more words (pages 82, 85).

EXAMPLES   storybook, showcase, bookmark

ice cream, dining room, high school

sister-in-law, seventh-grader, push-ups

compound predicate A compound predicate consists of two or more simple predicates, or verbs, that have the same subject. The verbs may be connected by *and, or, but, both . . . and, either . . . or,* or *neither . . . nor* (page 73).

EXAMPLE   Many students **read** the novel *Jane Eyre* and **enjoy** it.

compound sentence A compound sentence is a sentence that contains two or more main clauses joined by a comma and a coordinating conjunction or by a semicolon (pages 75, 181, 183–184, 192).

EXAMPLES **Eudora Welty is a novelist,** but **she also writes essays.**
[A comma and the coordinating conjunction *but* join the two main clauses, *Eudora Welty is a novelist* and *she also writes essays.*]

Eudora Welty is a novelist; she also writes essays.

compound subject A compound subject consists of two or more simple subjects that have the same predicate. The subjects may be joined by *and, or, both . . . and, either . . . or,* or *neither . . . nor* (pages 73, 181, 223–224).

EXAMPLE **Charlotte Brontë** and **Emily Brontë** were sisters.

compound verb *See compound predicate.*

concrete noun A concrete noun names something you can see or touch (page 82).

EXAMPLE **Julio** wore a **cap** on his **head** and a **scarf** around his **neck.**

conjunction A conjunction is a connecting word. *See coordinating conjunction, correlative conjunction, and subordinating conjunction.*

conjunctive adverb A conjunctive adverb may be used to join the simple sentences in a compound sentence (pages 183–184).

EXAMPLE The school cafeteria sometimes serves Chinese food; **however,** these meals are not very tasty.

contraction A contraction is a word formed from one or more words by omitting one or more letters and substituting an apostrophe (pages 87–88, 166, 274).

EXAMPLES We **can't** find the map. [*Can't* is a contraction of *cannot.*]

Carmella's visited every state. [*Carmella's* is a contraction of *Carmella has.*]

coordinating conjunction A coordinating conjunction is a word used to connect compound parts of a sentence. *And, but, or, nor,* and *for* are coordinating conjunctions. *So* and *yet* are also sometimes used as coordinating conjunctions (pages 181, 223–224).

EXAMPLE   Juan **or** Lisa collects the money **and** distributes the tickets.

correlative conjunction Correlative conjunctions are pairs of words used to connect compound parts of a sentence. Correlative conjunctions include *both . . . and, either . . . or, neither . . . nor,* and *not only . . . but also* (pages 181, 223–224).

EXAMPLE   Examples of great architecture exist in **both** New York **and** Paris.

dash A dash (—) is a punctuation mark. It's usually used in pairs to set off a sudden break or change in thought or speech (page 275).

EXAMPLE   Billy Adams—he lives next door—is our team manager.

declarative sentence A declarative sentence makes a statement. It ends with a period (pages 66, 261).

EXAMPLE   Edgar Allan Poe wrote suspenseful short stories.

demonstrative adjective A demonstrative adjective points out something and modifies a noun by answering the question *which one?* or *which ones? This, that, these,* and *those* are demonstrative adjectives when they modify nouns (page 147).

EXAMPLES   Take **this** umbrella with you.   **That** answer is wrong.
  Take **these** boots too.   **Those** clouds are lovely.

demonstrative pronoun A demonstrative pronoun is a pronoun that points out something. *This, that, these,* and *those* are demonstrative pronouns when they take the place of nouns (pages 136, 148).

EXAMPLES   Take **this** with you.   **That** is the wrong answer.

Take **these** too.   **Those** are lovely clouds.

dependent clause *See subordinate clause.*

direct address Direct address is a name used in speaking directly to a person. Direct address may also be a word or a phrase used in place of a name. Words used in direct address are set off by commas (page 263).

EXAMPLES   **Suzy,** please hand me a dish towel.

Here, **my dear mother,** is your birthday present.

Don't do that again, **Samson.**

direct object A direct object receives the action of a verb. It answers the question *whom?* or *what?* after an action verb (pages 98–100).

EXAMPLE   The actor rehearsed his **lines** from the play.

direct quotation A direct quotation gives a speaker's exact words (pages 248, 270).

EXAMPLE   **"Spiders,"** explained Raul, **"have eight legs."**

double negative A double negative is the use of two negative words to express the same idea. Only one negative word is necessary (pages 166–167).

EXAMPLES

INCORRECT   I **don't** have **no** homework.

CORRECT   I **don't** have **any** homework.

CORRECT   I have **no** homework.

end mark An end mark is a punctuation mark used at the end of a sentence. Periods, question marks, and exclamation points are end marks (pages 66–67, 261).

EXAMPLES Tell me a story.

Where have you been?

What a hot day this has been!

essential clause An essential clause is a clause that is necessary to make the meaning of a sentence clear. Don't use commas to set off essential clauses (page 197).

EXAMPLE The girl **who is standing beside the coach** is our best swimmer.

essential phrase An essential phrase is a phrase that is necessary to make the meaning of a sentence clear. Don't use commas to set off essential phrases (page 207).

EXAMPLE The boy **seated at the piano** is Erik.

exclamation point An exclamation point (!) is a punctuation mark used to end a sentence that shows strong feeling (exclamatory). It's also used after strong interjections (pages 67, 261).

EXAMPLES My! What a hot day it is!

exclamatory sentence An exclamatory sentence expresses strong feeling. It ends with an exclamation point (pages 67, 261).

EXAMPLES What a great writer Poe was!

How I enjoy his stories!

future perfect tense The future perfect tense of a verb expresses action that will be completed before another future event begins (page 110).

EXAMPLE   The production **will have closed** by next week.

future tense The future tense of a verb expresses action that will take place in the future (page 110).

EXAMPLE   Mr. and Mrs. Pao **will attend** the performance.

G

gender The gender of a noun may be masculine (male), feminine (female), or neuter (referring to things) (page 130).

EXAMPLES   boy (male), woman (female), desk (neuter)

gerund A gerund is a verb form that ends in -*ing* and is used as a noun (pages 208–209).

EXAMPLE   **Exercising** builds strength, endurance, and flexibility.

gerund phrase A gerund phrase is a group of words that includes a gerund and other words that complete its meaning (pages 208–209).

EXAMPLE   **Exercising on a bike** is fun for all ages.

helping verb A helping verb is a verb that helps the main verb express action or make a statement (pages 104–106, 217).

EXAMPLES   Telma **is acting** in another play today. [*Is* is the helping verb; *acting* is the main verb.]

Emilio **has written** a story. [*Has* is the helping verb; *written* is the main verb.]

hyphen A hyphen (-) is a punctuation mark that's used in some compound words (page 275).

EXAMPLE   Mrs. Gilmore's **mother-in-law** is **sixty-two** years old.

imperative sentence An imperative sentence gives a command or makes a request. It ends with a period (pages 66, 72, 261).

EXAMPLE   Read "The Pit and the Pendulum."

indefinite pronoun An indefinite pronoun is a pronoun that does not refer to a particular person, place, or thing (pages 132–133, 222, 274).

SOME INDEFINITE PRONOUNS

SINGULAR			PLURAL
another	everybody	no one	both
anybody	everyone	nothing	few
anyone	everything	one	many
anything	much	somebody	others
each	neither	someone	several
either	nobody	something	

SINGULAR OR PLURAL   all, any, most, none, some

indirect object An indirect object answers the question *to whom?* or *for whom?* or *to what?* or *for what?* an action is done (page 100).

EXAMPLE   Friends sent the **actors** flowers.

indirect quotation An indirect quotation does not give a speaker's exact words (page 248).

EXAMPLE   Raul said **that spiders have eight legs.**

infinitive An infinitive is formed with the word *to* and the base form of a verb. Infinitives are often used as nouns in sentences (pages 210–211).

EXAMPLE **To write** is Alice's ambition.

infinitive phrase An infinitive phrase is a group of words that includes an infinitive and other words that complete its meaning (pages 210–211).

EXAMPLE **To write a great novel** was Alice's ambition.

intensive pronoun An intensive pronoun ends with *-self* or *-selves* and is used to draw special attention to a noun or a pronoun already named (page 134).

EXAMPLE Yolanda **herself** repaired the engine.

interjection An interjection is a word or group of words that expresses emotion. It has no grammatical connection to other words in a sentence (pages 185–186, 261).

EXAMPLE **Good grief!** My favorite restaurant has closed.

interrogative pronoun An interrogative pronoun is a pronoun used to introduce an interrogative sentence. *Who, whom, which, what,* and *whose* are interrogative pronouns (pages 135–136).

EXAMPLE **Who** borrowed the book?

interrogative sentence An interrogative sentence asks a question. It ends with a question mark (pages 66, 71–72, 219, 261).

EXAMPLE Did Poe also write poetry?

intransitive verb An intransitive verb is a verb that does not have a direct object (pages 98–99).

EXAMPLE The audience **applauds** loudly.

inverted sentence An inverted sentence is a sentence in which the subject follows the verb (pages 72, 218–219).

EXAMPLES There **are** many **immigrants** among my ancestors.

Across the ocean **sailed** the three **ships.**

irregular verb An irregular verb is a verb whose past tense and past participle are formed in a way other than by adding -*d* or -*ed* to the base form (pages 113–116).

SOME IRREGULAR VERBS

BASE	PAST	PAST PARTICIPLE
go	went	gone
write	wrote	written
begin	began	begun

italics Italics are printed letters that slant to the right. *This sentence is printed in italic type.* Italics are used for the titles of certain kinds of published works and works of art. In handwriting, underlining is a substitute for italics (page 272).

EXAMPLE On the desk were a copy of *Robinson Crusoe* and several issues of *Time* magazine.

linking verb A linking verb connects the subject of a sentence with a noun or an adjective in the predicate (pages 101–102).

EXAMPLE Juana Ortiz **was** the director.

main clause A main clause has a subject and a predicate and can stand alone as a sentence (pages 192–194).

EXAMPLE After the storm passed, **the governor surveyed the damage.**

main verb A main verb is the last word in a verb phrase. If a verb stands alone, it's a main verb (pages 104–106, 217).

EXAMPLES The professor is **studying** ancient history.

The professor **studies** ancient history.

negative word A negative word expresses the idea of "no" or "not" (pages 166–167).

SOME COMMON NEGATIVE WORDS

barely	no	no one	nowhere
hardly	nobody	not	scarcely
never	none	nothing	

nonessential clause A nonessential clause is a clause that is not necessary to make the meaning of a sentence clear. Use commas to set off nonessential clauses (pages 197, 265).

EXAMPLE Janice, **who is standing beside the coach,** is our best swimmer.

nonessential phrase A nonessential phrase is a phrase that is not necessary to make the meaning of a sentence clear. Use commas to set off nonessential phrases (pages 207, 263, 264).

EXAMPLE Erik, **dreaming of fame,** sits at the piano.

nonrestrictive clause *See nonessential clause.*

nonrestrictive phrase *See nonessential phrase.*

noun A noun is a word that names a person, a place, a thing, or an idea (pages 81–90).

NOUNS

PERSONS	sister, mayor, player, coach, pianist, children
PLACES	park, zoo, lake, school, playground, desert, city
THINGS	magazine, boots, rose, pencil, peach, baseball, car
IDEAS	honesty, truth, democracy, pride, maturity, progress

noun clause A noun clause is a subordinate clause used as a noun (pages 200–201).

EXAMPLE **Whoever plays hockey** wears protective equipment.

number Number is the form of a word that shows whether it's singular or plural (page 130).

EXAMPLES **This book is a mystery.** [singular words]

These books are mysteries. [plural words]

O

object An object is a noun or a pronoun that follows a verb or a preposition. *See direct object, indirect object, and object of a preposition.*

EXAMPLE **Mario gave the horse a carrot for a treat.** [*Horse* is an indirect object; *carrot* is a direct object; *treat* is the object of a preposition.]

object of a preposition The object of a preposition is the noun or pronoun that ends a prepositional phrase (pages 175, 176–177).

EXAMPLE **Hang the painting outside the auditorium.**

object pronoun *Me, us, you, him, her, it, them,* and *whom* are object pronouns. Object pronouns are used as direct objects, indirect objects, and objects of prepositions (pages 125–127, 176–177).

EXAMPLE **Sally gave her and me a picture of them.**

parentheses Parentheses ( ) are punctuation marks used to set off words that define or explain another word (page 276).

EXAMPLE **This container holds one gallon (3.785 liters).**

participial phrase A participial phrase is a group of words that includes a participle and other words that complete its meaning (pages 206–207, 263).

EXAMPLE **Sitting at the piano,** Erik loses himself in the music.

participle A participle is a verb form that can act as the main verb in a verb phrase or as an adjective to modify a noun or a pronoun (pages 206–207, 263). *See also past participle and present participle.*

EXAMPLES Erik has **played** several pieces on the piano. [main verb]

His **playing** skill improves daily. [adjective]

passive voice A verb is in the passive voice when the subject receives the action of the verb (pages 111–112).

EXAMPLE That play **was composed** by Thornton Wilder.

past participle A past participle is usually formed by adding -*d* or -*ed* to the base form of a verb. Some past participles are formed irregularly. When the past participle acts as a verb, one or more helping verbs are always used before the past participle. A past participle may also be used as an adjective (pages 104–105, 113–116, 145, 206–207).

EXAMPLES Kimi has **baked** cookies for us. [*Baked* is the past participle of *bake.*]

Mrs. Gonzales had **planted** tomatoes in the spring. [*Planted* is the past participle of *plant.*]

Two students have **written** a play. [*Written* is the past participle of *write.*]

Erik practices on a **rented** piano. [*Rented* is an adjective modifying *piano.*]

past perfect tense The past perfect tense of a verb expresses action that happened before another action or event in the past (page 109).

EXAMPLES The actors **had rehearsed** for many weeks.

We **had** just **arrived** when the play started.

past progressive The past progressive form of a verb expresses action or a condition that was continuing at some time in the past (page 107).

EXAMPLE We **were watching** a scary show.

past tense The past tense of a verb expresses action that already happened (pages 103, 113–116).

EXAMPLE The actors **rehearsed.**

perfect tenses The perfect tenses are the present perfect tense, the past perfect tense, and the future perfect tense. The perfect tenses consist of a form of the verb *have* and a past participle (pages 108–110).

EXAMPLES Lynn **has played** the trumpet for three years. **[present perfect]**

His father **had played** the trumpet as a boy. **[past perfect]**

By the end of high school, Lynn **will have played** the trumpet for seven years. **[future perfect]**

period A period (.) is a punctuation mark used to end a sentence that makes a statement (declarative) or gives a command (imperative). It's also used at the end of many abbreviations (pages 66, 261, 276–278).

EXAMPLES The day was hot and humid. **[declarative]**

Bring me some lemonade. **[imperative]**

personal pronoun A personal pronoun is a pronoun that refers to people or things. *I, me, you, he, she, him, her, it, we, us, they,* and *them* are personal pronouns (pages 125–126).

EXAMPLE **I** saw **you** with **her** and **him.**

phrase A phrase is a group of words that is used as a single part of speech and does not contain a verb and its subject. *See adjective phrase, adverb phrase, appositive phrase, gerund phrase, infinitive phrase, participial phrase, prepositional phrase, and verb phrase.*

EXAMPLE Three students **wearing backpacks were hiking through the woods.** [*Wearing backpacks* **is a participial phrase acting as an adjective to modify the noun** *students.* *Were hiking* **is a verb phrase.** *Through the woods* **is a prepositional phrase acting as an adverb to modify the verb** *were hiking.*]

plural noun A plural noun is a noun that means more than one of something (pages 83–88).

EXAMPLE The **students** and their **parents** heard the **candidates** give their **speeches.**

possessive noun A possessive noun is a noun that shows ownership (pages 86–88, 273).

EXAMPLE **Tiffany's** friend distributed the **children's** toys.

possessive pronoun A possessive pronoun is a pronoun that shows ownership. *My, mine, our, ours, your, yours, his, her, hers, its, their, theirs,* and *whose* are possessive pronouns (pages 131, 274).

predicate The predicate part of a sentence tells what the subject does or has. It can also tell what the subject is or is like. The **complete predicate** includes all the words in the predicate of a sentence. The **simple predicate** is the main word or word group in the complete predicate. The simple predicate is always a verb (pages 68–73).

EXAMPLE Emily Dickinson **wrote hundreds of poems.** [The complete predicate is *wrote hundreds of poems.* The simple predicate is *wrote.*]

predicate adjective A predicate adjective is an adjective that follows a linking verb and modifies the subject of the sentence (pages 101–102, 145).

EXAMPLE   Ms. Ortiz is **stern** but **fair.**

predicate noun A predicate noun is a noun that follows a linking verb and renames or identifies the subject of the sentence (pages 101–102).

EXAMPLE   Ms. Ortiz is the **director.**

preposition A preposition is a word that relates a noun or a pronoun to another word in a sentence (pages 174–180).

EXAMPLE   A boy **with** red hair stood **near** the window.

prepositional phrase A prepositional phrase is a group of words that begins with a preposition and ends with a noun or a pronoun, which is called the **object of the preposition** (pages 174–180, 218–219, 263).

EXAMPLE   Hang the painting **outside the new auditorium.**

present participle A present participle is formed by adding *-ing* to the base form of a verb. A helping verb is always used with the present participle when it acts as a verb. A present participle may also be used as an adjective (pages 104–105, 145, 206–207).

EXAMPLES   Mr. Omara is **teaching** algebra this year. [*Teaching* **is the present participle of** *teach.*]

The students were **making** decorations. [*Making* **is the present participle of** *make.*]

Erik's **playing** skill improves daily. [*Playing* **is an adjective modifying** *skill.*]

present perfect tense The present perfect tense of a verb expresses action that happened at an indefinite time in the past (page 108).

EXAMPLE   The actors **have rehearsed** for many hours.

present progressive The present progressive form of a verb expresses action or a condition that is continuing in the present (pages 106–107, 110).

EXAMPLE Althea **is finishing** her song.

present tense The present tense of a verb expresses action that happens regularly. It can also express a general truth (pages 103, 110).

EXAMPLE A great actor **wins** awards.

principal parts of a verb The principal parts of a verb are the base form, the present participle, the past, and the past participle. The principal parts are used to form verb tenses (pages 104, 113–116).

BASE	PRESENT PARTICIPLE	PAST	PAST PARTICIPLE
play	playing	played	played
go	going	went	gone

progressive forms Progressive forms of verbs express continuing action. They consist of a form of the verb *be* and a present participle (pages 106–107). *See also past progressive and present progressive.*

EXAMPLES Carla **is leaving**, but Mr. and Mrs. Tsai **are staying**.

Ahmed **was studying**, but his brothers **were playing** basketball.

pronoun A pronoun is a word that takes the place of one or more nouns (pages 125–136).

EXAMPLE Max likes books. **He** particularly enjoys novels. [The pronoun *He* takes the place of the noun *Max*.]

proper adjective A proper adjective is an adjective formed from a proper noun. It begins with a capital letter (pages 145–146, 254).

EXAMPLE The **Florida** sun beat down on the **Japanese** tourists.

proper noun A proper noun names a particular person, place, thing, or idea. The first word and all other important words in a proper noun are capitalized (pages 81–82, 250–254).

EXAMPLE Did **Edgar Allan Poe** ever see the **Statue of Liberty**?

Q

question mark A question mark (?) is a punctuation mark used to end a sentence that asks a question (interrogative) (pages 66, 261).

EXAMPLE Do you like green eggs and ham**?**

quotation marks Quotation marks (" ") are punctuation marks used to enclose the exact words of a speaker. They're also used for certain titles (pages 270–271).

EXAMPLES "A spider," said Sean, "has eight legs."
Have you read the story "To Build a Fire"?

R

reflexive pronoun A reflexive pronoun ends with -*self* or -*selves* and refers to the subject of a sentence. In a sentence with a reflexive pronoun, the action of the verb returns to the subject (page 134).

EXAMPLE Yolanda bought **herself** a book on engine repair.

regular verb A regular verb is a verb whose past tense and past participle are formed by adding -*d* or -*ed* (page 103).

EXAMPLES I **believed** her.
The twins **have learned** a lesson.

relative pronoun A relative pronoun is a pronoun that may be used to introduce an adjective clause (page 195).

EXAMPLE Divers prefer equipment **that** is lightweight.

restrictive clause *See essential clause.*

restrictive phrase *See essential phrase.*

run-on sentence A run-on sentence is two or more sentences incorrectly written as one sentence (page 75).

EXAMPLES Welty wrote novels, she wrote essays. [run-on]

Welty wrote novels she wrote essays. [run-on]

Welty wrote novels. She wrote essays. [correct]

Welty wrote novels, and she wrote essays. [correct]

Welty wrote novels; she wrote essays. [correct]

S

salutation A salutation is the greeting in a letter. The first word and any proper nouns in a salutation should be capitalized (pages 249, 267).

EXAMPLES My dear aunt Julia,   Dear Professor Higgins:

semicolon A semicolon (;) is a punctuation mark used to join the main clauses of a compound sentence (pages 268–269).

EXAMPLE Kendra weeded the garden; Geronimo mowed the lawn.

sentence A sentence is a group of words that expresses a complete thought (pages 66–68).

EXAMPLE Edgar Allan Poe wrote many short stories.

sentence fragment A sentence fragment does not express a complete thought. It may also be missing a subject, a predicate, or both (page 68).

EXAMPLES The poems. [fragment]

Lay in Dickinson's bureau for years. [fragment]

The poems lay in Dickinson's bureau for years. [sentence]

simple predicate *See predicate.*

simple sentence A simple sentence has one subject and one predicate (pages 74, 192).

EXAMPLE Eudora Welty lived in Jackson, Mississippi.

simple subject *See subject.*

singular noun A singular noun is a noun that means only one of something (pages 83–86).

EXAMPLE   The **child** and his **father** saw a **rabbit** in the **garden.**

subject The subject part of a sentence names whom or what the sentence is about. The **complete subject** includes all the words in the subject of a sentence. The **simple subject** is the main word or word group in the complete subject (pages 68–73, 216–224).

EXAMPLE   **A large ship with many sails** appeared on the horizon. [The complete subject is *A large ship with many sails.* The simple subject is *ship.*]

subject pronoun *I, we, you, he, she, it, they,* and *who* are subject pronouns. Subject pronouns are used as subjects and predicate pronouns (pages 125–127).

EXAMPLE   **He** and **I** know **who you** are.

subordinate clause A subordinate clause is a group of words that has a subject and a predicate but does not express a complete thought and cannot stand alone as a sentence. A subordinate clause is always combined with a main clause in a sentence (pages 193–201).

EXAMPLE   Mariah, **who moved here from Montana,** is very popular.

subordinating conjunction A subordinating conjunction is a word that is used to introduce a subordinate clause (page 199).

SUBORDINATING CONJUNCTIONS

after	because	though	whenever
although	before	till	where
as	if	unless	whereas
as if	since	until	wherever
as though	than	when	while

superlative form The superlative form of an adjective compares one person or thing with several others. The superlative form of an adverb compares one action with several others (pages 149–152, 162–163).

EXAMPLES Is Brazil the **richest** country in South America? **[adjective]**

The drummer arrived **earliest** of all the players. **[adverb]**

tense Tense shows the time of the action of a verb (pages 103–110).

EXAMPLES The team often **wins** games. **[present tense]**

The team **won** the game. **[past tense]**

The team **will win** this game. **[future tense]**

transitive verb A transitive verb is an action verb that transfers action to a direct object (pages 98–99).

EXAMPLE The audience **applauds** the actors.

verb A verb is a word that expresses action or a state of being (pages 97–116, 216–224).

EXAMPLES Juanita **plays** soccer.

Kwami **is** a good student.

verbal A verbal is a verb form used as a noun, an adjective, or an adverb. Participles, gerunds, and infinitives are verbals (pages 206–211).

EXAMPLES The **swimming** instructor showed us **diving** techniques. **[participles used as adjectives]**

Mr. McCoy teaches **swimming** and **diving**. **[gerunds used as nouns]**

Mr. McCoy taught us **to swim** and **to dive**. **[infinitives used as nouns]**

verb phrase A verb phrase consists of one or more helping verbs followed by a main verb (page 105).

EXAMPLE Telma **is acting** in another play today. **[*Is* is the helping verb; *acting* is the main verb.]**

voice *See active voice and passive voice.*

USAGE GLOSSARY

This glossary will guide you in choosing between words that are often confused. It will also tell you about certain words and expressions you should avoid when you speak or write for school or business.

a, an Use *a* before words that begin with a consonant sound. Use *an* before words that begin with a vowel sound.

EXAMPLES **a** poem, **a** house, **a** yacht, **a** union, **a** one-track mind

an apple, **an** icicle, **an** honor, **an** umbrella, **an** only child

accept, except *Accept* is a verb that means "to receive" or "to agree to." *Except* is a preposition that means "but." *Except* may also be a verb that means "to leave out or exclude."

EXAMPLES Please **accept** this gift.

Will you **accept** our decision?

Everyone will be there **except** you. **[preposition]**

Some students may be **excepted** from taking physical education. **[verb]**

advice, advise *Advice,* a noun, means "an opinion offered as a guide." *Advise,* a verb, means "to give advice."

EXAMPLE Why should I **advise** you when you never accept my **advice**?

affect, effect *Affect* is a verb that means "to cause a change in" or "to influence the emotions of." *Effect* may be a noun or a verb. As a noun, it means "result." As a verb, it means "to bring about or accomplish."

EXAMPLES The mayor's policies have **affected** every city agency.

The mayor's policies have had a positive **effect** on every city agency. **[noun]**

The mayor has **effected** positive changes in every city agency. [verb]

ain't *Ain't* is unacceptable in speaking and writing unless you're quoting someone's exact words or writing dialogue. Use *I'm not; you, we,* or *they aren't; he, she,* or *it isn't.*

all ready, already *All ready* means "completely ready." *Already* means "before" or "by this time."

EXAMPLE The band was **all ready** to play its last number, but the fans were **already** leaving the stadium.

all right, alright The spelling *alright* is not acceptable in formal writing. Use *all right.*

EXAMPLE Don't worry; everything will be **all right.**

all together, altogether Use *all together* to mean "in a group." Use *altogether* to mean "completely" or "in all."

EXAMPLES Let's cheer **all together.**

You are being **altogether** silly.

I have three dollars in quarters and two dollars in dimes; that's five dollars **altogether.**

almost, most Don't use *most* in place of *almost.*

EXAMPLE Marty **almost** [*not* most] always makes the honor roll.

a lot, alot *A lot* should always be written as two words. It means "a large number or amount." Avoid using *a lot* in formal writing; be specific.

EXAMPLES **A lot** of snow fell last night.

Ten inches of snow fell last night.

altar, alter An *altar* is a raised structure at which religious ceremonies are performed. *Alter* means "to change."

EXAMPLES   The bride and groom approached the **altar.**

Mom **altered** my old coat to fit my little sister.

among, between   Use *among* to show a relationship in which more than two persons or things are considered as a group.

EXAMPLES   The committee will distribute the used clothing **among** the poor families in the community.

There was confusion **among** the players on the field.

In general, use *between* to show a relationship involving two persons or things, to compare one person or thing with an entire group, or to compare more than two items within a single group.

EXAMPLES   Mr. and Mrs. Ohara live halfway **between** Seattle and Portland. **[relationship involving two places]**

What was the difference **between** Elvis Presley and other singers of the twentieth century? **[one person compared with a group]**

Emilio could not decide **between** the collie, the cocker spaniel, and the beagle. **[items within a group]**

anxious, eager   *Anxious* means "fearful." It is not a synonym for *eager*, which means "filled with enthusiasm."

EXAMPLES   Jean was **anxious** about her test results.

Kirk was **eager** [*not* anxious] to visit his cousin.

anyways, anywheres, everywheres, nowheres, somewheres Write these words without the final *s: anyway, anywhere, everywhere, nowhere, somewhere.*

a while, awhile   Use *a while* after a preposition. Use *awhile* as an adverb.

EXAMPLES   She read for **a while.**

She read **awhile.**

Usage Glossary   **31**

bad, badly *Bad* is an adjective; use it before nouns and after linking verbs to modify the subject. *Badly* is an adverb; use it to modify action verbs.

EXAMPLES   Clara felt **bad** about the broken vase.

The team performed **badly** in the first half.

bare, bear *Bare* means "naked." A *bear* is an animal.

EXAMPLES   Don't expose your **bare** skin to the sun.

There are many **bears** in Yellowstone National Park.

base, bass One meaning of *base* is "a part on which something rests or stands." *Bass* pronounced to rhyme with *face* is a type of voice. When *bass* is pronounced to rhyme with *glass*, it's a kind of fish.

EXAMPLES   Who is playing first **base**?

We need a **bass** singer for the part.

We caught several **bass** on our fishing trip.

beside, besides *Beside* means "at the side of" or "next to." *Besides* means "in addition to."

EXAMPLES   Katrina sat **beside** her brother at the table.

Besides apples and bananas, the lunchroom serves dry cereal and doughnuts.

blew, blue *Blue* is the color of a clear sky. *Blew* is the past tense of *blow*.

EXAMPLES   She wore a **blue** shirt.

The dead leaves **blew** along the driveway.

boar, bore A *boar* is a male pig. *Bore* means "to tire out with dullness"; it can also mean "a dull person."

Wild **boars** are common in parts of Africa.

Please don't **bore** me with your silly jokes.

bow When *bow* is pronounced to rhyme with *low*, it means "a knot with two loops" or "an instrument for shooting arrows." When *bow* rhymes with *how*, it means "to bend at the waist."

EXAMPLES Can you tie a good **bow**?

Have you ever shot an arrow with a **bow**?

Actors **bow** at the end of a play.

brake, break As a noun, a *brake* is a device for stopping something or slowing it down. As a verb, *brake* means "to stop or slow down"; its principal parts are *brake, braking, braked,* and *braked.* The noun *break* has several meanings: "the result of breaking," "a fortunate chance," "a short rest." The verb *break* also has many meanings. A few are "to smash or shatter," "to destroy or disrupt," "to force a way through or into," "to surpass or excel." Its principal parts are *break, breaking, broke,* and *broken.*

EXAMPLES Rachel, please put a **brake** on your enthusiasm. **[noun]**

He couldn't **brake** the car in time to avoid the accident. **[verb]**

To fix the **break** in the drainpipe will cost a great deal of money. **[noun]**

Don't **break** my concentration while I'm studying. **[verb]**

bring, take *Bring* means "to carry from a distant place to a closer one." *Take* means "to carry from a nearby place to a more distant one."

EXAMPLES Will you **bring** me some perfume when you return from Paris?

Remember to **take** your passport when you go to Europe.

bust, busted Don't use these words in place of *break, broke, broken,* or *burst.*

EXAMPLES Don't **break** [*not* bust] that vase!

Who **broke** [*not* busted] this vase?

Someone has **broken** [*not* busted] this vase.

The balloon **burst** [*not* busted] with a loud pop.

The child **burst** [*not* busted] into tears.

buy, by *Buy* is a verb. *By* is a preposition.

EXAMPLES I'll **buy** the gift tomorrow.

Stand **by** me.

can, may *Can* indicates ability. *May* expresses permission or possibility.

EXAMPLES I **can** tie six kinds of knots.

"You **may** be excused," said Dad. [permission]

Luanna **may** play in the band next year. [possibility]

capital, capitol A *capital* is a city that is the seat of a government. *Capitol,* on the other hand, refers only to a building in which a legislature meets.

EXAMPLES What is the **capital** of Vermont?

The **capitol** has a gold dome.

cent, scent, sent A *cent* is a penny. A *scent* is an odor. *Sent* is the past tense and past participle of *send.*

EXAMPLES I haven't got one **cent** in my pocket.

The **scent** of a skunk is unpleasant.

I **sent** my grandma a birthday card.

choose, chose *Choose* is the base form; *chose* is the past tense. The principal parts are *choose, choosing, chose,* and *chosen.*

EXAMPLES Please **choose** a poem to recite in class.

Brian **chose** to recite a poem by Emily Dickinson.

cite, sight, site *Cite* means "to quote an authority." *Sight* is the act of seeing or the ability to see; it can also mean "to see" and "something seen." A *site* is a location; it also means "to place or locate."

EXAMPLES Consuela **cited** three sources of information in her report.

My **sight** is perfect.

The board of education has chosen a **site** for the new high school.

clothes, cloths *Clothes* are what you wear. *Cloths* are pieces of fabric.

EXAMPLES Please hang all your **clothes** in your closet.

Use these **cloths** to wash the car.

coarse, course *Coarse* means "rough." *Course* can mean "a school subject," "a path or way," "order or development," or "part of a meal." *Course* is also used in the phrase *of course*.

EXAMPLES To begin, I'll need some **coarse** sandpaper.

I'd like to take a photography **course.**

The hikers chose a difficult **course** through the mountains.

complement, complementary; compliment, complimentary As a noun, *complement* means "something that completes"; as a verb, it means "to complete." As a noun, *compliment* means "a flattering remark"; as a verb, it means "to praise." *Complementary* and *complimentary* are the adjective forms of the words.

EXAMPLES This flowered scarf will be the perfect **complement** for your outfit. **[noun]**

This flowered scarf **complements** your outfit perfectly. **[verb]**

Phyllis received many **compliments** on her speech. **[noun]**

Many people **complimented** Phyllis on her speech. **[verb]**

consul; council, councilor; counsel, counselor A *consul* is a government official living in a foreign city to protect his or her country's interests and citizens. A *council* is a group of people gathered for the purpose of giving advice. A *councilor* is one who serves on a council. As a noun, *counsel* means "advice." As a verb, *counsel* means "to give advice." A *counselor* is one who gives counsel.

EXAMPLES The **consul** protested to the foreign government about the treatment of her fellow citizens.

The city **council** met to discuss the lack of parking facilities at the sports field.

The defendant received **counsel** from his attorney. **[noun]**

The attorney **counseled** his client to plead innocent. **[verb]**

could of, might of, must of, should of, would of After the words *could, might, must, should,* and *would,* use the helping verb *have* or its contraction, *'ve,* not the word *of.*

EXAMPLES **Could** you **have** prevented the accident?

You **might have** swerved to avoid the other car.

You **must have** seen it coming.

I **should've** warned you.

dear, deer *Dear* is a word of affection and is used to begin a letter. It can also mean "expensive." A *deer* is an animal.

EXAMPLES Talia is my **dear** friend.

We saw a **deer** at the edge of the woods.

desert, dessert *Desert* has two meanings. As a noun, it means "dry, arid land" and is stressed on the first syllable. As a verb, it means "to leave" or "to abandon" and is stressed on the second syllable. A *dessert* is something sweet eaten after a meal.

EXAMPLES This photograph shows a sandstorm in the **desert.** [noun]

I won't **desert** you in your time of need. [verb]

Strawberry shortcake was served for **dessert.**

diner, dinner A *diner* is someone who dines or a place to eat. A *dinner* is a meal.

EXAMPLES The **diners** at the corner **diner** enjoy the friendly atmosphere.

Dinner will be served at eight.

doe, dough A *doe* is a female deer. *Dough* is a mixture of flour and a liquid.

EXAMPLES A **doe** and a stag were visible among the trees.

Knead the **dough** for three minutes.

doesn't, don't *Doesn't* is a contraction of *does not.* It is used with *he, she, it,* and all singular nouns. *Don't* is a contraction of *do not.* It is used with *I, you, we, they,* and all plural nouns.

EXAMPLES She **doesn't** know the answer to your question.

The twins **don't** like broccoli.

eye, I An *eye* is what you see with; it's also a small opening in a needle. *I* is a personal pronoun.

EXAMPLE **I** have something in my **eye.**

fewer, less Use *fewer* with nouns that can be counted. Use *less* with nouns that can't be counted.

EXAMPLES There are **fewer** students in my English class than in my math class.

I used **less** sugar than the recipe recommended.

flour, flower *Flour* is used to bake bread. A *flower* grows in a garden.

EXAMPLES Sift two cups of **flour** into a bowl.

A daisy is a **flower.**

for, four *For* is a preposition. *Four* is a number.

EXAMPLES Wait **for** me.

I have **four** grandparents.

formally, formerly *Formally* is the adverb form of *formal,* which has several meanings: "according to custom, rule, or etiquette," "requiring special ceremony or fancy clothing," "official." *Formerly* means "previously."

EXAMPLES The class officers will be **formally** installed on Thursday.

Mrs. Johnson was **formerly** Miss Malone.

G

go, say Don't use forms of *go* in place of forms of *say*.

EXAMPLES I tell her the answer, and she **says** [*not* goes], "I don't believe you."

I told her the news, and she **said** [*not* went], "Are you serious?"

good, well *Good* is an adjective; use it before nouns and after linking verbs to modify the subject. *Well* is an adverb; use it to modify action verbs. *Well* may also be an adjective meaning "in good health."

EXAMPLES You look **good** in that costume.

Joby plays the piano **well.**

You're looking **well** in spite of your cold.

grate, great A *grate* is a framework of bars set over an opening. *Grate* also means "to shred by rubbing against a rough surface." *Great* means "wonderful" or "large."

EXAMPLES The little girl dropped her lollipop through the **grate.**

Will you **grate** this cheese for me?

You did a **great** job!

H

had of Don't use *of* between *had* and a past participle.

EXAMPLE I wish I **had known** [*not* had of known] about this sooner.

had ought, hadn't ought, shouldn't ought *Ought* never needs a helping verb. Use *ought* by itself.

EXAMPLES You **ought** to win the match easily.

You **ought** not to blame yourself. *or* You **shouldn't** blame yourself.

hardly, scarcely *Hardly* and *scarcely* have negative meanings. They shouldn't be used with other negative words, like *not* or the contraction *n't,* to express the same idea.

EXAMPLES I **can** [*not* can't] **hardly** lift this box.

The driver **could** [*not* couldn't] **scarcely** see through the thick fog.

he, she, it, they Don't use a pronoun subject immediately after a noun subject, as in *The **girls they** baked the cookies.* Omit the unnecessary pronoun: *The **girls** baked the cookies.*

hear, here *Hear* is a verb meaning "to be aware of sound by means of the ear." *Here* is an adverb meaning "in or at this place."

EXAMPLES I can **hear** you perfectly well.

Please put your books **here.**

how come In formal speech and writing, use *why* instead of *how come.*

EXAMPLE **Why** weren't you at the meeting? [*not* **How come you weren't at the meeting?**]

in, into, in to Use *in* to mean "inside" or "within." Use *into* to show movement from the outside to a point within. Don't write *into* when you mean *in to.*

EXAMPLES Jeanine was sitting outdoors **in** a lawn chair.

When it got too hot, she went **into** the house.

She went **in to** get out of the heat.

its, it's *Its* is the possessive form of *it*. *It's* is a contraction of *it is* or *it has.*

EXAMPLES The dishwasher has finished **its** cycle.

It's [It is] raining again.

It's [It has] been a pleasure to meet you, Ms. Donatello.

kind of, sort of Don't use these expressions as adverbs. Use *somewhat* or *rather* instead.

EXAMPLE We were **rather** sorry to see him go. [*not* We were kind of sorry to see him go.]

knead, need *Knead* means "to mix or work into a uniform mass." As a noun, a *need* is a requirement. As a verb, *need* means "to require."

EXAMPLES **Knead** the clay to make it soft.

I **need** a new jacket.

knew, new *Knew* is the past tense of *know. New* means "unused" or "unfamiliar."

EXAMPLES I **knew** the answer.

I need a **new** pencil.

There's a **new** student in our class.

knight, night A *knight* was a warrior of the Middle Ages. *Night* is the time of day during which it is dark.

EXAMPLES A handsome **knight** rescued the fair maiden.

Night fell, and the moon rose.

lay, lie *Lay* means "to put" or "to place." Its principal parts are *lay, laying, laid,* and *laid.* Forms of *lay* are usually followed by a direct object. *Lie* means "to recline" or "to be positioned." Its principal parts are *lie, lying, lay,* and *lain.* Forms of *lie* are never followed by a direct object.

EXAMPLES **Lay** your coat on the bed.

The children are **laying** their beach towels in the sun to dry.

Dad **laid** the baby in her crib.

Myrna had **laid** the book beside her purse.

Lie down for a few minutes.

The lake **lies** to the north.

The dog is **lying** on the back porch.

This morning I **lay** in bed listening to the birds.

You have **lain** on the couch for an hour.

lead, led As a noun, *lead* has two pronunciations and several meanings. When it's pronounced to rhyme with *head,* it means "a metallic element." When it's pronounced to rhyme with *bead,* it can mean "position of being in first place in a race or contest," "example," "clue," "leash," or "the main role in a play."

EXAMPLES **Lead** is no longer allowed as an ingredient in paint.

Jason took the **lead** as the runners entered the stadium.

Follow my **lead.**

The detective had no **leads** in the case.

Only dogs on **leads** are permitted in the park.

Who will win the **lead** in the play?

As a verb, *lead* means "to show the way," "to guide or conduct," "to be first." Its principal parts are *lead, leading, led,* and *led.*

EXAMPLES Ms. Bachman **leads** the orchestra.

The trainer was **leading** the horse around the track.

An usher **led** us to our seats.

Gray has **led** the league in hitting for two years.

learn, teach *Learn* means "to receive knowledge." *Teach* means "to give knowledge."

EXAMPLES Manny **learned** to play the piano at the age of six.

Ms. Guerrero **teaches** American history.

leave, let *Leave* means "to go away." *Let* means "to allow to."

EXAMPLES I'll miss you when you **leave.**

Let me help you with those heavy bags.

like, as, as if, as though *Like* can be a verb or a preposition. It should not be used as a subordinating conjunction. Use *as, as if,* or *as though* to introduce a subordinate clause.

EXAMPLES I **like** piano music. [verb]

Teresa plays the piano **like** a professional. [preposition]

Moira plays **as** [*not* like] her teacher taught her to play.

He looked at me **as if** [*not* like] he'd never seen me before.

loose, lose The adjective *loose* means "free," "not firmly attached," or "not fitting tightly." The verb *lose* means "to misplace" or "to fail to win."

EXAMPLES Don't **lose** that **loose** button on your shirt.

If we **lose** this game, we'll be out of the tournament.

mail, male *Mail* is what turns up in your mailbox. *Mail* also means "send." A *male* is a boy or a man.

EXAMPLES We received four pieces of **mail** today.

Sunny **mailed** a gift to her aunt Netta.

The **males** in the chorus wore red ties.

main, mane *Main* means "most important." A *mane* is the long hair on the neck of certain animals.

EXAMPLES What is your **main** job around the house?

The horse's **mane** was braided with colorful ribbons.

many, much Use *many* with nouns that can be counted. Use *much* with nouns that can't be counted.

EXAMPLES **Many** of the events are entertaining.

Much of the money goes to charity.

meat, meet *Meat* is food from an animal. Some meanings of *meet* are "to come face to face with," "to make the acquaintance of," and "to keep an appointment."

EXAMPLES Some people don't eat **meat.**

Meet me at the library at three o'clock.

minute The word *minute* (min´it) means "sixty seconds" or "a short period of time." The word *minute* (mī no͞ot´) means "very small."

EXAMPLES I'll be with you in a **minute.**

Don't bother me with **minute** details.

object *Object* is stressed on the first syllable when it means "a thing." *Object* is stressed on the second syllable when it means "oppose."

EXAMPLES Have you ever seen an unidentified flying **object**?

Mom **objected** to the proposal.

of Don't use *of* after the prepositions *off, inside,* and *outside.*

EXAMPLES He jumped **off** [*not* **off of**] the diving board.

The cat found a mouse **inside** [*not* **inside of**] the garage.

Outside [*not* **outside of**] the school, there is an old-fashioned drinking fountain.

off Don't use *off* in place of *from.*

EXAMPLE I'll borrow some money **from** [*not* **off**] my brother.

ought to of Don't use *of* in place of *have* after *ought to.*

EXAMPLE You **ought to have** [*not* **ought to of**] known better.

pair, pare, pear A *pair* is two. *Pare* means "to peel." A *pear* is a fruit.

EXAMPLES I bought a new **pair** of socks.

Pare the potatoes and cut them in quarters.

Would you like a **pear** or a banana?

passed, past *Passed* is the past tense and the past participle of the verb *pass. Past* can be an adjective, a preposition, an adverb, or a noun.

EXAMPLES We **passed** your house on the way to school. [verb]

The **past** week has been a busy one for me. [adjective]

We drove **past** your house. [preposition]

At what time did you drive **past**? [adverb]

I love Great-grandma's stories about the **past.** [noun]

pause, paws A *pause* is a short space of time. *Pause* also means "to wait for a short time." *Paws* are animal feet.

EXAMPLES We **pause** now for station identification.

I wiped the dog's muddy **paws.**

peace, piece *Peace* means "calmness" or "the absence of conflict." A *piece* is a part of something.

EXAMPLES We enjoy the **peace** of the countryside.

The two nations have finally made **peace.**

May I have another **piece** of pie?

plain, plane *Plain* means "not fancy," "clear," or "a large area of flat land." A *plane* is an airplane or a device for smoothing wood; it can also mean "a two-dimensional figure."

EXAMPLES   He wore a **plain** blue tie.

The solution is perfectly **plain** to me.

Buffalo once roamed the **plains.**

We took a **plane** to Chicago.

Jeff used a **plane** to smooth the rough wood.

How do you find the area of a **plane** with four equal sides?

precede, proceed *Precede* means "to go before" or "to come before." *Proceed* means "to continue" or "to move along."

EXAMPLE   Our band **preceded** the decorated floats as the parade **proceeded** through town.

principal, principle As a noun, *principal* means "head of a school." As an adjective, *principal* means "main" or "chief." *Principle* is a noun meaning "basic truth or belief" or "rule of conduct."

EXAMPLES   Mr. Washington, our **principal,** will speak at the morning assembly. **[noun]**

What was your **principal** reason for joining the club? **[adjective]**

The **principle** of fair play is important in sports.

Q

quiet, quit, quite The adjective *quiet* means "silent" or "motionless." The verb *quit* means "to stop" or "to give up or resign." The adverb *quite* means "very" or "completely."

EXAMPLES   Please be **quiet** so I can think.

Shirelle has **quit** the swim team.

We were **quite** sorry to lose her.

raise, rise *Raise* means "to cause to move upward." It can also mean "to breed or grow" and "to bring up or rear." Its principal parts are *raise, raising, raised,* and *raised.* Forms of *raise* are usually followed by a direct object. *Rise* means "to move upward." Its principal parts are *rise, rising, rose,* and *risen.* Forms of *rise* are never followed by a direct object.

EXAMPLES **Raise** your hand if you know the answer.

My uncle is **raising** chickens.

Grandma and Grandpa Schwartz **raised** nine children.

Steam **rises** from boiling water.

The sun is **rising.**

The children **rose** from their seats when the principal entered the room.

In a short time, Loretta had **risen** to the rank of captain.

rap, wrap *Rap* means "to knock." *Wrap* means "to cover."

EXAMPLES **Rap** on the door.

Wrap the presents.

read, reed *Read* means "to understand the meaning of something written" or "to speak aloud something that is written or printed." A *reed* is a stalk of tall grass.

EXAMPLES Will you **read** Jimmy a story?

We found a frog in the **reeds** beside the lake.

real, really *Real* is an adjective; use it before nouns and after linking verbs to modify the subject. *Really* is an adverb; use it to modify action verbs, adjectives, and other adverbs.

EXAMPLES Winona has **real** musical talent.

She is **really** talented.

real, reel *Real* means "actual." A *reel* is a spool to wind something on, such as a fishing line.

EXAMPLES I have a **real** four-leaf clover.

My dad bought me a new fishing **reel.**

reason is because Don't use *because* after *reason is.* Use *that* after *reason is,* or use *because* alone.

EXAMPLES The **reason** I'm tired is **that** I didn't sleep well last night.

I'm tired **because** I didn't sleep well last night.

row When *row* is pronounced to rhyme with *low,* it means "a series of things arranged in a line" or "to move a boat by using oars." When *row* is pronounced to rhyme with *how,* it means "a noisy quarrel."

EXAMPLES We sat in the last **row** of the theater.

Let's **row** across the lake.

My sister and I had a serious **row** yesterday, but today we've forgotten about it.

S

sail, sale A *sail* is part of a boat. It also means "to travel in a boat." A *sale* is a transfer of ownership in exchange for money.

EXAMPLES As the boat **sails** away, the crew raise the **sails.**

The **sale** of the house was completed on Friday.

sea, see A *sea* is a body of water. *See* means "to be aware of with the eyes."

EXAMPLES The **sea** is rough today.

I can **see** you.

set, sit *Set* means "to place" or "to put." Its principal parts are *set, setting, set,* and *set.* Forms of *set* are usually followed by a direct object. *Sit* means "to place oneself in a seated position." Its principal parts are *sit, sitting, sat,* and *sat.* Forms of *sit* are not followed by a direct object.

EXAMPLES   Lani **set** the pots on the stove.

The children **sit** quietly at the table.

sew, sow   *Sew* means "to work with needle and thread." When *sow* is pronounced to rhyme with *how*, it means "a female pig." When *sow* is pronounced to rhyme with *low*, it means "to plant."

EXAMPLES   Can you **sew** a button on a shirt?

The **sow** has five piglets.

Some farmers **sow** corn in their fields.

shined, shone, shown   Both *shined* and *shone* are past tense forms and past participles of *shine.* Use *shined* when you mean "polished"; use *shone* in all other instances.

EXAMPLES   Clete **shined** his shoes.

The sun **shone** brightly.

Her face **shone** with happiness.

Shown is the past participle of *show;* its principal parts are *show, showing, showed,* and *shown.*

EXAMPLES   You **showed** me these photographs yesterday.

You have **shown** me these photographs before.

some, somewhat   Don't use *some* as an adverb in place of *somewhat.*

EXAMPLE   The team has improved **somewhat [*not* some]** since last season.

son, sun   A *son* is a male child. A *sun* is a star.

EXAMPLES   Kino is Mr. and Mrs. Akawa's **son.**

Our **sun** is 93 million miles away.

stationary, stationery *Stationary* means "fixed" or "unmoving." *Stationery* is writing paper.

EXAMPLES   This classroom has **stationary** desks.

Rhonda likes to write letters on pretty **stationery.**

sure, surely *Sure* is an adjective; use it before nouns and after linking verbs to modify the subject. *Surely* is an adverb; use it to modify action verbs, adjectives, and other adverbs.

EXAMPLES   Are you **sure** about that answer?

You are **surely** smart.

tail, tale A *tail* is what a dog wags. A *tale* is a story.

EXAMPLES   The dog's **tail** curled over its back.

Everyone knows the **tale** of Goldilocks and the three bears.

tear When *tear* is pronounced to rhyme with *ear,* it's a drop of fluid from the eye. When *tear* is pronounced to rhyme with *bear,* it means "a rip" or "to rip."

EXAMPLES   A **tear** fell from the child's eye.

Tear this rag in half.

than, then *Than* is a conjunction used to introduce the second part of a comparison. *Then* is an adverb meaning "at that time."

EXAMPLES   LaTrisha is taller **than** LaToya.

My grandmother was a young girl **then.**

that, which, who *That* may refer to people or things. *Which* refers only to things. *Who* refers only to people.

EXAMPLES   The poet **that** wrote *Leaves of Grass* is Walt Whitman.

I have already seen the movie **that** is playing at the Palace.

The new play, **which** closed after a week, received poor reviews.

Students **who** do well on the test will receive scholarships.

that there, this here Don't use *there* or *here* after *that, this, those,* or *these.*

EXAMPLES I can't decide whether to read **this** [*not* this here] magazine or **that** [*not* that there] book.

Fold **these** [*not* these here] towels and hang **those** [*not* those there] shirts in the closet.

their, there, they're *Their* is a possessive form of *they;* it's used to modify nouns. *There* means "in or at that place." *They're* is a contraction of *they are.*

EXAMPLES A hurricane damaged **their** house.

Put your books **there.**

They're our next-door neighbors.

theirs, there's *Theirs* is a possessive form of *they* used as a pronoun. *There's* is a contraction of *there is* or *there has.*

EXAMPLES **Theirs** is the white house with the green shutters.

There's [There is] your friend Chad.

There's [There has] been an accident.

them Don't use *them* as an adjective in place of *those.*

EXAMPLE I'll take one of **those** [*not* them] hamburgers.

this kind, these kinds Use the singular forms *this* and *that* with the singular nouns *kind, sort,* and *type.* Use the plural forms *these* and *those* with the plural nouns *kinds, sorts,* and *types.*

EXAMPLES Use **this kind** of lightbulb in your lamp.

Do you like **these kinds** of lamps?

Many Pakistani restaurants serve **that sort** of food.

Those sorts of foods are nutritious.

This type of dog makes a good pet.

These types of dogs are good with children.

thorough, through *Thorough* means "complete." *Through* is a preposition meaning "into at one side and out at another."

EXAMPLES We gave the bedrooms a **thorough** cleaning.

A breeze blew **through** the house.

threw, through *Threw* is the past tense of *throw. Through* is a preposition meaning "into at one side and out at another." *Through* can also mean "finished."

EXAMPLES Lacey **threw** the ball.

Ira walked **through** the room.

At last I'm **through** with my homework.

to, too, two *To* means "in the direction of"; it is also part of the infinitive form of a verb. *Too* means "very" or "also." *Two* is the number after *one*.

EXAMPLES Jaleela walks **to** school.

She likes **to** study.

The soup is **too** salty.

May I go **too**?

We have **two** kittens.

try and Use *try to*.

EXAMPLE Please **try to** [*not* try and] be on time.

unless, without Don't use *without* in place of *unless*.

EXAMPLE **Unless** [*not* Without] I clean my room, I can't go to the mall.

used to, use to The correct form is *used to.*

EXAMPLE We **used to** [*not* use to] live in Cleveland, Ohio.

waist, waste Your *waist* is where you wear your belt. As a noun, *waste* means "careless or unnecessary spending" or "trash." As a verb, it means "to spend or use carelessly or unnecessarily."

EXAMPLES She tied a colorful scarf around her **waist.**

Buying that computer game was a **waste** of money.

Put your **waste** in the dumpster.

Don't **waste** time worrying.

wait, weight *Wait* means "to stay or remain." *Weight* is a measurement.

EXAMPLES **Wait** right here.

Her **weight** is 110 pounds.

wait for, wait on *Wait for* means "to remain in a place looking forward to something expected." *Wait on* means "to act as a server."

EXAMPLES **Wait for** me at the bus stop.

Nat and Tammy **wait on** diners at The Golden Griddle.

way, ways Use *way,* not *ways,* in referring to distance.

EXAMPLE It's a long **way** [*not* ways] to Tipperary.

weak, week *Weak* means "feeble" or "not strong." A *week* is seven days.

EXAMPLE She felt **weak** for a **week** after the operation.

weather, whether *Weather* is the condition of the atmosphere. *Whether* means "if"; it is also used to introduce the first of two choices.

EXAMPLES The **weather** in Portland is mild and rainy.

Tell me **whether** you can go.

I can't decide **whether** to go or stay.

when, where Don't use *when* or *where* incorrectly in writing a definition.

EXAMPLES A compliment is a flattering remark. [*not* A compliment is when you make a flattering remark.]

Spelunking is the hobby of exploring caves. [*not* Spelunking is where you explore caves.]

where Don't use *where* in place of *that*.

EXAMPLE I see **that** [*not* where] the Yankees are in first place in their division.

where . . . at Don't use *at* after *where*.

EXAMPLE **Where** is your mother? [*not* Where is your mother at?]

who's, whose *Who's* is a contraction of *who is* or *who has*. *Whose* is the possessive form of *who*.

EXAMPLES **Who's [Who is]** conducting the orchestra?

Who's [Who has] read this book?

Whose umbrella is this?

wind When *wind* has a short-*i* sound, it means "moving air." When *wind* has a long-*i* sound, it means "to wrap around."

EXAMPLES The **wind** is strong today.

Wind the bandage around your ankle.

wood, would *Wood* comes from trees. *Would* is a helping verb.

EXAMPLE **Would** you prefer a **wood** bookcase or a metal one?

wound When *wound* is pronounced to rhyme with *sound*, it is the past tense of *wind*. The word *wound* (wo͞ond) means "an injury in which the skin is broken."

EXAMPLE I **wound** the bandage around my ankle to cover the **wound.**

your, you're *Your* is a possessive form of *you*. *You're* is a contraction of *you are*.

EXAMPLES **Your** arguments are convincing.

You're doing a fine job.

ABBREVIATIONS

An abbreviation is a short way to write a word or a group of words. Abbreviations should be used sparingly in formal writing except for a few that are actually more appropriate than their longer forms. These are *Mr., Mrs.,* and *Dr. (doctor)* before names, *A.M.* and *P.M.,* and *B.C.* and *A.D.*

Some abbreviations are written with capital letters and periods, and some with capital letters and no periods; some are written with lowercase letters and periods, and some with lowercase letters and no periods. A few may be written in any one of these four ways and still be acceptable. For example, to abbreviate *miles per hour,* you may write *MPH, M.P.H., mph,* or *m.p.h.*

Some abbreviations may be spelled in more than one way. For example, *Tuesday* may be abbreviated *Tues.* or *Tue. Thursday* may be written *Thurs.* or *Thu.* In the following lists, only the most common way of writing each abbreviation is given.

When you need information about an abbreviation, consult a dictionary. Some dictionaries list abbreviations in a special section in the back. Others list them in the main part of the book.

MONTHS

Jan.	January	none	July
Feb.	February	Aug.	August
Mar.	March	Sept.	September
Apr.	April	Oct.	October
none	May	Nov.	November
none	June	Dec.	December

DAYS

Sun.	Sunday	Thurs.	Thursday
Mon.	Monday	Fri.	Friday
Tues.	Tuesday	Sat.	Saturday
Wed.	Wednesday		

TIME AND DIRECTION

CDT	central daylight time
CST	central standard time
DST	daylight saving time
EDT	eastern daylight time
EST	eastern standard time
MDT	mountain daylight time
MST	mountain standard time
PDT	Pacific daylight time
PST	Pacific standard time
ST	standard time
NE	northeast
NW	northwest
SE	southeast
SW	southwest
A.D.	in the year of the Lord (Latin *anno Domini*)
B.C.	before Christ
B.C.E.	before the common era
C.E.	common era
A.M.	before noon (Latin *ante meridiem*)
P.M.	after noon (Latin *post meridiem*)

MEASUREMENT

The same abbreviation is used for both the singular and the plural meaning of measurements. Therefore, *ft.* stands for both *foot* and *feet,* and *in.* stands for both *inch* and *inches.* Note that abbreviations of metric measurements are commonly written without periods. U.S. measurements, on the other hand, are usually written with periods.

Metric System

Mass and Weight

t	metric ton
kg	kilogram
g	gram
cg	centigram
mg	milligram

Capacity

kl	kiloliter
l	liter
cl	centiliter
ml	milliliter

Length

km	kilometer
m	meter
cm	centimeter
mm	millimeter

U.S. Weights and Measures

Weight

wt.	weight
lb.	pound
oz.	ounce

Capacity

gal.	gallon
qt.	quart
pt.	pint
c.	cup
tbsp.	tablespoon
tsp.	teaspoon
fl. oz.	fluid ounce

Length

mi.	mile
rd.	rod
yd.	yard
ft.	foot
in.	inch

MISCELLANEOUS MEASUREMENTS

p.s.i.	pounds per square inch
MPH	miles per hour
MPG	miles per gallon
rpm	revolutions per minute
C	Celsius, centigrade
F	Fahrenheit
K	Kelvin
kn	knot

COMPUTER AND INTERNET

CPU	central processing unit
CRT	cathode ray tube
DOS	disk operating system
e-mail	electronic mail
K	kilobyte
URL	uniform resource locator
DVD	digital video disc
d.p.i.	dots per inch
WWW	World Wide Web
ISP	Internet service provider
DNS	domain name system

ADDITIONAL ABBREVIATIONS

ac	alternating current
dc	direct current
AM	amplitude modulation
FM	frequency modulation
ASAP	as soon as possible
e.g.	for example (Latin *exempli gratia*)
etc.	and others, and so forth (Latin *et cetera*)
i.e.	that is (Latin *id est*)
Inc.	incorporated
ISBN	International Standard Book Number

lc	lowercase
misc.	miscellaneous
p.	page
pp.	pages
R.S.V.P.	please reply (French *répondez s'il vous plaît*)
SOS	international distress signal
TM	trademark
uc	uppercase
vs.	versus
w/o	without

UNITED STATES (U.S.)

In most cases, state names and street addresses should be spelled out. The postal abbreviations in the following list should be used with ZIP codes in addressing envelopes. They may also be used with ZIP codes for return addresses and inside addresses in business letters. The traditional state abbreviations are seldom used nowadays, but occasionally it's helpful to know them.

State	Traditional	Postal
Alabama	Ala.	AL
Alaska	none	AK
Arizona	Ariz.	AZ
Arkansas	Ark.	AR
California	Calif.	CA
Colorado	Colo.	CO
Connecticut	Conn.	CT
Delaware	Del.	DE
District of Columbia	D.C.	DC
Florida	Fla.	FL
Georgia	Ga.	GA
Hawaii	none	HI
Idaho	none	ID
Illinois	Ill.	IL
Indiana	Ind.	IN

Iowa	none	IA
Kansas	Kans.	KS
Kentucky	Ky.	KY
Louisiana	La.	LA
Maine	none	ME
Maryland	Md.	MD
Massachusetts	Mass.	MA
Michigan	Mich.	MI
Minnesota	Minn.	MN
Mississippi	Miss.	MS
Missouri	Mo.	MO
Montana	Mont.	MT
Nebraska	Nebr.	NE
Nevada	Nev.	NV
New Hampshire	N.H.	NH
New Jersey	N.J.	NJ
New Mexico	N. Mex.	NM
New York	N.Y.	NY
North Carolina	N.C.	NC
North Dakota	N. Dak.	ND
Ohio	none	OH
Oklahoma	Okla.	OK
Oregon	Oreg.	OR
Pennsylvania	Pa.	PA
Rhode Island	R.I.	RI
South Carolina	S.C.	SC
South Dakota	S. Dak.	SD
Tennessee	Tenn.	TN
Texas	Tex.	TX
Utah	none	UT
Vermont	Vt.	VT
Virginia	Va.	VA
Washington	Wash.	WA
West Virginia	W. Va.	WV
Wisconsin	Wis.	WI
Wyoming	Wyo.	WY

Part Two

Grammar, Usage, and Mechanics

Your first discipline is your vocabulary; then your grammar and your punctuation....Then you add rhyme and meter. And your delight is in that power.

—Robert Frost

(you) | Wri

People | write

people | Do wri

Diagrams | are \ useful

Subjects, Predicates, and Sentences

PRETEST **Kinds of Sentences**

Write declarative, interrogative, imperative, *or* exclamatory *to identify each sentence.*

1. When did Michael Jordan join the Chicago Bulls?
2. Watch Jordan shoot free throws.
3. What a great jumper Jordan is!
4. My favorite team is the Boston Celtics.
5. Dad prefers baseball to basketball.

PRETEST **Sentences and Sentence Fragments**

Write sentence *or* fragment *for each item. Rewrite each fragment to make it a sentence.*

6. Edgar Allan Poe wrote poems and stories.
7. The American Revolution or the Civil War.

8. My dog is very smart.
9. Dan and Debi play softball in the summer.
10. Knows the answer to many questions.
11. Sally and her seven brothers.
12. Of the tall buildings.
13. Earthquakes occur in California.
14. Ancient Egyptians built boats from reeds.
15. Saw several movies about the Old West.

PRETEST Subjects and Predicates

Write each sentence. Underline the simple subjects once and the simple predicates twice.

16. There is a fly in your soup.
17. This dictionary has a red cover.
18. Yesterday Somally and Johanna tutored Monica for an hour.
19. Did the girls take the test and pass it?
20. Wait for them here.
21. Venus and Serena Williams play professional tennis.
22. Over the net flies the ball.
23. Here are a trophy and two ribbons from last year.
24. Are the five Great Lakes Huron, Ontario, Michigan, Erie, and Superior?
25. Find and name the capital of your state.

PRETEST Simple, Compound, and Run-on Sentences

Write simple, compound, *or* run-on *to identify each numbered item. If an item is a run-on, rewrite it correctly.*

26. The family vacations every summer in Myrtle Beach, South Carolina.
27. Heavy rains fell all day the river overflowed its banks.
28. All mammals are animals, but not all animals are mammals.

29. My sister and I pitched the tent and gathered wood for a fire.
30. Suyuan is a champion gymnast her brother doesn't enjoy sports.
31. Did you finish your homework, or did you talk on the phone for an hour?
32. The fire crackled and sputtered in the fireplace, and the clock struck twelve.
33. Some plants grow in poor soil and eat insects for food.
34. The Venus's-flytrap attracts insects, the leaves of the plant then snap shut around their prey.
35. The settlers planted corn and wheat, but bad weather and insect pests destroyed their crops.

1.1 KINDS OF SENTENCES CCSS L.7.1b

A **sentence** is a group of words that expresses a complete thought.

Different kinds of sentences have different purposes. A sentence can make a statement, ask a question, or give a command. A sentence can also express strong feeling. All sentences begin with a capital letter and end with a punctuation mark. The punctuation mark depends on the purpose of the sentence.

A **declarative sentence** makes a statement. It ends with a period.

EXAMPLE Edgar Allan Poe wrote suspenseful short stories.

An **interrogative sentence** asks a question. It ends with a question mark.

EXAMPLE Did Poe also write poetry?

An **imperative sentence** gives a command or makes a request. It ends with a period.

EXAMPLE Read "The Pit and the Pendulum."

An **exclamatory sentence** expresses strong feeling. It ends with an exclamation point.

EXAMPLE   What a great writer Poe was!

EXAMPLE   How I enjoy his stories!

PRACTICE **Identifying Kinds of Sentences**

Write declarative, interrogative, imperative, *or* exclamatory *to identify each sentence.*

1. Are elephants the largest land animals?
2. You can reach California by traveling west.
3. Don't forget your mother's birthday.
4. Bring me those papers on the desk.
5. How hot it is today!
6. Have you ever seen a live kangaroo?
7. What a great fireworks display that was!
8. Construction of the new school will begin in the spring.
9. My little brother's favorite movie is *The Lion King*.
10. Let me help you with those heavy suitcases.

1.2 SENTENCES AND SENTENCE FRAGMENTS

CCSS L.7.1b

Every sentence has two parts: a subject and a predicate.

EXAMPLE

┌──────────────── Sentence ────────────────┐
Emily Dickinson   wrote poetry.
└──── Subject ────┘   └── Predicate ──┘

The **subject part** of a sentence names whom or what the sentence is about.

The **predicate part** of a sentence tells what the subject does or has. It can also tell what the subject is or is like.

A **sentence fragment** does not express a complete thought. It may also be missing a subject, a predicate, or both.

CORRECTING SENTENCE FRAGMENTS

FRAGMENT	PROBLEM	SENTENCE
The poems.	The fragment lacks a predicate. *What did the poems do?*	The poems lay in Dickinson's bureau for years.
Wrote about her emotions.	The fragment lacks a subject. *Who wrote about her emotions?*	This famous poet wrote about her emotions.
Of meaning.	The fragment lacks a subject and a predicate.	Her poems contain many layers of meaning.

Write sentence *or* fragment *for each item. Write each sentence and underline the subject part once and the predicate part twice. For each fragment, add a subject or a predicate or both to make it a sentence.*

1. Mr. Wilson teaches life science at the middle school.
2. Over the river and through the woods.
3. Showed me a book about pioneers in Montana.
4. Am having a good time at summer camp.
5. Jacob writes a letter to his parents once a week.
6. Frogs begin life as tadpoles.
7. This unusual photograph shows a sandstorm in the desert.
8. Everywhere on this planet and throughout the solar system.
9. Won the game by just two points.
10. A huge green and white beach umbrella.

1.3 SUBJECTS AND PREDICATES CCSS L.7.1b

A sentence consists of a subject and a predicate that together express a complete thought. Both a subject and a predicate may consist of more than one word.

	Complete Subject	Complete Predicate
EXAMPLE	Charles Dickens's **novels**	**are** still popular today.
EXAMPLE	My English **teacher**	**wrote** an article about Dickens.

The **complete subject** includes all the words in the subject of a sentence.

The **complete predicate** includes all the words in the predicate of a sentence.

Not all words in the subject or the predicate are equally important.

Complete Subject   Complete Predicate

The young **Charles Dickens**   **wrote** many articles.

Simple Subject   Simple Predicate

The **simple subject** is the main word or word group in the complete subject.

The simple subject is usually a noun or a pronoun. A **noun** is a word that names a person, a place, a thing, or an idea. A **pronoun** is a word that takes the place of one or more nouns.

The **simple predicate** is the main word or word group in the complete predicate.

The simple predicate is always a verb. A **verb** is a word that expresses action or a state of being.

Sometimes the simple subject is the same as the complete subject. Sometimes the simple predicate is the same as the complete predicate.

PRACTICE   Identifying Complete Subjects and Complete Predicates

Write each sentence. Underline the complete subject once and the complete predicate twice.

1. The purple mountains appeared misty in the distance.
2. Emilio cheered for his sister's teammates.
3. A big raccoon crawled out of the hole.
4. Ms. Hayashida is our math teacher.
5. I like strawberry shortcake with cream.
6. The Snake River flows through southern Idaho.
7. You seem sad today.

8. This dictionary has 1,559 pages.
9. The young detective searched the room for clues.
10. The fresh yellow butter melted.

Identifying Simple Subjects and Simple Predicates

Write each sentence. Underline the simple subject once and the simple predicate twice.

1. Thirteen pink candles decorated Lisa's birthday cake.
2. This collie's name is Misty Moonlight.
3. Some teachers assign homework every day.
4. The boys' soccer team lost only one game this season.
5. His bushy beard stretched to his waistline.
6. Daffodils swayed in the brisk breeze.
7. Jefferson Middle School has a new principal.
8. That tall blond boy plays a trombone in the band.
9. My library book disappeared.
10. Computer games give me many hours of fun and entertainment.

1.4 IDENTIFYING THE SUBJECT CCSS L.7.1b

In most sentences, the subject comes before the predicate.

┌─────── Subject ───────┐   ┌─────────── Predicate ───────────┐
EXAMPLE Washington Irving   described New York in his stories.

Other kinds of sentences, such as questions, begin with part or all of the predicate. The subject comes next, followed by the rest of the predicate.

Predicate   Subject   ┌──────────Predicate──────────┐
EXAMPLE Are   people   still reading his stories?

To locate the subject of a question, rearrange the words to form a statement.

PREDICATE	SUBJECT	PREDICATE
Did	Irving	write many funny stories?
	Irving	did write many funny stories.

The predicate also comes before the subject in sentences with inverted word order and in declarative sentences that begin with *Here is, Here are, There is,* and *There are.*

EXAMPLE

┌───── Predicate ─────┐ ┌── Subject ──┐

Over the paper raced Irving's pen.

EXAMPLE

┌ Predicate ┐ ┌───────── Subject ─────────┐

There is Irving's original manuscript.

In imperative sentences (requests and commands), the subject is usually not stated. The predicate is the entire sentence. The word *you* is understood to be the subject.

EXAMPLE

Understood Subject ┌──────── Predicate ────────┐

(You) Look for the author's name on the cover.

PRACTICE **Identifying the Subject**

Write each sentence. Underline the complete subject. Write (You) *before any sentence with an understood subject.*

1. Does your brother deliver the morning paper?
2. Into the tall grass crawled the little garter snake.
3. Call me this afternoon at three o'clock.
4. Has the mail arrived yet?
5. The Beatles introduced many popular songs.
6. Here is a famous painting by Grant Wood.
7. From the bottom of the sea rose a hideous monster.
8. Define the words *numerator* and *denominator.*
9. A personal computer is a useful tool for a writer.
10. There are rules for this game.

1.5 COMPOUND SUBJECTS AND COMPOUND PREDICATES   CCSS L.7.1b

A sentence may have more than one simple subject or simple predicate.

A **compound subject** consists of two or more simple subjects that have the same predicate. The subjects may be joined by *and, or, both . . . and, either . . . or,* or *neither . . . nor.*

                      Compound Subject

EXAMPLE   **Charlotte Brontë** and **Emily Brontë**   were sisters.

When the two simple subjects are joined by *and* or by *both . . . and,* the compound subject is plural. Use the plural form of the verb to agree with the plural compound subject.

When simple subjects are joined by *or, either . . . or,* or *neither . . . nor,* the verb must agree with the nearer simple subject.

EXAMPLE   Neither **Charlotte** nor **Emily is** my favorite author.

EXAMPLE   Neither her **sisters** nor **Charlotte was** outgoing.

EXAMPLE   Neither **Charlotte** nor her **sisters were** outgoing.

In the first sentence, *Emily* is the nearer subject, so the singular form of the verb is used. In the second sentence, *Charlotte* is the nearer subject, so the singular form of the verb is used here too. In the third sentence, *sisters* is the nearer subject, so the plural form of the verb is used.

A **compound predicate** consists of two or more simple predicates, or verbs, that have the same subject. The verbs may be connected by *and, or, but, both . . . and, either . . . or,* or *neither . . . nor.*

                     Compound Predicate

EXAMPLE   Many students   **read** and **enjoy** novels.

The compound predicate in this sentence consists of *read* and *enjoy.* Both verbs agree with the plural subject, *students.*

Chapter 1   Subjects, Predicates, and Sentences   **73**

Write each sentence, using the correct form of the verb in parentheses. Then underline the compound subjects once and the compound predicates twice.

1. Rita Dove and Robert Frost (is, are) two famous American poets.
2. The hotel guests either (reads, read) or (naps, nap) in the afternoon.
3. Both owls and raccoons (hunts, hunt) at night.
4. The chef or his assistants (bakes, bake) and (decorates, decorate) the wedding cakes.
5. Althea (works, work) hard during the week but (relaxes, relax) on Saturday and Sunday.
6. The players or the coach (thanks, thank) the cheerleaders.
7. Some students neither (revises, revise) nor (proofreads, proofread) their compositions.
8. The brothers and sisters both (plays, play) and (sings, sing) together.
9. Either Ruth or Betty (feeds, feed) the children and (puts, put) them to bed.
10. Neither the three sisters nor their brother (weeds, weed) the garden or (mows, mow) the lawn.

1.6 SIMPLE, COMPOUND, AND RUN-ON SENTENCES CCSS L.7.1b

A **simple sentence** has one subject and one predicate.

EXAMPLE ┌─────────── Simple Sentence ───────────┐
Eudora Welty   lived in Jackson, Mississippi.

A simple sentence may have a compound subject, a compound predicate, or both, as in the following example.

EXAMPLE ┌─────────── Simple Sentence ───────────┐
Jeff and I   read and enjoy Welty's stories.
     Compound Subject   Compound Predicate

A **compound sentence** is a sentence that contains two or more simple sentences joined by a comma and a coordinating conjunction (*and, but, or*) or by a semicolon.

<table>
<tr><td>EXAMPLE</td><td colspan="2">┌─── Compound Sentence ───┐
Welty is a novelist, but she also writes essays.</td></tr>
<tr><td>EXAMPLE</td><td>Welty is a novelist; she also writes essays.</td></tr>
</table>

┌─ Simple Sentence ─┐ ┌─ Simple Sentence ─┐

A run-on sentence is two or more sentences incorrectly written as one sentence. To correct a run-on, write separate sentences or combine the sentences.

CORRECTING RUN-ON SENTENCES

RUN-ON	CORRECT
Welty wrote novels she wrote essays. Welty wrote novels, she wrote essays.	Welty wrote novels. **S**he wrote essays. Welty wrote novels, **and** she wrote essays. Welty wrote novels; she wrote essays.

PRACTICE **Identifying Simple, Compound, and Run-on Sentences**

Write simple, compound, *or* run-on *to identify each numbered item. If an item is a run-on, rewrite it correctly.*

1. The school bus stops at the corner of my street.
2. LaToya missed the basket, but Laura caught the rebound.
3. We went to a movie then we stopped for a snack.
4. Ms. Martin's class made the posters, and Mr. Rossi's class sold tickets.
5. Lawyers prepare their cases and defend their clients in court.

6. Cars and trucks stream across the bridge and disappear into the tunnel.
7. Did George Washington really chop down his father's cherry tree, or is that story just a legend?
8. Dad washes dishes by hand Mom puts them in the dishwasher.
9. The wind howls, and the hikers huddle in their tents and drink hot soup.
10. The engine sputters and coughs, the car jerks forward and then stops.

PRACTICE Proofreading

Rewrite the following passage, correcting errors in spelling, capitalization, grammar, and usage. Add any missing punctuation. Write legibly to be sure one letter is not mistaken for another. There are ten errors.

Arnold Adoff

[1]Arnold Adoff grew up in New York City. [2]As a boy, he liked books and Jewish poetry. [3]What did Adoff study in college [4]He received a degree in history and government, then he went to Columbia University for further study. [5]for many years, he was a teacher in the public schools of New York. [6]Now he travel, lectures, and writes poetry. [7]His poetry has received an award from the National Council of Teachers of English. [8]According to Adoff, a poem should be read three times and you should listen for its music and rhythm. [9]Two of his books are *Sports Pages* and *All the Colors of the Race.*

[10]Adoff married the writer Virginia Hamilton, author of *M. C. Higgins, the Great,* in 1960. [11]Mr. and Mrs. Adoff lives in Yellow Springs, Ohio. [12]A small college town. [13]They have two grown-up children, Leigh and Jaime

[14]Adoff's wife writes her books on a computer but Adoff prefers his old familiar typewriter. [15]Many of his poems have a definate physical shape. [16]Perhaps he can compose such poems more easily with a typewriter.

Write declarative, interrogative, imperative, *or* exclamatory *to identify each sentence.*

1. Some dinosaurs may have weighed a hundred tons!
2. A large car weighs about a ton and a half.
3. How much does a rhinoceros weigh?
4. Take me to the zoo.
5. You can see many unusual animals in a zoo.

POSTTEST Sentences and Sentence Fragments

Write sentence *or* fragment *for each item. Rewrite each fragment to make it a sentence.*

6. Beneath the surface of the lake.
7. The story of a dog.
8. A volcanic eruption destroyed the city.
9. Lived there all his life.
10. The tall, thin boy is my cousin.
11. The three tiny kittens have a new home.
12. The icy track down the mountain.
13. Geraldo washed the car.
14. In the beautiful blue sky.
15. Practices every morning.

POSTTEST Subjects and Predicates

Write each sentence. Underline the simple subjects once and the simple predicates twice.

16. Have Kawa and Tyrone studied American history this year?
17. In 1842 pioneers and their animals traveled on the Oregon Trail.
18. Then came the railroads.
19. Through the mountains sped the trains.

GRAMMAR / USAGE / MECHANICS

20. In 1925 Nellie Tayloe Ross became the governor of Wyoming.
21. She was the first female governor in the United States.
22. Name another female governor.
23. Annie Oakley performed in Buffalo Bill's Wild West Show in 1885 and amazed the crowds with her rifle.
24. Here is a model of her rifle.
25. When did this performer die?

POSTTEST Simple, Compound, and Run-on Sentences

Write simple, compound, *or* run-on *to identify each numbered item. If an item is a run-on, rewrite it correctly.*

26. Seventy-six trombones led the big parade.
27. My mother works as a dental assistant, and my father drives a truck.
28. I made an outline for my report then I wrote the introduction.
29. Several aunts and uncles and all my grandparents live in other states.
30. Jake and Sally grilled hot dogs and made a salad.
31. Perry makes his bed every morning Sandra always leaves her room in a mess.
32. The dog barked and growled, the thief turned and ran.
33. Did Serena prepare this meal by herself, or did her brother help her?
34. Silvia lost her watch, but Jeremiah found it and returned it.
35. Mr. and Mrs. Montoya raise Irish setters, and their son and daughter feed and exercise the animals.

Chapter 2

Nouns

··

PRETEST **Kinds of Nouns**

Write each noun. Label the common nouns C *and the proper nouns* P.

1. In the tiny house in Cleveland, Grandma Palavinskas baked strudel with her daughter.
2. The success of the project will depend on hard work by all members of the team.
3. The friendship between the two girls from Orlando began in kindergarten.
4. Men and women throughout the world wear makeup for different reasons.
5. A vacation at Disney World will be fun for the whole family.

PRETEST **Possessive Nouns**

Write the possessive form of the noun in parentheses.

6. This store sells only (women) shoes.
7. My (mom) responsibilities allow her little free time.

8. (Chris) father works in a bakery.
9. The doctor set (Jessica) broken leg.
10. What is the (store) policy on returns?
11. The (Williamses) house is on the north side of Buffalo Road.
12. Did you hear the (judge) instructions to the jury?
13. The counselors scheduled the (campers) activities in advance.
14. Mrs. (Cassirer) daughter designed her own Web page.
15. The airline delivered the (passengers) baggage to the wrong city.

PRETEST Recognizing Plurals, Possessives, and Contractions

Identify the italicized word in each sentence by writing plural noun, singular possessive noun, plural possessive noun, *or* contraction.

16. The *Women's* National Basketball Association allowed women into professional basketball.
17. How shall we celebrate *Mei-Ling's* birthday?
18. *Edwin's* won three races today.
19. There will be a dinner for the *volunteers* on Thursday.
20. Will you attend the *writers'* conference?
21. Please clean the *cat's* litter box.
22. John *Dixon's* the president of the company.
23. The *mall's* location is convenient.
24. Workers clean the *horses'* stables twice a day.
25. The *Smiths* have three children in high school.

PRETEST Appositives

Write the appositive or appositive phrase in each sentence.

26. Soccer's world championship, the World Cup occurs every four years.
27. The scientific community admired Albert Einstein, a United States immigrant.

28. The rock group Fudd will perform tonight in the high school auditorium.
29. A mighty volcano, Kilauea destroys homes and plant life with its lava flows.
30. Harold talks constantly about computer games, his favorite subject.
31. Have you ever read the short story "Rikki-tikki-tavi"?
32. A champion golfer, Babe Didrikson Zaharias is probably the greatest female athlete of all time.
33. Tamika visited her cousin Bernard.
34. Harry Houdini, a famous magician, specialized in escape tricks.
35. The poet Shel Silverstein wrote *Where the Sidewalk Ends.*

2.1 KINDS OF NOUNS

A **noun** is a word that names a person, a place, a thing, or an idea.

NOUNS	
PERSONS	sister, mayor, player, coach, pianist, children
PLACES	park, zoo, lake, school, playground, desert, city
THINGS	magazine, boots, rose, pencil, peach, baseball, car
IDEAS	honesty, truth, democracy, pride, maturity, progress

A **common noun** names *any* person, place, thing, or idea.
A **proper noun** names a *particular* person, place, thing, or idea.

The first word and all other important words in a proper noun are capitalized: *Edgar Allan Poe, Statue of Liberty.*

Common nouns can be either concrete or abstract.

Concrete nouns name things you can see or touch.
Abstract nouns name ideas, qualities, and feelings that can't be seen or touched.

KINDS OF NOUNS		
COMMON NOUNS		**PROPER NOUNS**
Abstract	**Concrete**	
truth	document	Supreme Court
courage	crown	Queen Elizabeth I
time	snow	December
history	museum	Museum of Modern Art
entertainment	actor	Meryl Streep
education	school	Howard University
comedy	comedian	Jerry Seinfeld
friendship	friend	Jessica
tragedy	ship	*Titanic*

Compound nouns are nouns made of two or more words.

A compound noun can be one word, like *storybook*, or more than one word, like *ice cream.* A compound noun can also be joined by one or more hyphens, like *runner-up.*

COMPOUND NOUNS	
ONE WORD	housekeeper, showcase, bookmark, outdoors, teammate
MORE THAN ONE WORD	post office, dining room, maid of honor, high school
HYPHENATED	sister-in-law, great-aunt, kilowatt-hour, walkie-talkie

PRACTICE Identifying Common and Proper Nouns

Write each noun. Label the common nouns C *and the proper nouns* P.

1. Paul rolled his wheelchair up the ramp and into the Weston Municipal Building.
2. The Empire State Building in New York City was once the tallest structure in the world.
3. Friendship and loyalty are two qualities most people admire.
4. Buy your fruits and flowers at Friendly Farm Market in Clarkville.
5. Abraham Lincoln served as president during the Civil War.
6. Harry bought several souvenirs during his visit to Disney World.
7. The United Nations encourages peace and cooperation among nations.
8. My mom sometimes calls Pizza Pantry for a quick delivery.
9. Grandma Faith often describes memories of her youth on a farm in Kansas.
10. The librarian recommended *Treasure Island,* a book by Robert Louis Stevenson.

2.2 SINGULAR AND PLURAL NOUNS

A **singular noun** names one person, place, thing, or idea. A **plural noun** names more than one.

To form the plural of most nouns, you simply add -*s*. Other plural nouns are formed in different ways.

NOUNS ENDING WITH	TO FORM PLURAL	EXAMPLES		
s, z, ch, sh, x	Add **-es.**	bus bus**es**	buzz buzz**es**	box box**es**
o preceded by a vowel	Add **-s.**	rodeo rodeo**s**	studio studio**s**	radio radio**s**
o preceded by a consonant	Usually add **-es.**	hero hero**es**	potato potato**es**	echo echo**es**
	Sometimes add **-s.**	zero zero**s**	photo photo**s**	piano piano**s**
y preceded by a vowel	Add **-s.**	day day**s**	turkey turkey**s**	toy toy**s**
y preceded by a consonant	Usually change **y** to **i** and add **-es.**	city cit**ies**	diary diar**ies**	penny penn**ies**
f or **fe**	Usually change **f** to **v** and add **-s** or **-es.**	wife wi**ves**	leaf lea**ves**	half hal**ves**
	Sometimes add **-s.**	roof roof**s**	chief chief**s**	belief belief**s**

GRAMMAR / USAGE / MECHANICS

To form the plural of compound nouns written as one word, usually add *-s* or *-es*. To form the plural of compound nouns that are written as more than one word or are hyphenated, make the main noun in the compound word plural, or check a dictionary.

COMPOUND NOUNS	
ONE WORD	doorbells, necklaces, rosebushes; *Exception:* passersby
MORE THAN ONE WORD	post offices, dining rooms, maids of honor, high schools
HYPHENATED	brothers-in-law, great-aunts, eighth-graders, push-ups

Words such as *family* and *team* are called collective nouns.

A **collective noun** names a group of people, animals, or things.

A collective noun subject may be followed by a singular verb or a plural verb, depending on the meaning. The subject is singular when the members of the group act as a single unit. The subject is plural when each member of the group acts separately. Other words in a sentence can sometimes help you decide whether a collective noun is singular or plural.

EXAMPLE   The **team shares** the field with **its** opponent.
[shares, its, singular]

EXAMPLE   The **team share their** jokes with one another.
[share, their, plural]

PRACTICE Forming Plural Nouns

Write the plural form of each noun.

1. mailbox
2. belief
3. country
4. banana
5. leaf

6. valley
7. bush
8. mother-in-law
9. potato
10. radio

Write each collective noun. Label it S *if it's singular and* P *if it's plural.*

1. The science club meets after school.
2. The jury vote by secret ballot.
3. The Sanchez family goes to all the football games.
4. The teaching staff plans the graduation ceremonies.
5. The team take their positions on the field.
6. The committee interview community leaders.
7. The crowd cheers.
8. The class give their reports.
9. The herd enters the barn.
10. The orchestra tune their instruments.

2.3 POSSESSIVE NOUNS

A noun can show ownership or possession of things or qualities. This kind of noun is called a possessive noun.

A **possessive noun** tells who or what owns or has something.

Possessive nouns may be common nouns or proper nouns. They may also be singular or plural. Notice the possessive nouns in the following sentences:

SINGULAR NOUN	**Rita** has a book about baseball.
SINGULAR POSSESSIVE NOUN	**Rita's** book is about baseball.
PLURAL NOUN	Several **cities** have baseball teams.
PLURAL POSSESSIVE NOUN	These **cities'** teams attract fans.

Possessive nouns are formed in one of two ways. To form the possessive of singular nouns and plural nouns not ending in *s*, add an apostrophe and *s* (*'s*). To form the possessive of plural nouns ending in *s*, add just an apostrophe at the end of the word.

FORMING POSSESSIVE NOUNS

NOUNS	TO FORM POSSESSIVE	EXAMPLES
All singular nouns; plural nouns not ending in *s*	Add an apostrophe and *s* (*'s*).	a girl—a girl**'s** name Germany—Germany**'s** exports the bus—the bus**'s** capacity Ms. Ames—Ms. Ames**'s** class children—children**'s** toys women—women**'s** coats
Plural nouns ending in *s*	Add just an apostrophe (') at the end of the plural noun.	babies—babies**'** birth weight the Joneses—the Joneses**'** car

GRAMMAR / USAGE / MECHANICS

PRACTICE Writing Possessive Nouns

Write the possessive form of the noun in parentheses.

1. The teacher read (Doris) composition.
2. I took my little brother to the (children) story hour at the library.
3. The (Barkleys) house stands on the corner.
4. Is (Dallas) climate hot enough for you?
5. My (parents) cars are parked in the driveway.
6. The (judge) decision is final.
7. You will find (men) suits on the third floor.
8. Return this key to the (boys) locker room.
9. I have seen many of (Florida) tourist attractions.
10. I got (Tiger Woods) autograph!

2.4 RECOGNIZING PLURALS, POSSESSIVES, AND CONTRACTIONS

Most plural nouns, all possessive nouns, and certain contractions end with the sound of *s*. These words may sound alike, but their spellings and meanings are different.

Chapter 2 Nouns **87**

NOUN FORMS AND CONTRACTIONS

	EXAMPLE	MEANING
Plural Noun	The **students** wrote a play.	more than one student
Plural Possessive Noun	The **students'** play is good.	the play by several students
Singular Possessive Noun	I saw the **student's** performance.	the performance of one student
Contraction	This **student's** the author. This **student's** written other plays.	This student is the author. This student has written other plays.

A **contraction** is a word made by combining two words and leaving out one or more letters. An apostrophe shows where the letters have been omitted.

Plural nouns don't have an apostrophe. Contractions and singular possessive nouns look exactly alike. Some plural possessive nouns end with 's, and some end with just an apostrophe. You can tell these words apart by the way they're used in a sentence.

NOUN FORMS AND CONTRACTIONS

PLURAL NOUNS	CONTRACTIONS	SINGULAR POSSESSIVE NOUNS	PLURAL POSSESSIVE NOUNS
speakers	speaker's	speaker's	speakers'
women	woman's	woman's	women's
echoes	echo's	echo's	echoes'
countries	country's	country's	countries'

Identify the italicized word in each sentence by writing plural noun, singular possessive noun, plural possessive noun, *or* contraction.

1. The *nurses'* committee will meet on Monday.
2. *Keely's* parents attend all her softball games.
3. My *aunt's* left for a trip to China.
4. Many *students* volunteer throughout the community.
5. No opponent has defeated the *girls'* basketball team.
6. Have you found the *dog's* leash?
7. *Harrison's* washing the family car.
8. The principal called the *boy's* parents.
9. The *astronauts'* voyage to the moon was a success.
10. The *Pattons* moved to Santa Fe last month.

2.5 APPOSITIVES   CCSS L.7.1a, c

An **appositive** is a noun that is placed next to another noun to identify it or add information about it.

EXAMPLE   James Madison's wife, **Dolley,** was a famous first lady.

The noun *Dolley* identifies the noun next to it, *wife.* In this sentence, *Dolley* is an appositive.

An **appositive phrase** is a group of words that includes an appositive and other words that modify the appositive.

EXAMPLE   Madison, **our fourth president,** held many other offices.

The words *our* and *fourth* modify the appositive *president.* The phrase *our fourth president* is an appositive phrase. It identifies the noun *Madison.*

An appositive or an appositive phrase can appear anywhere in a sentence as long as it appears next to the noun it identifies.

GRAMMAR / USAGE / MECHANICS

Our fourth president, Madison held many other offices.

Many historians have studied the life of Madison, **our fourth president.**

Appositives and appositive phrases are usually set off with commas. If the appositive is essential to the meaning of the sentence, however, commas are not used.

EXAMPLE Madison's friend **Thomas Jefferson** was president before Madison.

EXAMPLE Madison's father, **James Madison,** was a plantation owner.

Obviously, Madison had more than one friend, so the appositive, *Thomas Jefferson,* is needed to identify this particular friend. No commas are needed. However, Madison had only one father. The father's name is not needed to identify him. Therefore, commas are needed.

PRACTICE **Identifying Appositives**

Write each sentence. Underline the appositive or appositive phrase and add appropriate commas. Circle the noun the appositive identifies.

1. Manuel Ortiz an artist will display his works at the library.
2. Jane Nakamura the president's assistant spoke at the banquet.
3. The entertainer Will Rogers was famous for his political jokes.
4. In euchre a lively card game jacks are the high cards.
5. Mr. Wells explained his latest invention a time machine.
6. A mystery writer Agatha Christie composed clever plots.
7. Aunt Carmella my mother's sister is a veterinarian in San Antonio.
8. My favorite athlete is the baseball player Ken Griffey Jr.
9. Harry's dog a cocker spaniel won a blue ribbon.
10. An industrious young man Jimmy already runs his own business.

Proofreading

Rewrite the following passage, correcting errors in spelling, capitalization, grammar, and usage. Add any missing punctuation. Write legibly to be sure one letter is not mistaken for another. There are ten errors.

Gary Soto

¹Gary Soto grew up in Fresno, California. ²Sotos grandparents were born in Mexico and worked in the United States. ³His parent's were born in the United States. ⁴Soto often heard his family and friends speak Spanish, but Soto never learned Spanish in school.

⁵Soto read a poem, "Unwanted," by the poet edward field. ⁶Then he wrote poetry. ⁷Soto also wrote storys. ⁸At the age of twenty, he enrolled at California State University. ⁹At the university, Philip Levine another poet taught Soto more about poetry.

¹⁰Soto has achieved sucess as a poet. ¹¹This poets won many awards for his writing. ¹²The Academy of American Poets award prizes every year. ¹³Soto won a prize in 1975. ¹⁴Another organization the Guggenheim Foundation gave him money for a year in Mexico. ¹⁵Gabriel García Márquez a Colombian writer influenced Gary Soto.

Kinds of Nouns

Write each noun. Label the common nouns C *and the proper nouns* P.

1. The monarch butterfly travels four thousand miles during its migration.
2. Many sporting events are held at the Meadowlands in New Jersey.
3. Anika values the love of her family, her friendship with Ricardi, and the relaxation of an afternoon without homework.
4. Susan B. Anthony fought for the rights of women.
5. A psychiatrist is a medical doctor with four additional years of preparation in a hospital.

Write the possessive form of the noun in parentheses.

6. Do you like this (artist) style?

7. We went directly to the (boys) shoe department.

8. The (Harrises) van is parked in the driveway.

9. (Mwanakweli) flower business showed a profit in the first year.

10. The heavy rain seeped through the (tents) fabric.

11. One of (Arkansas) tourist attractions is Mammoth Springs.

12. The (children) toys were scattered everywhere.

13. Did you enjoy (Ross) report on turtles?

14. The (photographer) subject, a three-year-old girl, smiled at her puppy.

15. Ms. Montaldo belongs to the (nurses) association.

POSTTEST Recognizing Plurals, Possessives, and Contractions

Identify the italicized word in each sentence by writing plural noun, singular possessive noun, plural possessive noun, *or* contraction.

16. We're collecting *children's* toys for the hospital.

17. *Tecumseh's* diplomatic skills unified tribes from Florida to the Great Lakes.

18. *Dad's* worked at the same job for fifteen years.

19. Which of these *singers* is your favorite?

20. The *workers'* helmets were bright yellow.

21. I put some food in the *hamster's* cage.

22. Ms. *Esteban's* our new principal.

23. The *car's* brakes are in need of repair.

24. I found three *robins'* nests in the garden.

25. The *Wilsons* have two dalmation puppies.

GRAMMAR / USAGE / MECHANICS

Write the appositive or appositive phrase in each sentence.

26. Everyone likes Mr. Swallow, our band director.

27. The third store from the corner, a bakery, is our destination.

28. Our best player, Jason Tran, broke his ankle.

29. A round tent, the yurt is a Mongolian house.

30. The architect Frank Lloyd Wright designed a house over a waterfall.

31. An "unsinkable" ship, the *Titanic* hit an iceberg on its first voyage and sank.

32. The popular singer Linda Ronstadt performs in a variety of musical styles.

33. The city of Shanghai lies at the mouth of China's longest river, the Yangtze.

34. The American colonist David Bushnell built a submarine in 1776.

35. A starchy vegetable, the potato is also a source of vitamins.

Verbs

··

PRETEST   Action Verbs and Linking Verbs

Write each verb. Label the action verbs A *and the linking verbs* L.

1. The temperature rose to a hundred.
2. Dorothy remembered the dream.
3. The actor's face looks familiar.
4. Enrico looked into the next room.
5. The children were quiet.
6. Every culture has its own myths, legends, and fairy tales.
7. The weather grew cold.
8. The twins are visiting their grandparents.
9. Maria Tallchief became a famous ballerina.
10. Our cat has disappeared again.

PRETEST Direct Objects, Indirect Objects, Predicate Nouns, and Predicate Adjectives

Identify the italicized word in each sentence by writing direct object, indirect object, predicate noun, *or* predicate adjective.

11. Ants at a picnic are *pests.*
12. The workers built a *house.*
13. A tornado's winds are *dangerous.*
14. The new mother fed her seven *infants* formula from a bottle.
15. Tiger Woods has shown the *world* his talent.
16. The science field trip was *sensational.*
17. Follow your favorite *sports* on this channel.
18. Mother Teresa was a religious *woman.*
19. We rode a *train* from Boston to Providence.
20. The ancient Roman gladiator was a powerful *fighter.*

PRETEST Present and Past Tenses and Progressive Forms

Write the verb. Then write present tense, past tense, present progressive, *or* past progressive *to identify it.*

21. Tom Whittaker, a man with an artificial right foot, was climbing Mount Everest.
22. Athletes in ancient Greece participated in the first Olympic Games.
23. The human hyoid bone, a bone above the larynx, touches no other bone.
24. Sumiko and her brother were building a tree house.
25. Kou was making a pumpkin pie with his father.
26. These birds fly south for the winter.
27. Someone measured the depth of the Pacific Ocean.
28. We are recording our thoughts in our journals.
29. Ogun, a seventh-grader, is acting in plays.
30. I am enjoying my vacation.

Write the verb. Then write present perfect, past perfect, future, *or* future perfect *to identify it.*

31. By two o'clock, we had finished our chores.
32. We shall visit the dinosaur display at the museum.
33. Emily's neighbor has raised cattle all her life.
34. The student council has decorated the gymnasium.
35. Who will win the next election?
36. The Egyptian mummy had vanished from the tomb.
37. By this time tomorrow, I shall have finished my report.
38. The train will have departed by ten o'clock tonight.
39. We have attended every football game this season.
40. The two actors had rehearsed the play for five weeks.

PRETEST **Irregular Verbs**

Write the correct verb form from the choices in parentheses.

41. We (flew, flown) our kites on the windiest day in March.
42. All the campers (swam, swum) a mile on Friday afternoon.
43. The sprinter had (sprang, sprung) out of the blocks in record time.
44. The boxer has (hit, hitted) the punching bag one hundred times this morning.
45. A dreadful storm (began, begun) just after midnight.
46. The small fangs of the centipede have (stinged, stung) me.
47. Antony had (cut, cutted) the lawn with the lawnmower.
48. The Morgan twins have (sang, sung) in the choir for three years.
49. Oniwaki has (spoke, spoken) three languages in one conversation!
50. The balloon (burst, bursted).

3.1 ACTION VERBS

You may have heard the movie director's call for "lights, camera, *action!*" The actions in movies and plays can be expressed by verbs. If a word expresses action and tells what a subject does, it's an action verb.

An **action verb** is a word that expresses action. An action verb may be made up of more than one word.

Notice the action verbs in the following sentences.

EXAMPLE   The director **shouts** at the members of the cast.

EXAMPLE   The lights **are flashing** above the stage.

EXAMPLE   The audience **arrived** in time for the performance.

EXAMPLE   Several singers **have memorized** the lyrics of a song.

Action verbs can express physical actions, such as *shout* and *arrive.* They can also express mental activities, such as *memorize* and *forget.*

ACTION VERBS	
PHYSICAL	shout, flash, arrive, talk, applaud, act, sing, dance
MENTAL	remember, forget, think, memorize, read, dream, appreciate

Have, has, and *had* are often used before other verbs. They can also be used as action verbs when they tell that the subject owns or holds something.

EXAMPLE   The actors already **have** their costumes.

EXAMPLE   The director **has** a script in her back pocket.

EXAMPLE   Rosa **had** a theater program from 1920.

Write the action verbs.

1. Mom and Dad play golf on Saturday.
2. Six juicy hamburgers sizzled on the grill.
3. The workers cleaned the pool last week.
4. David had scored twelve points.
5. Our neighbors have a new car.
6. The ceremony began at two o'clock.
7. The cafeteria staff prepares lunch for the entire school.
8. Serena has read thirty books this year.
9. The icy rain blew through the open window.
10. Josh and his sister are arranging the flowers.

3.2 TRANSITIVE AND INTRANSITIVE VERBS

In some sentences, the predicate consists of only an action verb.

EXAMPLE   The actor **rehearsed.**

Most sentences provide more information. The predicate often names who or what receives the action of the verb.

EXAMPLE   The actor rehearsed his **lines** from the play.

The word *lines* tells what the actor rehearsed. *Lines* is a direct object.

A **direct object** receives the action of a verb. It answers the question *whom?* or *what?* after an action verb.

A sentence may have a compound direct object. That is, a sentence may have more than one direct object.

EXAMPLE   We saw **Maurice** and **Inez** in the audience.

When an action verb transfers action to a direct object, the verb is transitive. When an action verb has no direct object, the verb is intransitive.

A **transitive verb** has a direct object.
An **intransitive verb** does not have a direct object.

Most action verbs can be transitive or intransitive. A verb can be labeled transitive or intransitive only by examining its use in a particular sentence.

EXAMPLE   The audience **applauds** the actors. [transitive]

EXAMPLE   The audience **applauds** loudly. [intransitive]

PRACTICE Recognizing Transitive and Intransitive Verbs

For each sentence, write the action verb. Then write T *if the verb is transitive or* I *if the verb is intransitive. If the verb is transitive, write the direct object or objects.*

1. A transitive verb has a direct object.
2. Jason forgot his homework.
3. Three plastic deer stood in the garden.
4. Horatio achieved his success with hard work and luck.
5. The stone goose wore a bright yellow raincoat.
6. The porpoises jump through hoops.
7. The high school drama club performed the play for the middle school students.
8. The baby cried loudly from her crib in the next room.
9. Jackie ordered a vanilla shake and a hot dog with mustard.
10. Little Miss Muffet sat on a tuffet.

3.3 INDIRECT OBJECTS

A direct object answers the question *whom?* or *what?* after an action verb.

EXAMPLE Friends sent **flowers.**

In some sentences, an indirect object also follows an action verb.

An **indirect object** answers the question *to whom?* or *for whom?* or *to what?* or *for what?* an action is done.

EXAMPLE Friends sent the **actors** flowers.

The direct object in the sentence is *flowers.* The indirect object is *actors. Actors* answers the question *to whom?* after the action verb *sent.*

A sentence may have a compound indirect object. In the sentence below, *cast* and *orchestra* are indirect objects. The direct object is *thanks.*

EXAMPLE Ms. Ortiz gave the **cast** and the **orchestra** her thanks.

An indirect object appears only in a sentence that has a direct object. Two clues can help you recognize an indirect object. First, an indirect object always comes between the verb and the direct object. Second, you can put the word *to* or *for* before an indirect object and change its position. The sentence will still have the same meaning, but it will no longer have an indirect object.

EXAMPLE Friends **sent** the **director flowers.** [*Director* **is an indirect object.**]

EXAMPLE Friends sent flowers **to the director.** [*Director* **is not an indirect object.**]

You know that in the first sentence *director* is the indirect object because it comes between the verb and the direct object and because it can be placed after the word *to,* as in the second sentence.

Write the indirect objects and underline them. Then write the direct objects.

1. Kareem gave the crowd a big smile.
2. The eager salesperson sold the couple a new car.
3. The company promises its employees annual pay increases.
4. Ms. Nishimura served her guests a traditional meal.
5. Sharlene made her brother and his friend costumes for the play.
6. Mrs. Kowalski fed her favorite horse a carrot.
7. The Harrisons have left the university their art collection.
8. The parents' club bought the school three new computers.
9. Muhammad writes his cousin a letter once a month.
10. Satch threw the last batter a slow curveball.

3.4 LINKING VERBS AND PREDICATE WORDS

A **linking verb** connects the subject of a sentence with a noun or an adjective in the predicate.

EXAMPLE Juana Ortiz **was** the **director.**

EXAMPLE Ms. Ortiz **is imaginative.**

In the first sentence, the verb *was* links the noun *director* to the subject. *Director* identifies the subject. In the second sentence, the verb *is* links the adjective *imaginative* to the subject. *Imaginative* describes the subject.

A **predicate noun** is a noun that follows a linking verb. It renames or identifies the subject.

A **predicate adjective** is an adjective that follows a linking verb. It describes, or modifies, the subject.

A sentence may contain a compound predicate noun or a compound predicate adjective.

EXAMPLE   Ms. Ortiz is a **teacher** and a **musician.** [compound predicate noun]

EXAMPLE   Ms. Ortiz is **stern** but **fair.** [compound predicate adjective]

COMMON LINKING VERBS			
be (am, is, are, was, were) become	seem appear look	taste feel smell	sound grow turn

Most of these verbs can also be used as action verbs.

EXAMPLE   The director **sounded** angry. [linking verb]

EXAMPLE   The director **sounded** the alarm. [action verb]

NOTE   Two other linking verbs are *remain* and *stay*.

PRACTICE   **Identifying Verbs, Predicate Nouns, and Predicate Adjectives**

For each sentence, write the verb. Label the verb A if it's an action verb or L if it's a linking verb. If it's a linking verb, write the predicate noun or the predicate adjective. Label a predicate noun PN. Label a predicate adjective PA.

1. Douglas looks handsome in his pirate costume.
2. Carly is a singer and a dancer.
3. A shadowy figure appeared in the gloom.
4. The band sounds wonderful today.
5. Suddenly Zelda smelled smoke.
6. Ouida Sebestyen became a writer late in life.

7. Mr. Menendez grows huge pumpkins in his garden.

8. Sereta felt nervous before her performance.

9. Harry's horse seems a sure winner in the next race.

10. The leaves turn red and yellow in the fall.

3.5 PRESENT AND PAST TENSES

The verb in a sentence expresses action. It also tells when the action takes place. The form of a verb that shows the time of the action is called the **tense** of the verb.

The **present tense** of a verb expresses action that happens regularly. It can also express a general truth.

EXAMPLE   A great actor **wins** awards.

In the present tense, the base form of a verb is used with all plural subjects and the pronouns *I* and *you.* For singular subjects other than *I* and *you, -s* or *-es* is usually added to the base form of the verb. Remember that a verb must agree in number with its subject.

PRESENT TENSE FORMS	
SINGULAR	**PLURAL**
I **walk.**	We **walk.**
You **walk.**	You **walk.**
He, she, *or* it **walks.**	They **walk.**

The **past tense** of a verb expresses action that already happened.

The past tense of many verbs is formed by adding *-d* or *-ed* to the base form of the verb.

EXAMPLE   The actors **rehearsed.** Ms. Ortiz **directed.**

For each sentence, write the verb. Then write present *or* past *to identify its tense.*

1. I like pizza with everything.
2. James and Betsy waited twenty minutes for the bus.
3. Millions of people around the world are poor.
4. You borrowed too many books from the library.
5. Tulips and daffodils bloom in the spring.
6. I enjoyed my visit to Aunt Ethel's horse farm.
7. The cruise passengers dine between six and eight.
8. Captain James Cook explored the South Pacific in the eighteenth century.
9. Amos or Tara mows the lawn once a week.
10. The Pattersons moved here in April.

3.6 MAIN VERBS AND HELPING VERBS

Verbs have four principal parts that are used to form all tenses. Notice how the principal parts of a verb are formed.

PRINCIPAL PARTS OF VERBS			
BASE FORM	**PRESENT PARTICIPLE**	**PAST**	**PAST PARTICIPLE**
act	acting	acted	acted

You can use the base form and the past alone to form the present and past tenses. The present participle and the past participle can be combined with helping verbs to form other tenses.

A **helping verb** helps the main verb express action or make a statement.

A **verb phrase** consists of one or more helping verbs followed by a main verb.

EXAMPLE Telma **is acting** in another play today.

The word *is* is the helping verb, and the present participle *acting* is the main verb. Together they form a verb phrase.

The most common helping verbs are *be, have,* and *do.* Forms of the helping verb *be* are *am, is,* and *are* in the present and *was* and *were* in the past. These helping verbs often combine with the present participle of the main verb.

BE AND THE PRESENT PARTICIPLE

SINGULAR	PLURAL	SINGULAR	PLURAL
I **am** learning.	We **are** learning.	I **was** learning.	We **were** learning.
You **are** learning.	You **are** learning.	You **were** learning.	You **were** learning.
She **is** learning.	They **are** learning.	He **was** learning.	They **were** learning.

The helping verb *have* combines with the past participle of the main verb. Forms of the helping verb *have* are *have* and *has* in the present and *had* in the past.

HAVE AND THE PAST PARTICIPLE

SINGULAR	PLURAL	SINGULAR	PLURAL
I **have** learned.	We **have** learned.	I **had** learned.	We **had** learned.
You **have** learned.	You **have** learned.	You **had** learned.	You **had** learned.
She **has** learned.	They **have** learned.	He **had** learned.	They **had** learned.

Forms of the helping verb *do* are *do* and *does* in the present and *did* in the past. The helping verb *do* combines with the base form of a verb: *I do believe you. She does believe you. They did believe you.*

NOTE   Other helping verbs are *can, could, may, might, must, should,* and *would.*

PRACTICE **Identifying Main Verbs and Helping Verbs**

Write each verb phrase. Underline the helping verb. Write base form, present participle, *or* past participle *to identify the main verb.*

1. DeeDee is planning her science project.
2. Silvia Chin has solved several mysteries for the police.
3. The students were measuring the area of their classroom.
4. The pioneers had journeyed over two thousand miles.
5. Did you feed the dog?
6. I am reading a good baseball story.
7. We do need your help, Jason.
8. A boy with red hair was walking across the football field.
9. The mayor and the city council are cooperating on the project.
10. Have you discovered the secret of success?

3.7 PROGRESSIVE FORMS

You know that the present tense of a verb can express action that occurs repeatedly. To express action that is taking place at the present time, use the present progressive form of the verb.

The **present progressive form** of a verb expresses action or a condition that is continuing in the present.

EXAMPLE   Althea **is finishing** her song.

The present progressive form of a verb consists of the helping verb *am*, *are*, or *is* and the present participle of the main verb.

PRESENT PROGRESSIVE FORMS	
SINGULAR	**PLURAL**
I **am watching.**	We **are watching.**
You **are watching.**	You **are watching.**
He, she, *or* it **is watching.**	They **are watching.**

The **past progressive form** of a verb expresses action or a condition that was continuing at some time in the past.

EXAMPLE   We **were watching** a scary show.

The past progressive form of a verb consists of the helping verb *was* or *were* and the present participle of the main verb.

PAST PROGRESSIVE FORMS	
SINGULAR	**PLURAL**
I **was working.**	We **were working.**
You **were working.**	You **were working.**
He, she, *or* it **was working.**	They **were working.**

Rewrite the sentence using the progressive form of the verb. If the verb is in the present tense, change it to the present progressive form. If the verb is in the past tense, change it to the past progressive form.

1. Sean plays computer games.
2. The horses trotted around the track.
3. This machine worked yesterday.
4. Serena hurried to her dance class.
5. Harry and Sally take piano lessons.
6. The Ryans vacation at the beach.
7. Sharon and Joel cleaned the garage.
8. Courtney visits her grandmother.
9. I watch television with my best friend.
10. Billy typed a letter to his cousin.

3.8 PRESENT PERFECT AND PAST PERFECT TENSES

The **present perfect tense** of a verb expresses action that happened at an indefinite time in the past.

EXAMPLE   The actor **has rehearsed** for many hours.

EXAMPLE   Lori and Pam **have watched** *Grease* five times.

The present perfect tense consists of the helping verb *have* or *has* and the past participle of the main verb.

PRESENT PERFECT TENSE	
SINGULAR	**PLURAL**
I **have watched.**	We **have watched.**
You **have watched.**	You **have watched.**
He, she, *or* it **has watched.**	They **have watched.**

The **past perfect tense** of a verb expresses action that happened before another action or event in the past.

The past perfect tense is often used in sentences that contain a past-tense verb in another part of the sentence.

EXAMPLE   The actors **had rehearsed** for many weeks.

EXAMPLE   We **had** just **arrived** when the play **started.**

The past perfect tense of a verb consists of the helping verb *had* and the past participle of the main verb.

PAST PERFECT TENSE	
SINGULAR	**PLURAL**
I **had started.**	We **had started.**
You **had started.**	You **had started.**
He, she, *or* it **had started.**	They **had started.**

PRACTICE   Identifying Perfect Tenses

Write the verb. Then write present perfect *or* past perfect *to identify the tense.*

1. Harry has saved a hundred dollars for a new bike.
2. The chef had decorated the wedding cake earlier in the day.
3. I have wanted a camera of my own for a long time.
4. Jerry has checked his spelling twice.
5. You have mentioned your fabulous aunt Harriet many times.
6. I had packed my lunch during the evening news.
7. Kay and Ben have collected several hundred aluminum cans.
8. Davis had bunted on his last trip to the plate.

9. Mitsuko has combed her hair three times.

10. Around midnight the butler had locked all the doors and windows.

3.9 EXPRESSING FUTURE TIME

The **future tense** of a verb expresses action that will take place in the future.

EXAMPLE   We **shall attend** the performance.

EXAMPLE   The actors **will show** their talents.

The future tense of a verb is formed by using the helping verb *will* before the base form of a verb. The helping verb *shall* is sometimes used when the subject is *I* or *we*.

There are other ways to show that an action will happen in the future. *Tomorrow, next year,* and *later* are all words that indicate a future time. These words are called **time words,** and they may be used with the present tense to express future time.

EXAMPLE   Our show **opens next week.**

EXAMPLE   **Tomorrow** we **start** rehearsals.

The present progressive form can also be used with time words to express future actions.

EXAMPLE   Our show **is opening next week.**

EXAMPLE   **Tomorrow** we **are starting** rehearsals.

Another way to talk about the future is with the future perfect tense.

The **future perfect tense** of a verb expresses action that will be completed before another future event begins.

EXAMPLE   By Thursday I **shall have performed** six times.

EXAMPLE   The production **will have closed** by next week.

The future perfect tense is formed by using *will have* or *shall have* before the past participle of a verb.

Identifying Verb Tenses

Write the verb. Then write present, future, present progressive, *or* future perfect *to identify the verb tense.*

1. We shall arrive in Denver around noon.
2. The new comedy show *Oscar and Larry* begins next Monday night on Channel 3.
3. Bonita's flute lessons are ending in April.
4. By October the construction workers will have finished the new school.
5. Workers in the downtown area will watch the parade from their office windows.
6. Dad is interviewing for a new job tomorrow.
7. I go to the dentist's office at three o'clock today.
8. I shall have applied three coats of paint to these walls by tomorrow afternoon.
9. Marge and Homer will be the team leaders.
10. By the end of this course, you will have learned the foxtrot and the waltz.

GRAMMAR / USAGE / MECHANICS

3.10 ACTIVE AND PASSIVE VOICE

A verb is in the **active voice** when the subject performs the action of the verb.

EXAMPLE   Thornton Wilder **composed** that play.

A verb is in the **passive voice** when the subject receives the action of the verb.

EXAMPLE   That play **was composed** by Thornton Wilder.

In the first example, the author, Thornton Wilder, seems more important because *Thornton Wilder* is the subject of the sentence. In the second example, the play seems more important because *play* is the subject of the sentence.

Notice that verbs in the passive voice consist of a form of *be* and the past participle. Often a phrase beginning with *by* follows the verb in the passive voice.

EXAMPLE   I am puzzled **by your question. [passive voice]**

EXAMPLE   Your question puzzles me. **[active voice]**

EXAMPLE   The puppy is frightened **by loud noises. [passive voice]**

EXAMPLE   Loud noises frighten the puppy. **[active voice]**

EXAMPLE   Plays are performed **by actors. [passive voice]**

EXAMPLE   Actors perform plays. **[active voice]**

EXAMPLE   This painting was purchased **by Ms. Jones. [passive voice]**

EXAMPLE   Ms. Jones purchased this painting. **[active voice]**

The active voice is usually a stronger, more direct way to express ideas. Use the passive voice if you want to stress the receiver of the action or if you don't know who performed the action.

EXAMPLE   *Our Town* **was performed. [You may want to stress the play.]**

EXAMPLE   The actors **were fired. [You may not know who fired the actors.]**

PRACTICE   Using Active and Passive Voice

Rewrite each sentence, changing the verb from active to passive or from passive to active.

1. Most of the town was destroyed by a tornado.
2. Elias Howe invented the sewing machine.
3. Radium and polonium were discovered by Marie Curie.
4. The speech was delivered by Dr. Galbraith.
5. Mario Mendoza played a minuet by Mozart.
6. Irving Berlin composed the song "God Bless America."
7. The song was performed many times by Kate Smith.
8. Voters often reject tax proposals.
9. The judge settles all disputes.
10. These flowers were planted by our 4-H club.

3.11 IRREGULAR VERBS

The irregular verbs listed here are grouped according to the way their past tense and past participle are formed.

IRREGULAR VERBS			
PATTERN	BASE FORM	PAST	PAST PARTICIPLE
One vowel changes to form the past and the past participle.	begin	began	begun
	drink	drank	drunk
	ring	rang	rung
	shrink	shrank *or* shrunk	shrunk
	sing	sang	sung
	sink	sank	sunk
	spring	sprang *or* sprung	sprung
	swim	swam	swum
The past and the past participle are the same.	bring	brought	brought
	build	built	built
	buy	bought	bought
	catch	caught	caught
	creep	crept	crept
	feel	felt	felt
	fight	fought	fought
	find	found	found
	get	got	got *or* gotten
	have	had	had
	hold	held	held
	keep	kept	kept
	lay	laid	laid
	lead	led	led
	leave	left	left
	lend	lent	lent
	lose	lost	lost
	make	made	made
	meet	met	met
	pay	paid	paid
	say	said	said

PATTERN	BASE FORM	PAST	PAST PARTICIPLE
The past and	seek	sought	sought
the past	sell	sold	sold
participle are	send	sent	sent
the same.	sit	sat	sat
	sleep	slept	slept
	spend	spent	spent
	spin	spun	spun
	stand	stood	stood
	sting	stung	stung
	swing	swung	swung
	teach	taught	taught
	tell	told	told
	think	thought	thought
	win	won	won

PRACTICE Using Irregular Verbs I

Write the correct verb form from the choices in parentheses.

1. The center fielder (catched, caught) several fly balls.
2. The chorus (sang, sung) three selections from *My Fair Lady.*
3. The last bell (rang, rung) at three o'clock.
4. How many people have (swam, swum) the English Channel?
5. The jockey (lead, led) his horse to the winner's circle.
6. Ms. Delgado has (teached, taught) us many useful things about photography.
7. Mary Lou had (brung, brought) treats for everyone.
8. This wool sweater has (shrank, shrunk) two sizes.
9. Lars (drank, drunk) a quart of milk after the game.
10. The Tigers had (winned, won) the championship for the last three years.

3.12 MORE IRREGULAR VERBS

Here are some more irregular verbs.

	IRREGULAR VERBS		
PATTERN	BASE FORM	PAST	PAST PARTICIPLE
The base form and the past participle are the same.	become	became	become
	come	came	come
	run	ran	run
The past ends in *ew,* and the past participle ends in *wn.*	blow	blew	blown
	draw	drew	drawn
	fly	flew	flown
	grow	grew	grown
	know	knew	known
	throw	threw	thrown
The past participle ends in *en.*	bite	bit	bitten *or* bit
	break	broke	broken
	choose	chose	chosen
	drive	drove	driven
	eat	ate	eaten
	fall	fell	fallen
	freeze	froze	frozen
	give	gave	given
	ride	rode	ridden
	rise	rose	risen
	see	saw	seen
	shake	shook	shaken
	speak	spoke	spoken
	steal	stole	stolen
	take	took	taken
	write	wrote	written

GRAMMAR / USAGE / MECHANICS

PATTERN	BASE FORM	PAST	PAST PARTICIPLE
The past and	be	was, were	been
the past	do	did	done
participle don't	go	went	gone
follow any	lie	lay	lain
pattern.	tear	tore	torn
	wear	wore	worn
The base form,	burst	burst	burst
the past, and	cost	cost	cost
the past	cut	cut	cut
participle are	hit	hit	hit
the same.	hurt	hurt	hurt
	let	let	let
	put	put	put
	read	read	read
	set	set	set
	spread	spread	spread

GRAMMAR / USAGE / MECHANICS

PRACTICE Using Irregular Verbs II

Write the correct verb form from the choices in parentheses.

1. The answer (came, come) to me in a flash.
2. The twins have (broke, broken) Mom's favorite teacup.
3. Nathan (ran, run) the three blocks to the library.
4. I (saw, seen) that movie last week.
5. The math team has (went, gone) to a competition in River City.
6. Cinderella had finally (became, become) a princess.
7. Dad has (wore, worn) the same suit for five years.
8. The children (bursted, burst) all the balloons.
9. I never (did, done) a back dive before.
10. Little Freddy had (fell, fallen) into a mud puddle.

Rewrite the following passage, correcting errors in spelling, capitalization, grammar, and usage. Add any missing punctuation. Write legibly to be sure one letter is not mistaken for another. There are ten errors.

Carl Sandburg

[1]Carl Sandburg liked simple poems [2]His parents came from Sweden. [3]They had chose the United States as their home. [4]Sandburg grew up in Illinois. [5]By the age of eighteen, he had leaved home. [6]He traveled across the country, and he often catched rides on trains.

[7]At the age of twenty, Sandburg joined the army. [8]He served breifly in Puerto Rico. [9]Then he returned home and attended Lombard College.

[10]As a boy, Sandburg had thunk about the name Carl. [11]It sounded too foreign, so he taked the name Charles. [12]At the age of thirty, he married a teacher. [13]She liked the name Carl. [14]He used this name again, and he become proud of his Swedish ancestors.

[15]Sandburg won the Pulitzer Prize for poetry in 1951. [16]He did not just write poems. [17]He also gone across the country. [18]He collected and sung American folk songs.

Write each verb. Label the action verbs A and the linking verbs L.

1. Chuon Chuon jogs for her health.
2. My uncle is a plumber.
3. Tomorrow Chuon Chuon and Verta have a softball practice.
4. Shelby feels unhappy.
5. Nick felt the dog's tongue on his hand.
6. Grass needs rain.
7. Without rain, grass turns yellow.
8. Mom is watering her plants.
9. Jaime has written his cousin a letter.
10. Antonia seems a friendly person.

POSTTEST Direct Objects, Indirect Objects, Predicate Nouns, and Predicate Adjectives

Identify the italicized word in each sentence by writing direct object, indirect object, predicate noun, *or* predicate adjective.

11. A screwdriver seems a useful *tool.*
12. The kindergarten student made his *mother* a present.
13. The heat grew *unbearable.*
14. The children catch *fireflies* on summer nights.
15. A crocodile is a large *reptile* with many teeth.
16. The students suddenly became *serious.*
17. This banana feels *mushy.*
18. The guide showed the *class* the new dinosaur exhibit.
19. Many movies and television series have dramatized western *heroes.*
20. The western hero often has a favorite *horse.*

Present and Past Tenses and Progressive Forms

Write the verb. Then write present tense, past tense, present progressive, *or* past progressive *to identify it.*

21. Developers planned the route of the first transcontinental road, the Lincoln Highway, in 1913.
22. The band members are practicing in the gym.
23. I am writing a report on hot-air balloons.
24. The fire destroyed the neighborhood flower shop.
25. In a single contraction, the heart pumps about two ounces of blood.
26. The stoplight was causing traffic problems.
27. The professional athletes were boasting about their talent.
28. Workers make bulletproof glass with two sheets of plate glass and a layer of resin.
29. Jake was studying for an important test.
30. The dinosaur exhibit is traveling from city to city.

POSTTEST **Perfect and Future Tenses**

Write the verb. Then write present perfect, past perfect, future, *or* future perfect *to identify it.*

31. Wildlife has disappeared from this area.
32. I shall greet the guests at the door.
33. I had finished my homework by six o'clock.
34. In the excitement, Mr. Parmesi had misplaced his key.
35. By next week, I will have memorized all my lines for the play.
36. The offer for a free can of dog food will expire next Monday.
37. The chef has selected the perfect ingredients for the taco salad.

38. By Thursday evening, the workers will have signed a new contract.

39. The passengers had boarded the ship early in the morning.

40. I have tested the trombone, the saxophone, the flute, and the trumpet.

POSTTEST **Irregular Verbs**

Write the correct verb form from the choices in parentheses.

41. The awards program (began, begun) at eight o'clock.

42. The Milwaukee Brewers (won, winned) the baseball game in the eighteenth inning!

43. Christopher Pike has (wrote, written) a number of scary stories.

44. The enormous Hoover Dam has (holded, held) back the waters of the Colorado River for more than fifty years.

45. I (drank, drunk) too many soft drinks.

46. The detective (catched, caught) the computer thief with a clever trap.

47. She had (wore, worn) her best dress to the awards ceremony.

48. A soft pad (broke, breaked) the fall of the pole-vaulter.

49. I (leaved, left) my umbrella on the bus.

50. Mom has (keeped, kept) every one of my letters.

Pronouns

....

PRETEST **Personal Pronouns**

Write each personal pronoun. Then write one of the following phrases to identify the pronoun: subject pronoun as subject, subject pronoun as predicate pronoun, object pronoun as direct object, object pronoun as indirect object.

1. The girl in the picture is I.
2. We saw her at the mall.
3. She handed me the notes from yesterday's science class.
4. You gave them a chance, but they wasted it.
5. The mysterious stranger was he, and I thanked him for the help.

Write the correct word or phrase from the choices in parentheses.

6. (You and I, You and me, I and you, Me and you) make a good team.
7. Su and (he, him) explored the cave together.
8. The store owner gave (he and I, I and he, him and me, me and him) part-time jobs.
9. (She, Her) and Mrs. Cranston share the garden chores and the vegetables.
10. Mr. Lusalah gave (he and she, him and her, he and her, him and she) several old comic books.
11. (We, Us) newspaper carriers struggle with the heavy Sunday edition.
12. (Clare and I, Clare and me, I and Clare, Me and Clare) took photographs of the race, and (Samantha and they, Samantha and them) developed the pictures in a tiny darkroom.
13. Mom tested Charlie and (she, her) on their spelling words.
14. The most exciting actor was (he, him).
15. The scientist showed Zainab and (they, them) the fossil of a trilobite.

PRETEST Pronouns and Antecedents

Write each personal pronoun and its antecedent. If a pronoun doesn't have a clear antecedent, rewrite the numbered item to make the meaning clear.

16. The people light lamps during one festival to honor the man. They think he is important.
17. Prehistoric food gatherers tied logs together for rafts. Then they fished from them.

18. Eric and Carl met Rocknie and Romeo at the skating rink. They were late.
19. Black Shawl rented a movie. She watched it in the living room.
20. They have strict safety rules at the local swimming pool.

PRETEST Identifying Pronouns

Write each pronoun. Then write possessive, indefinite, reflexive, intensive, interrogative, *or* demonstrative *to identify it.*

21. Grace drew this herself.
22. Whose are these?
23. Has anyone found mine?
24. Ms. Grimes takes her trash to the alley, but several leave theirs in the hallway.
25. The musicians themselves took their instruments to the repair shop.
26. All know the decision about that is yours.
27. Mr. McFadden bought himself a new tractor for his fields.
28. The great horned owl has fourteen bones in its neck.
29. What did the thieves steal?
30. The professional ballet dancers treated themselves to a rare night without a practice.

PRETEST Indefinite Pronouns

Write the subjects and the correct words from the choices in parentheses.

31. Everyone (wonder, wonders) about the accuracy of the story in the newspaper.
32. In my opinion, all of the action movies this summer (are, is) unrealistic.

33. Both of the doctors (tell, tells) the nurses about new procedures.
34. This morning everything (have, has) gone wrong.
35. (Do, Does) either of the magicians ask you for assistance?
36. Few of the students (have, has) volunteered yet.
37. All of the sugar (are, is) spilling onto the floor.
38. Why (were, was) none of the long jumpers ready for the event?
39. Anybody in the spelling bee (get, gets) only one chance for a correct spelling.
40. Several of the flooded areas (receive, receives) help from the government.

PRETEST Personal, Reflexive, Intensive, Interrogative, and Demonstrative Pronouns

Write the correct word from the choices in parentheses.

41. The young cowboy drove the cattle (hisself, himself).
42. Esi and (I, myself) learned about Neil Armstrong.
43. (Who, Whom) did the coach choose for the varsity squad?
44. (These, This) is a great day for the outdoor scavenger hunt.
45. Ms. Hammersmith promised Talika and (me, myself) some fruit from her cherry tree.
46. (Whose, Who's) is this?
47. The engineers (theirselves, themselves) examined the bridge.
48. Do (that, those) belong to you?
49. (Whose, Who's) brought refreshments?
50. The crossword puzzle stumped (us, ourselves).

4.1 PERSONAL PRONOUNS

A **pronoun** is a word that takes the place of one or more nouns.

EXAMPLE   Max likes books. **He** particularly enjoys novels.

EXAMPLE   Max and Irma like books. **They** particularly enjoy novels.

In the first example, the pronoun *He* replaces the noun *Max* as the subject of the sentence. In the second example, *They* replaces *Max and Irma.*

Pronouns that refer to people or things are called **personal pronouns.**

Some personal pronouns are used as the subjects of sentences. Others are used as the objects of verbs.

A **subject pronoun** is used as the subject of a sentence. It may also be used like a predicate noun, in which case it's called a predicate pronoun.

EXAMPLE   **I** enjoy a good book in my spare time. [subject]

EXAMPLE   **We** belong to a book club. [subject]

EXAMPLE   **She** gave a good book report. [subject]

EXAMPLE   **It** was about Andrew Jackson. [subject]

EXAMPLE   **They** especially like adventure stories. [subject]

EXAMPLE   The most popular author was **he.** [predicate pronoun]

An **object pronoun** may be a direct object or an indirect object.

EXAMPLE   The teacher praised **us.** [direct object]

EXAMPLE   Tell **me** a story. [indirect object]

EXAMPLE   The movie frightened **them.** [direct object]

EXAMPLE   The class wrote **her** a letter. [indirect object]

EXAMPLE   The story amuses **you.** [direct object]

EXAMPLE   The plot gives **him** an idea. [indirect object]

PERSONAL PRONOUNS		
	SINGULAR	**PLURAL**
Subject Pronouns	I you he, she, it	we you they
Object Pronouns	me you him, her, it	us you them

PRACTICE **Identifying Personal Pronouns**

Write each personal pronoun. Then write one of the following phrases to identify the pronoun: subject pronoun as subject, subject pronoun as predicate pronoun, object pronoun as direct object, object pronoun as indirect object.

1. They awarded her the prize.
2. We drove them to the airport.
3. I fixed him a tuna sandwich.
4. The person in the chicken costume was you!
5. They saw you and him at the mall.
6. He and she found it on the beach.
7. The winner of the essay contest was I.
8. It showed us the location of the treasure.
9. She helped you with the dishes.
10. You are giving me a headache.

4.2 USING PRONOUNS

Use subject pronouns in compound subjects. Use object pronouns in compound objects.

EXAMPLE **He** and Carmen wrote the report. [not *Him and Carmen*]

EXAMPLE Tell John and **me** about the report. [not *John and I*]

If you're not sure which form of the pronoun to use, read the sentence with only the pronoun as the subject or the object. Your ear will tell you which form is correct.

When the pronoun *I, we, me,* or *us* is part of a compound subject or object, *I, we, me,* or *us* should come last. (It's simply courteous to name yourself or the group of which you are a part last.)

EXAMPLE Lee and **I** played some new tunes. [not *I and Lee*]

EXAMPLE Country music interests Lee and **me.** [not *me and Lee*]

In formal writing and speech, use a subject pronoun after a linking verb.

EXAMPLE The writer of this report was **she.**

EXAMPLE It is **I.**

A pronoun and a noun may be used together. The form of the pronoun depends on its use in the sentence.

EXAMPLE **We** students read the book. [*We* is the subject.]

EXAMPLE The book delighted **us** readers. [*Us* is a direct object.]

Some sentences make incomplete comparisons. The form of the pronoun can affect the meaning of such sentences. In any incomplete comparison, use the form of the pronoun that would be correct if the comparison were complete.

EXAMPLE You like pizza better than **I** [like pizza].

EXAMPLE You like pizza better than [you like] **me.**

PRACTICE Using Subject and Object Pronouns

Write the correct word or phrase from the choices in parentheses.

1. Kareem will save Mr. Jerome and (we, us) seats in the bleachers.
2. (Jed and I, I and Jed, Me and Jed, Jed and me) fixed the bicycle ourselves.
3. The drama director assigned (we, us) volunteers jobs as ushers.

4. The coach told (Sally and I, I and Sally, me and Sally, Sally and me) the results of the tryouts for the volleyball team.
5. Ziggy and (we, us) took the subway to the zoo.
6. The principal asked Sheryl and (he, him) for help with the middle school handbook.
7. Mrs. Santini sent (she and I, I and she, me and her, her and me) to the office for supplies.
8. The contestants were (they and we, them and we, they and us, them and us).
9. (We, Us) volunteers will meet at the hospital after school.
10. Mrs. Feinstein fixed Isaac and (they, them) a snack.

4.3 PRONOUNS AND ANTECEDENTS

Read the following sentences. Can you tell to whom the pronoun *She* refers?

EXAMPLE   Louisa May Alcott wrote a novel about a young woman. **She** had three sisters.

The sentence is not clear because the word *She* could refer to either *Louisa May Alcott* or *a young woman*. Sometimes you must repeat a noun or rewrite a sentence to avoid confusion.

EXAMPLE   Louisa May Alcott wrote a novel about a young woman. **The young woman** had three sisters.

The word a pronoun refers to is called its **antecedent.** The word *antecedent* means "going before."

EXAMPLE   **Jo March** is the main character in *Little Women.* **She** writes stories. [*Jo March* **is the antecedent of the pronoun** *She.*]

EXAMPLE   **Meg, Beth,** and **Amy** are Jo's sisters. Jo writes **them** stories. [*Meg, Beth,* **and** *Amy* **are the antecedents of** *them.*]

When you use a pronoun, be sure it refers to its antecedent clearly. Be especially careful when you use the pronoun *they*. Read the following sentence.

EXAMPLE **They** have five books by Alcott at the school library.

The meaning of *They* is unclear. The sentence can be improved by rewriting it in the following way.

EXAMPLE The school library has five books by Alcott.

When you use pronouns, be sure they agree with their antecedents in **number** (singular or plural) and **gender.** The gender of a noun may be masculine (male), feminine (female), or neuter (referring to things).

EXAMPLE The Marches must face a death in the family. **They** face **it** with courage.

They is plural; it agrees with the plural antecedent *Marches*. *It* is singular and agrees with the singular antecedent *death*.

Write each personal pronoun and its antecedent. If a pronoun doesn't have a clear antecedent, rewrite the numbered item to make the meaning clear.

1. Ms. Johnson spoke to Mary about the science fair. She was enthusiastic.
2. Jody's grandparents are experts in motorcycle repair. They often talk to Jody about it.
3. They have no books about women in chemistry at the library.
4. Malcolm went to the mall with Jaleel. He needed some new shoes.
5. Myrna collects books about baseball history. She keeps them in a special bookcase.
6. They charge too much for the latest albums at Music Madness.
7. The Lloyds have adopted a boy and a girl. They love him and her equally.
8. In this geography book, they don't have up-to-date maps of Africa.
9. Todd has an expensive new bike. He takes good care of it.
10. The students filled the vases with flowers for the sick. Mrs. Shelby sent them to the nursing center.

4.4 POSSESSIVE PRONOUNS

You often use personal pronouns to replace nouns that are subjects or objects in sentences. You can use pronouns in place of possessive nouns, too.

A **possessive pronoun** is a pronoun that shows who or what has something. A possessive pronoun may take the place of a possessive noun.

Read the following sentences. Notice the possessive nouns and the possessive pronouns that replace them.

EXAMPLE   Lisa's class put on a play. **Her** class put on a play.

EXAMPLE   The idea was Lisa's. The idea was **hers.**

Possessive pronouns have two forms. One form is used before a noun. The other form is used alone.

POSSESSIVE PRONOUNS		
	SINGULAR	**PLURAL**
Used Before Nouns	my	our
	your	your
	her, his, its	their
Used Alone	mine	ours
	yours	yours
	hers, his, its	theirs

Possessive pronouns are not written with apostrophes. Don't confuse the possessive pronoun *its* with the word *it's*. *It's* is a contraction, or shortened form, of *it is* or *it has.*

EXAMPLE   **Its** popularity is growing. [possessive pronoun]

EXAMPLE   **It's** popular with many students. [contraction of *It is*]

EXAMPLE   **It's** succeeded on the stage. [contraction of *It has*]

Write the possessive pronouns.

1. These are their tickets. Where are ours?
2. This is his equipment. Theirs is in the lab.
3. Did you prefer her performance or his?
4. It's been a pleasure to meet your parents.
5. Is this jacket yours, or is it hers?
6. Will your mother or your dad pick us up after our game?
7. My best friend is staying at our house.
8. The dishwasher has finished its cycle.
9. Where are your coats? Here is mine.
10. Their new house will be smaller than yours.

4.5 INDEFINITE PRONOUNS

An **indefinite pronoun** is a pronoun that does not refer to a particular person, place, or thing.

EXAMPLE **Everybody** thinks about the plot.

Some indefinite pronouns are always singular. Others are always plural. A few may be either singular or plural.

SOME INDEFINITE PRONOUNS			
ALWAYS SINGULAR			**ALWAYS PLURAL**
another	everybody	no one	both
anybody	everyone	nothing	few
anyone	everything	one	many
anything	much	somebody	others
each	neither	someone	several
either	nobody	something	

The indefinite pronouns *all, any, most, none,* and *some* may be singular or plural, depending on the phrase that follows them.

When an indefinite pronoun is used as the subject of a sentence, the verb must agree with it in number.

EXAMPLE   **Everyone reads** part of the novel. **[singular]**

EXAMPLE   **Several enjoy** it very much. **[plural]**

EXAMPLE   **Most** of the story **happens** in England. **[singular]**

EXAMPLE   **Most** of the characters **seem** real. **[plural]**

Possessive pronouns often have indefinite pronouns as their antecedents. In such cases, the pronouns must agree in number. Note that in the first example below the words that come between the subject and the verb don't affect the agreement.

EXAMPLE   **Each** of the actors memorizes **his** or **her** lines.

EXAMPLE   **Many** are enjoying **their** roles in the play.

PRACTICE   Using Indefinite Pronouns

Write the indefinite pronouns and the correct words from the choices in parentheses.

1. Some of the students (has, have) formed a science club.
2. Some of the food (is, are) cold.
3. Everyone (makes, make) a mistake occasionally.
4. Several of the band members (is, are) suggesting a picnic.
5. Someone left (his or her, their) umbrella in the hall.
6. Most of the voters (wants, want) more information.
7. Both (has, have) asked (his or her, their) parents for permission.
8. Nobody (likes, like) ants in (his or her, their) picnic lunch.
9. Everything in these three cupboards (is, are) dirty.
10. Few (gives, give) (his or her, their) most valuable possessions to charity.

4.6 REFLEXIVE AND INTENSIVE PRONOUNS

A **reflexive pronoun** ends with -*self* or -*selves* and refers to the subject of a sentence. In a sentence with a reflexive pronoun, the action of the verb returns to the subject.

EXAMPLE   Yolanda bought **herself** a book on engine repair.
Reflexive Pronoun

Don't use a reflexive pronoun in place of a personal pronoun.

EXAMPLE   Yolanda asked Pat and **me** for help. [**not** *Pat and myself*]

EXAMPLE   Yolanda and **I** read the book. [**not** *Yolanda and myself*]

An **intensive pronoun** ends with -*self* or -*selves* and is used to draw special attention to a noun or a pronoun already named.

EXAMPLE   Yolanda **herself** repaired the engine.
Intensive Pronoun

EXAMPLE   Yolanda repaired the engine **herself.**
Intensive Pronoun

Reflexive and intensive pronouns are formed by adding -*self* or -*selves* to certain personal and possessive pronouns.

REFLEXIVE AND INTENSIVE PRONOUNS	
SINGULAR	**PLURAL**
myself	ourselves
yourself	yourselves
himself, herself, itself	themselves

Don't use *hisself* or *theirselves* in place of *himself* and *themselves.*

Write the correct word from the choices in parentheses. Then write personal, reflexive, *or* intensive *to identify the word you chose.*

1. Ms. Statler gave Moisha and (me, myself) the good news.
2. The volunteers were proud of (themselves, theirselves).
3. Progress brings (us, ourselves) advantages and disadvantages.
4. Jim repaired the old grandfather clock (himself, hisself).
5. The drama director chose Peyton and (me, myself) for the lead roles.
6. The students (themselves, theirselves) made all the decorations.
7. The twins and (I, myself) prepared the entire meal.
8. We found (us, ourselves) in an awkward situation.
9. The coach (himself, hisself) presented the trophies.
10. I promised (me, myself) a reward for all my hard work.

4.7 INTERROGATIVE AND DEMONSTRATIVE PRONOUNS

An **interrogative pronoun** is a pronoun used to introduce an interrogative sentence.

The interrogative pronouns *who* and *whom* refer to people. *Who* is used when the interrogative pronoun is the subject of the sentence. *Whom* is used when the interrogative pronoun is an object.

EXAMPLE **Who** borrowed the book? **[subject]**

EXAMPLE **Whom** did the librarian call? **[direct object]**

Which and *what* refer to things and ideas.

EXAMPLES **Which** is it?   **What** interests you?

GRAMMAR / USAGE / MECHANICS

Whose shows possession.

EXAMPLE   I found a copy of the play. **Whose** is it?

Don't confuse *whose* with *who's*. *Who's* is a contraction of *who is* or *who has*.

A **demonstrative pronoun** is a pronoun that points out something.

The demonstrative pronouns are *this, that, these,* and *those. This* (singular) and *these* (plural) refer to things nearby. *That* (singular) and *those* (plural) refer to things at a distance.

EXAMPLE   **This** is an interesting book. **[singular, nearby]**

EXAMPLE   **These** are interesting books. **[plural, nearby]**

EXAMPLE   **That** was a good movie. **[singular, at a distance]**

EXAMPLE   **Those** were good movies. **[plural, at a distance]**

PRACTICE **Using Interrogative and Demonstrative Pronouns**

Write the correct word from the choices in parentheses.

1. (Who, Whom) left these muddy shoes in the living room?

2. (Who, Whom) did you meet at the mall this afternoon?

3. (Whose, Who's) that bald man with the yellow umbrella?

4. Is (that, those) the most comfortable chair?

5. (Whose, Who's) broken my new camera?

6. (Whose, Who's) looking for me?

7. Do (this, these) make suitable gifts for young men?

8. (Whose, Who's) are the red sneakers with the pink shoelaces?

9. (Who, Whom) have your parents invited for dinner?

10. (Who, Whom) has won the election?

Rewrite the following passage, correcting errors in spelling, grammar, and usage. Write legibly to be sure one letter is not mistaken for another. There are ten errors.

Sandra Cisneros

[1]Us students have just read the short stories "Bums in the Attic" and "A Smart Cookie." [2]Both is by Sandra Cisneros. [3]Whom is Sandra Cisneros? [4]She is a Mexican American writer. [5]She writes short stories and poems.

[6]At the age of fifteen, Cisneros moved to a new house. [7]Her and her family moved into a red house in a Puerto Rican neighborhood. [8]There is a simlar house in *The House on Mango Street,* Cisneros's most famous book. [9]It's main character is Esperanza.

[10]Sandra Cisneros is a well-known writer. [11]They probably have her books at your local library. [12]Juan and myself read her short story "Eleven." [13]I enjoyed the story more than him. [14]Esperanza reminded me of my friend Alice. [15]She is a very strong girl.

GRAMMAR / USAGE / MECHANICS

POSTTEST Personal Pronouns

Write each personal pronoun. Then write one of the following phrases to identify the pronoun: subject pronoun as subject, subject pronoun as predicate pronoun, object pronoun as direct object, object pronoun as indirect object.

1. I told them the news.
2. They saw her and us at the library.
3. You are asking me too many questions.
4. She and he carried it into the garage.
5. The guests of honor at the banquet were we.

POSTTEST Using Pronouns

Write the correct word or phrase from the choices in parentheses.

6. Mrs. Sindato and (we, us) students watched the free performance in the park.
7. (You and I, I and you, You and me, Me and you) tasted peaches in Georgia and ate crab in Maryland.
8. The astronomer told (she and he, she and him, her and he, her and him) about the meteor shower.
9. At the construction site, the supervisor gave Greg and (they, them) hammers, saws, and nails.
10. Hariza and (she, her) left the house early in the morning.
11. (Mr. Gilbert and we, We and Mr. Gilbert, Mr. Gilbert and us, Us and Mr. Gilbert) saw a bolt of lightning during the snowstorm.
12. The true winners of the race were (they, them).
13. Mr. Polinski coaches (she and I, I and she, her and me, me and her) in gymnastics.
14. That new adventure film thrilled (we, us) moviegoers.
15. The most enthusiastic band members are (she and I, I and she, her and me, me and her).

Write each personal pronoun and its antecedent. If a pronoun doesn't have a clear antecedent, rewrite the numbered item to make the meaning clear.

16. Many small parts make up a watch. They all fit together and make it work.

17. John and Mary look hungry. Give him or her the rest of the fruit salad.

18. Eagle Plume told Kim the news. She had made the volleyball team.

19. They serve delicious meals at the Chinese Dragon.

20. Shelley lost the tennis match. She was disappointed.

Write each pronoun. Then write possessive, indefinite, reflexive, intensive, interrogative, *or* demonstrative *to identify it.*

21. Who invented the legend of the Minotaur, a creature half man and half bull?

22. The blue shirts are theirs; the red shirts are ours.

23. Nothing, not even a large body of water, stops the lemming during its self-destructive journey.

24. The Perezes bought that and saved themselves some money.

25. Both appreciated the photo finish, but neither celebrated before the judges' ruling.

26. Yours is a story of courage.

27. The bargain hunter bought herself this and many of the gifts at the sale.

28. The trainer herself rubs down the horse after each of the practices.

29. Which are poisonous snakes?

30. The astronaut cares for his equipment himself.

GRAMMAR / USAGE / MECHANICS

Write the subjects and the correct words from the choices in parentheses.

31. Most of the mountain (are, is) under a watch for forest fires.

32. No one here (know, knows) the difference between stalagmites and stalactites.

33. We stroll along the river; others (walk, walks) to the new video arcade.

34. Somebody in my class (walk, walks) three miles every day.

35. (Are, Is) any of the clouds producing hail?

36. Many of the volcanoes in the Ring of Fire (have, has) erupted.

37. Some of the water in the fire hydrants (have, has) leaked.

38. Most of the old elm trees (have, has) died of disease.

39. (Is, Are) either of the children asking about the trip to the zoo?

40. Much of the activity (were, was) too difficult.

POSTTEST **Personal, Reflexive, Intensive, Interrogative, and Demonstrative Pronouns**

Write the correct word from the choices in parentheses.

41. Debra and (I, myself) watched the intense chess match.

42. (Whose, Who's) are these?

43. Is (this, these) your only pencil?

44. These spiders spun the enormous webs (themselves, theirselves) in a single hour.

45. (Who, Whom) told you about the danger of the sun's ultraviolet rays?

46. The astronaut gave (me, myself) a piece of moon rock.

47. Are (that, those) Habib's shoes?

48. (Who, Whom) did you ask to the dance?

49. (Whose, Who's) the new student in your math class?

50. The police officer warned (me, myself) about the dangers of jaywalking.

Chapter 5

Adjectives

PRETEST Identifying Adjectives

Write each adjective. Beside the adjective, write the noun it modifies.

1. The cougar is a large North American cat.
2. Bill Nye, a wacky scientist, performs goofy experiments on Saturday television.
3. An astronaut suit is a complex piece of scientific equipment with bright lights, a drinking bag, a cooling unit, and other devices.
4. Amahl felt happy about the test results.
5. Wilhelm Roentgen, a German scientist, discovered the amazing capabilities of the invisible X-ray.
6. The Komodo dragon, an endangered lizard, has a poisonous bite.
7. Many voters seemed angry or disappointed with the outcome of the last election.
8. The famous athlete visited the sick children at the local hospital after the big game.

9. Omar Vizquel picked up the ball with one bare hand, tagged second base, and threw out the speedy runner at first base.
10. The kitten was a soft, round ball of silky fur.

PRETEST Articles and Demonstratives

Write the correct word or phrase from the choices in parentheses.

11. (This, This here) dog is my constant companion.
12. (A, An) human can reason, but (a, an) animal cannot.
13. Don't sit in (this, that) chair on (an, the) other side of the room.
14. Is (that, that there) your brother?
15. (This, These) boomerang will return to me.
16. Name (a, the) person with the same first and last initials.
17. Rafael attends (a, an) university in (a, an) small town (a, an) hour from here.
18. Jane took (them, those) aluminum cans to the recycling center.
19. Are (that, those) your shoes on the back porch?
20. Look at (these, those) dark clouds on the horizon.

PRETEST Comparative and Superlative Adjectives

Write the correct comparative or superlative form of the adjective in parentheses.

21. Are wetlands (valuable) than forests?
22. Thomas Edison invented the light bulb, a (reliable) light than the gas light.
23. What is the (tall) plant on earth?
24. From the two pieces of pizza, I chose the (big) one.
25. I think he is the (funny) comedian on television.
26. In this story about a shy dancer, the main character is (lonely) than her sister.

27. There were six watches in the showcase. I bought the (expensive) one.
28. Which dog looks (sad)—the basset hound or the bulldog?
29. Of all my vegetables, the (large) one is my eggplant.
30. What is the (important) step in the process?

Irregular Comparative and Superlative Adjectives

Write the correct word or phrase from the choices in parentheses.

31. Of the three children, Buddy wanted the (more, most) attention.
32. Which of the three plans will cause the (less, least) trouble?
33. The (baddest, worst) actor forgot her lines, fell on the stage, and burst into tears.
34. Andreas took (less, least) gravy today than yesterday.
35. My grades in science are (better, more better) than my grades in English.
36. Out of one hundred paintings, the judges found the (better, best) one.
37. The untreated duster picks up (little, less) dust than the treated one.
38. This cold medication tastes (more worse, worse) than that one.
39. Don has (more, most) computer games than Harold.
40. I am feeling (gooder, better) today than yesterday.

5.1 ADJECTIVES

The words we use to describe people, places, and things are called adjectives.

An **adjective** is a word that describes, or modifies, a noun or a pronoun.

Adjectives modify nouns in three ways.

HOW ADJECTIVES MODIFY NOUNS	
WHAT KIND?	We studied **ancient** history.
HOW MANY?	I read **four** chapters.
WHICH ONE?	**That** invention changed history.

Most adjectives come before the nouns they modify. Some adjectives follow linking verbs and modify the noun or pronoun that is the subject of the sentence.

EXAMPLE **Some** architects are **skillful** and **imaginative.**

The adjective *some* precedes the noun *architects.* The adjectives *skillful* and *imaginative* follow the linking verb, *are,* and modify the subject, *architects.* They are called predicate adjectives.

A **predicate adjective** follows a linking verb and modifies the subject of a sentence.

Two verb forms are often used as adjectives and predicate adjectives. They are the present participle and the past participle.

EXAMPLE   The architect drew a **surprising** design. [present participle]

EXAMPLE   Visitors seem **impressed.** [past participle]

Some adjectives are formed from proper nouns and begin with a capital letter. They are called proper adjectives.

Proper adjectives are adjectives formed from proper nouns.

Some proper adjectives have the same form as the noun. Others are formed by adding an ending to the noun form.

FORMING PROPER ADJECTIVES	
PROPER NOUN	**PROPER ADJECTIVE**
oranges from **Florida**	**Florida** oranges
the history of **America**	**American** history

More than one adjective may modify the same noun.

EXAMPLE **These new frozen** *dinners* are **tasty** and **nutritious.**

These, new, frozen, tasty, and *nutritious* all modify *dinners.*

NOTE   Many words that are usually nouns can also be used as adjectives: ***stone** wall,* ***band** uniform,* ***baseball** game.*

PRACTICE   Identifying Adjectives

Write each adjective. Beside the adjective, write the noun it modifies.

1. The old green sprinkling can was rusty and dented.
2. Several stories about Spanish explorers are in this book.
3. Lazy people often lead dull lives.
4. Fragrant red roses bloomed beside the babbling brook.
5. Old coins from Roman ruins are valuable.
6. These portraits are familiar to many visitors from Italian cities.
7. Rock bands usually include some guitars.
8. I counted twenty-two mistakes in this composition.
9. French fashions are popular with American women.
10. Three broken dishes lay on the dirty floor.

5.2 ARTICLES AND DEMONSTRATIVES

The words *a, an,* and *the* make up a special group of adjectives called **articles.**

A and *an* are called **indefinite articles** because they refer to one of a general group of people, places, things, or ideas. *A* is used before words beginning with a consonant sound. *An* is used before words beginning with a vowel sound. Don't confuse sounds with spellings. In speaking, you would say *a university* but *an uncle, a hospital* but *an honor.*

EXAMPLES   a union   a picture   **an** hour   **an** easel

The is called the **definite article** because it identifies specific people, places, things, or ideas.

EXAMPLE   **The** picture beside **the** fireplace is **the** best one.

The words *this, that, these,* and *those* are called **demonstrative adjectives.** They are used to point out something.

DEMONSTRATIVE ADJECTIVES	
Take **this** umbrella with you.	**That** store is closed.
Take **these** boots too.	**Those** clouds are lovely.

Demonstrative adjectives point out something and modify nouns by answering the question *which one?* or *which ones?*

Use *this* and *that* with singular nouns. Use *these* and *those* with plural nouns. Use *this* and *these* to point out something close to you. Use *that* and *those* to point out something at a distance.

DEMONSTRATIVES		
	SINGULAR	**PLURAL**
NEAR	this	these
FAR	that	those

Demonstratives can be used with nouns or without them. When they're used without nouns, they're called **demonstrative pronouns.**

DEMONSTRATIVE PRONOUNS	
This is mine.	**These** are his.
That is hers.	**Those** are yours.

The words *here* and *there* should not be used with demonstrative adjectives or demonstrative pronouns. The words *this, these, that,* and *those* already point out the locations *here* and *there*.

EXAMPLE   Look at **this** photograph. [not *this here photograph*]

Don't use the object pronoun *them* in place of the demonstrative adjective *those*.

EXAMPLE   I took a photo of **those** buildings. [not *them buildings*]

PRACTICE Using Articles and Demonstratives

Write the correct word from the choices in parentheses.

1. (A, An) honest person will not tell (a, an) lie.
2. (This, These) are the posters I was telling you about.
3. Do you know (them, those) people across the street?
4. My father has joined (a, an) union.
5. (This, This here) is (a, the) house where I was born.
6. Can you think of (a, the) word with six syllables?
7. (This, These) house is exactly like (these, those) in your neighborhood.
8. (This, That) portrait on (a, the) opposite wall is a picture of my great-grandfather.
9. (A, An) animal has damaged (these, those) shrubs on the far side of the lawn.
10. (That, That there) is (a, an) historic battlefield.

5.3 COMPARATIVE AND SUPERLATIVE ADJECTIVES

The **comparative form** of an adjective compares one person or thing with another.

The **superlative form** of an adjective compares one person or thing with several others.

For most adjectives with one syllable and for some with two syllables, add *-er* to form the comparative and *-est* to form the superlative.

EXAMPLE Is Venezuela **larger** than Peru?

EXAMPLE Is Brazil the **richest** country in South America?

For most adjectives with two or more syllables, form the comparative by using *more* before the adjective. Form the superlative by using *most* before the adjective.

EXAMPLE Is Chile **more mountainous** than Bolivia?

EXAMPLE Was Simón Bolívar South America's **most successful** general?

COMPARATIVE AND SUPERLATIVE FORMS

BASE FORM	COMPARATIVE	SUPERLATIVE
small	small**er**	small**est**
big	big**ger**	big**gest**
pretty	prett**ier**	prett**iest**
fabulous	**more** fabulous	**most** fabulous

The words *less* and *least* are used before both short and long adjectives to form the negative comparative and superlative.

NEGATIVE COMPARATIVE AND SUPERLATIVE FORMS	
BASE FORM	The first dancer was **graceful.**
COMPARATIVE	The second dancer was **less graceful** than the first.
SUPERLATIVE	The third dancer was the **least graceful** one.

Don't use *more, most, less,* or *least* before adjectives that already end with *-er* or *-est.* This is called a double comparison.

PRACTICE Using Comparative and Superlative Adjectives I

Write the correct comparative or superlative form of the adjective in parentheses.

1. Who has the (easy) job—you or I?
2. This has been the (splendid) vacation of my life!
3. Do you think a screwdriver is (useful) than a hammer?
4. Are Tony's pizzas (spicy) than Gino's pizzas?
5. You're the (wonderful) friend I've ever had!
6. The downtown bus is (slow) than the crosstown bus.
7. This must be the (beautiful) spot in the world!
8. Is your pizza (delicious) than mine?
9. Is this the (short) route to the amusement park?
10. The (old) person in my family is Great-grandma Harris.

PRACTICE Using Comparative and Superlative Adjectives II

Write the correct word or phrase from the choices in parentheses.

1. The baby becomes (curiouser, more curious) every day.
2. Janine is the (more popular, most popular) girl in the seventh grade.
3. Science is my (less favorite, least favorite) subject.

150 *Grammar, Usage, and Mechanics*

GRAMMAR / USAGE / MECHANICS

4. Kenji is the (fastest, most fastest) runner on the track team.
5. Emmy is (less talkative, least talkative) than Margaret.
6. You have the (most unusualest, most unusual) dog I've ever seen.
7. This pizza is (less flavorful, least flavorful) than the one we had last weekend.
8. No one is (slower, slowest) than you!
9. This photograph of Mount Rushmore is the (more interesting, most interesting) picture in your entire album.
10. Is your brother Ted (younger, more younger) than your cousin Alisha?

5.4 IRREGULAR COMPARATIVE AND SUPERLATIVE ADJECTIVES

The comparative and superlative forms of some adjectives are not formed in the regular way.

EXAMPLE   Harriet Tubman believed in a **good** cause.

EXAMPLE   She knew that freedom was **better** than slavery.

EXAMPLE   The Underground Railroad was the **best** route to freedom.

Better is the comparative form of the adjective *good*. *Best* is the superlative form of *good*.

IRREGULAR COMPARATIVE AND SUPERLATIVE FORMS

BASE FORM	COMPARATIVE	SUPERLATIVE
good, well	better	best
bad	worse	worst
many, much	more	most
little	less	least

Don't use *more* or *most* before irregular adjectives that are already in the comparative or superlative form.

EXAMPLE   Tubman felt **better** at the end of the day. [not *more better*]

PRACTICE Using Irregular Adjectives

Write the correct word or phrase from the choices in parentheses.

  1. My parents pay (much, more) attention to my sister than to me.
  2. Of all the employees, Carol Ann has the (less, least) influence with the president.
  3. This cough syrup tastes (worse, more worse) than the other one.
  4. Which month has the (most, mostest) holidays?
  5. Yoko is a (good, gooder) tap dancer.
  6. Today is (good, better) than yesterday.
  7. My dad's job requires (less, least) physical labor than my mom's job.
  8. That was the (baddest, worst) joke I've ever heard!
  9. Tobias has (little, most little) sympathy for me.
  10. This was my (best, bestest) performance ever!

PRACTICE Proofreading

Rewrite the following passage, correcting errors in spelling, capitalization, grammar, and usage. Add any missing punctuation. Write legibly to be sure one letter is not mistaken for another. There are ten errors.

Maya Angelou

¹Maya Angelou is a author and a poet. ²Her parents named her Marguerite Johnson. ³She was born in St. Louis. ⁴These city is in Missouri. ⁵She had one brother, Bailey. ⁶Bailey was oldest than she was. ⁷He called Marguerite "Mya Sister," and her nickname became

Maya. [8]She was the goodest student in her eighth-grade class.

[9]Johnson became a dancer and changed her name to Maya Angelou. [10]She worked at the Purple Onion. [11]She was more better than some of the other dancers there. [12]She toured Europe in the african american musical *Porgy and Bess.*

[13]At the age of thirty, Angelou became a writer. [14]She learned from such writers as James Baldwin. [15]Their advice was benificial.

[16]Angelou also worked for civil rights. [17]She met one of the most famousest civil rights leaders, Martin Luther King Jr.

[18]Angelou wrote five books about her life. [19]One of them books is *I Know Why the Caged Bird Sings.* [20]She wrote the poem "On the Pulse of Morning," and she read it at the inauguration of President Clinton. [21]It was surely a honor for her.

POSTTEST Identifying Adjectives

Write each adjective. Beside the adjective, write the noun it modifies.

1. During the hot summer, the inventive youth sold large glasses of cold lemonade.
2. This year I learned the names of the nine planets.
3. A disabled vehicle stood at the northwest corner of the busy intersection.
4. Six visitors to the ancient ruins of the Roman Colosseum bought expensive souvenirs.
5. The golden eagle loves these mountainous areas.
6. The first president of the United States was George Washington, a man with a strong reputation for absolute honesty.
7. The hot Mexican chili was spicy and delicious.
8. The French gift of the copper Statue of Liberty stands on tiny Liberty Island.

9. Which wrestler wears the strange outfit with ostrich feathers?
10. An enormous sailing ship appeared against the misty glow of the full moon.

Articles and Demonstratives

Write the correct word or phrase from the choices in parentheses.

11. Is (this, that) your house on the opposite side of the street?
12. Ronald Reagan was (a, an) actor, (a, an) governor, and (a, an) president.
13. Are you preserving (that, that there) flower for (a, an) reason?
14. (This, These) dry weather makes my allergies worse.
15. Mischa received (a, an) honor at (a, the) last awards ceremony.
16. Do you know the name of (these, those) mountains in the distance?
17. In (this, this here) movie, (a, an) meteor hits (a, an, the) earth.
18. May I have some of (that, those) grapes?
19. (A, An) Olympic athlete needs (a, an) one-track mind.
20. (A, An, The) horrid bug is crawling among (them, those) flowers on your desk.

Comparative and Superlative Adjectives

Write the correct comparative or superlative form of the adjective in parentheses.

21. Is a curveball (fast) than a slider?
22. That was the (embarrassing) moment of my life.
23. Stocks are a (risky) investment than a savings account.

24. From the batch of thirty, the chef rejected the two (small) tomatoes.
25. Of the two disc jockeys, we hired the (expensive) one.
26. This has been the (hot) day of the summer.
27. Dreama chose the (sensible) of the two plans.
28. The (large) python in the wild can devour an entire crocodile.
29. Benson gave the (interesting) report in the class.
30. The river is now (high) than ever before.

POSTTEST Irregular Comparative and Superlative Adjectives

Write the correct word or phrase from the choices in parentheses.

31. John Deere made a (gooder, better) plow than others on the market in 1838.
32. Our team's record is (worse, worser) than your team's.
33. Yellowstone suffered (less, least) damage from the fire than other areas of the West.
34. That was the (worse, worst) mistake I've ever made.
35. Do you have a (better, more better) answer?
36. Of all Sean's friends, Don has the (most, mostest) computer games.
37. The exotic birds receive the (most, mostest) attention at the zoo.
38. I spent (more, most) time on the project than you.
39. Of the two travelers, Mei-Ling paid (less, least) attention to the map.
40. This is the (best, most best) day of my life.

Adverbs

PRETEST Identifying Adverbs

Write each adverb and the word it modifies. Then write whether the modified word is a verb, *an* adjective, *or an* adverb.

1. Susan B. Anthony fought tirelessly for women's voting rights.
2. The women often suffered defeats, but they continued their campaign.
3. In 1919 the Nineteenth Amendment finally gave women the vote.
4. Are women always treated fairly today?
5. We arrived really early for the concert.
6. The kittens were extremely tiny, and we handled them quite gently.
7. I completely admire gymnasts' amazingly complex performances.
8. Have you ever seen that movie anywhere?
9. Beth's handwriting is somewhat sloppy, but she expresses her ideas very well.
10. Do you play soccer here?

Write the correct word or phrase from the choices in parentheses.

11. Dad thinks (better, best) of all in peace and quiet.

12. Cars on the German autobahn travel (faster, more faster, fastest, most fastest) than vehicles on American highways.

13. Some students work (more independently, most independently) than others.

14. Of all my students, Sherman works (harder, hardest).

15. You play this game even (worse, worser, worst) than I.

16. Of the six families, which traveled (farther, more farther, farthest, most farthest) to the reunion?

17. Which of these two computer games do you like (better, best)?

18. Who practices (more frequently, most frequently)— Trisha, Moishi, or Teodoro?

19. Does André serve (more rapidly, most rapidly) than Pete?

20. Which of the three babies cries (less, least)?

PRETEST **Using Adjectives and Adverbs**

Write the correct word from the choices in parentheses.

21. Spiders cause (real, really) fear in some people.

22. I (most, almost) never take a walk after nine o'clock in the evening.

23. Jamaica is a (real, really) good artist.

24. After that enormous dinner, I don't feel (good, well).

25. Your brother (sure, surely) knows a great deal about computers.

26. The volleyball player with the sprained wrist played (bad, badly).

27. I felt (bad, badly) about the loss.

28. (Most, Almost) visitors to the zoo move (slow, slowly) through the exhibits.

29. A surgeon needs keen eyes and (sure, surely) hands.

30. You look (good, well) in that new hairstyle.

Correcting Double Negatives

Rewrite each sentence so it correctly expresses a negative idea.

31. Because of a Siberian tiger's colored stripes, you can't scarcely see it in the autumn.

32. Don't never ask me about that mistake again.

33. I wouldn't hardly call a crocodile a good pet!

34. Edwin Land wouldn't never have invented the Polaroid camera without a question from his daughter.

35. Can't I say nothing about the missing suitcase of money?

36. Without luck I couldn't never have caught that line drive.

37. In Red Bird's fifteen years, he hadn't gone nowhere outside the reservation.

38. Doesn't nobody here know about humans' eight wrist bones?

39. The train wreck wasn't no accident.

40. I haven't no homework tonight.

6.1 ADVERBS THAT MODIFY VERBS

Adjectives are words that modify nouns and pronouns. Adverbs are another type of modifier. They modify verbs, adjectives, and other adverbs.

An **adverb** is a word that modifies a verb, an adjective, or another adverb.

WHAT ADVERBS MODIFY	
VERBS	People *handle* old violins **carefully.**
ADJECTIVES	**Very** *old* violins are valuable.
ADVERBS	Orchestras **almost** *always* include violins.

An adverb may tell *how* or *in what manner* an action is done. It may tell *when* or *how often* an action is done. It may also tell *where* or *in what direction* an action is done.

WAYS ADVERBS MODIFY VERBS	
ADVERBS TELL	**EXAMPLES**
HOW	grandly, easily, completely, neatly, gratefully, sadly
WHEN	soon, now, immediately, often, never, usually, early
WHERE	here, there, everywhere, inside, downstairs, above, far

When an adverb modifies an adjective or another adverb, the adverb usually comes before the word it modifies. When an adverb modifies a verb, the adverb can sometimes occupy different positions in a sentence.

POSITION OF ADVERBS MODIFYING VERBS	
BEFORE THE VERB	Guests **often** dine at the White House.
AFTER THE VERB	Guests dine **often** at the White House.
AT THE BEGINNING	**often** guests dine at the White House.
AT THE END	Guests dine at the White House **often.**

Many adverbs are formed by adding *-ly* to adjectives. However, not all words that end in *-ly* are adverbs. The words *friendly, lively, kindly, lovely,* and *lonely* are usually adjectives. On the other hand, not all adverbs end in *-ly*.

SOME ADVERBS NOT ENDING IN -*LY*			
afterward	everywhere	near	short
already	fast	never	sometimes
always	forever	not	somewhere
anywhere	hard	now	soon
away	here	nowhere	straight
below	home	often	then
even	late	outside	there
ever	long	seldom	well

PRACTICE   Identifying Adverbs I

Write each adverb. Beside the adverb, write the verb it modifies.

1. Cinderella whisked her broom quickly across the floor.
2. She sighed heavily and stepped outside.
3. Cinderella wished desperately for an invitation to the ball.
4. Her mean stepsisters were already dressing for the event.
5. At the ball, Cinderella danced gracefully with the prince.
6. She left the ball late and arrived home without one of her glass slippers.
7. The prince searched eagerly for the owner of the slipper.
8. Cinderella and the prince lived happily for the rest of their days.
9. The newlyweds traveled everywhere throughout the kingdom.
10. The happy couple seldom invited the mean stepsisters for a visit.

6.2 ADVERBS THAT MODIFY ADJECTIVES AND OTHER ADVERBS

Adverbs are often used to modify adjectives and other adverbs. Notice how adverbs affect the meaning of the adjectives in the following sentences. Most often they tell *how* or *to what extent.*

EXAMPLE Harry Truman used **extremely** direct language.

EXAMPLE He became a **very** popular president.

In the first sentence, the adverb *extremely* modifies the adjective *direct. Extremely* tells to what extent Truman's language was direct. In the second sentence, the adverb *very* modifies the adjective *popular. Very* tells to what extent Truman was popular.

In the following sentences, adverbs modify other adverbs.

EXAMPLE Truman entered politics **unusually** late in life.

EXAMPLE He moved through the political ranks **quite** quickly.

In the first sentence, the adverb *unusually* modifies the adverb *late. Unusually* tells how late Truman entered politics. In the second sentence, the adverb *quite* modifies the adverb *quickly. Quite* tells how quickly Truman moved through the ranks.

When an adverb modifies an adjective or another adverb, the adverb almost always comes directly before the word it modifies. On the following page is a list of some adverbs that are often used to modify adjectives and other adverbs.

ADVERBS OFTEN USED TO MODIFY ADJECTIVES AND OTHER ADVERBS			
almost	just	rather	too
barely	nearly	really	totally
extremely	partly	so	unusually
hardly	quite	somewhat	very

PRACTICE Identifying Adverbs II

Write each adverb and the word it modifies. Then write whether the modified word is a verb, *an* adjective, *or an* adverb.

1. Anita almost never misses a foul shot.
2. Jason told a very silly joke.
3. That movie was just wonderful!
4. These coins are extremely rare and unusually valuable.
5. My parents nearly always vote on election day.
6. Norma Jean is really shy, but she is quite popular.
7. Harrison ate too fast and felt rather sick.
8. Tessa stacked the dishes somewhat carelessly in the sink.
9. Fred and Ginger glide so smoothly around the dance floor.
10. I have barely enough money for one hamburger, and I am totally hungry!

6.3 COMPARATIVE AND SUPERLATIVE ADVERBS

The **comparative form** of an adverb compares one action with another.

The **superlative form** of an adverb compares one action with several others.

Most short adverbs add -er to form the comparative and -est to form the superlative.

COMPARING ADVERBS WITH *-ER* AND *-EST*	
COMPARATIVE	The pianist arrived **earlier** than the violinist.
SUPERLATIVE	The drummer arrived **earliest** of all the players.

Long adverbs and a few short ones require the use of *more* or *most*.

COMPARING ADVERBS WITH *MORE* AND *MOST*	
COMPARATIVE	The violinist plays **more often** than the harpist.
SUPERLATIVE	Which musicians play **most often?**

Some adverbs have irregular comparative and superlative forms.

IRREGULAR COMPARATIVE AND SUPERLATIVE FORMS		
BASE FORM	**COMPARATIVE**	**SUPERLATIVE**
well	better	best
badly	worse	worst
little	less	least
far (distance)	farther	farthest
far (degree)	further	furthest

The words *less* and *least* are used before adverbs to form the negative comparative and superlative.

EXAMPLES I play **less well.** I play **least accurately.**

Don't use *more, most, less,* or *least* before adverbs that already end in -er or -est.

Using Comparative and Superlative Adverbs

Write the correct word or phrase from the choices in parentheses.

1. George finished his work (later, more later) than Stanley.
2. Of all the students, Bonita completed the assignment (more, most) successfully.
3. Which of these two books did you like (better, best)?
4. Eleanor draws (worse, worst) than Elizabeth.
5. Who walks (farther, farthest) to school—Jackson, Emerson, or Theo?
6. Which of the fifteen team members swims (faster, more faster, fastest, most fastest)?
7. Mr. Roberts works (less, least) energetically than his son.
8. Which of your six cousins do you see (more often, more oftener, most often, most oftenest)?
9. Of the three pianists, which one plays (better, best)?
10. Jan does her chores (more, most) cheerfully than her sister.

6.4 USING ADJECTIVES AND ADVERBS

Sometimes it's hard to decide whether a sentence needs an adjective or an adverb. Think carefully about how the word is used.

EXAMPLE   He was (**careful, carefully**) with the antique clock.

EXAMPLE   He worked (**careful, carefully**) on the antique clock.

In the first sentence, the missing word follows a linking verb and modifies the subject, *He.* Therefore, an adjective is needed. *Careful* is the correct choice. In the second sentence, the missing word modifies the verb, *worked.* Thus, an adverb is needed, and *carefully* is the correct choice.

The words *good* and *well* and the words *bad* and *badly* are sometimes confused. *Good* and *bad* are adjectives. Use them before nouns and after linking verbs. *Well* and *badly* are adverbs. Use them to modify verbs. *Well* may also be used as an adjective to mean "healthy": *You look well today.*

TELLING ADJECTIVES FROM ADVERBS

ADJECTIVE	ADVERB
The band sounds **good**.	The band plays **well**.
The band sounds **bad**.	The band plays **badly**.
The soloist is **well**.	The soloist sings **well**.

Use these modifiers correctly: *real* and *really, sure* and *surely, most* and *almost. Real* and *sure* are adjectives. *Really, surely,* and *almost* are adverbs. *Most* can be an adjective or an adverb.

TELLING ADJECTIVES FROM ADVERBS

ADJECTIVE	ADVERB
Music is a **real** art.	This music is **really** popular.
A pianist needs **sure** hands.	Piano music is **surely** popular.
Most pianos have eighty-eight keys.	Piano strings **almost** never break.

PRACTICE Using Adjectives and Adverbs

Write the correct word from the choices in parentheses.

1. Proceed (immediate, immediately) to the exit.
2. Stan (most, almost) always takes the garbage out.

3. That chicken sandwich tasted (bad, badly).
4. Those colors look (good, well) on you.
5. Mr. and Mrs. Kim have a (sure, surely) chance for a trophy.
6. Jolene has a (real, really) good sense of humor.
7. Dalila has a (real, really) talent for mathematics.
8. You are (sure, surely) right about that!
9. My little brother reads very (good, well) for his age.
10. The team played (bad, badly) in the first half.

6.5 CORRECTING DOUBLE NEGATIVES

The adverb *not* is a **negative word,** expressing the idea of "no." *Not* often appears in a short form as part of a contraction. When *not* is part of a contraction, as in the words in the chart below, *n't* is an adverb.

CONTRACTIONS WITH *NOT*		
are not = aren't	does not = doesn't	should not = shouldn't
cannot = can't	had not = hadn't	was not = wasn't
could not = couldn't	has not = hasn't	were not = weren't
did not = didn't	have not = haven't	will not = won't
do not = don't	is not = isn't	would not = wouldn't

In all but two of these words, the apostrophe replaces the *o* in *not*. In *can't* both an *n* and the *o* are omitted. *Will not* becomes *won't*.

Other negative words are listed in the following chart. Each negative word has several opposites. These are **affirmative words,** or words that show the idea of "yes."

SOME NEGATIVE AND AFFIRMATIVE WORDS

NEGATIVE	AFFIRMATIVE
never, scarcely, hardly, barely	always, ever
nobody	anybody, everybody, somebody
no, none	all, any, one, some
no one	anyone, everyone, one, someone
nothing	anything, something
nowhere	anywhere, somewhere

Don't use two negative words to express the same idea. This is called a **double negative.** Only one negative word is necessary to express a negative idea. You can correct a double negative by removing one of the negative words or by replacing one of the negative words with an affirmative word.

EXAMPLE   **INCORRECT**   I **don't** have **no** homework.

EXAMPLE   **CORRECT**   I have **no** homework.

EXAMPLE   **CORRECT**   I **don't** have **any** homework.

PRACTICE   **Expressing Negative Ideas**

Rewrite each sentence so it correctly expresses a negative idea.

1. George Washington wouldn't never tell a lie.
2. Wasn't nobody in the auditorium?
3. There isn't a better school nowhere than this one.
4. Mr. Perez couldn't find nothing wrong with the electrical system.
5. None of this stuff doesn't belong in the living room.

6. We can't tell you nothing about the surprise.
7. No one doesn't never go to the wrestling matches.
8. There weren't no eggs in the refrigerator.
9. Didn't you never see a real circus before?
10. I haven't no money for lunch.

PRACTICE Proofreading

Rewrite the following passage, correcting errors in spelling, grammar, and usage. Write legibly to be sure one letter is not mistaken for another. There are ten errors.

Langston Hughes

[1]Langston Hughes was real popular in his time. [2]He wrote really good. [3]Hughes's father moved to Mexico. [4]Hughes was only one year old at the time. [5]His mother didn't never go with him. [6]She stayed behind in the United States, and Hughes lived with his grandmother in Kansas.

[7]At the age of five, Hughes went to a libary with his mother. [8]He fell deep in love with books. [9]At Central High School in Cleveland, Ohio, he wrote poems and edited the school yearbook. [10]He also ran more faster than many athletes in his class. [11]His school won a city championship in track.

[12]At the age of eighteen, Hughes wrote "The Negro Speaks of Rivers" on a train to Mexico. [13]He crossed the Mississippi River and wrote the poem quick on the back of an envelope. [14]Students most always read this poem by Hughes.

[15]Hughes included jazz and blues rhythms in his poetry more oftener than many other poets. [16]With his poetry, novels, and plays, Hughes sure became one of the most important writers of his day.

Write each adverb and the word it modifies. Then write whether the modified word is a verb, *an* adjective, *or an* adverb.

1. I occasionally read books about the Egyptian pyramids.
2. These enormous monuments rise grandly from the sands.
3. Outside they almost always look very simple.
4. In one horror movie, an Egyptian mummy came to life and extremely quickly terrified an entire city.
5. Sometimes nature accidentally produces a mummy.
6. Two hikers in the Alps found a partially frozen body.
7. Someone had died there between 3350 and 3300 B.C.
8. The baseball season will soon end.
9. Today will be partly sunny, but it will be too cold for a picnic.
10. A rather chilly wind blew quite fiercely through the trees.

POSTTEST Comparative and Superlative Adverbs

Write the correct word or phrase from the choices in parentheses.

11. Which of those two Disney movies did you like (better, best)?
12. I studied (less, least) for this test than for the last one.
13. Which of the five instruments measured the distance (more exactly, most exactly)?
14. This new modem connects me to the Internet (faster, more faster, fastest, most fastest) than the old one.
15. Hetty plays the violin (worse, worst) than anyone else in the orchestra.
16. I eat hot dogs (more frequently, most frequently) than hamburgers.
17. Of all the test-takers, Ashley left the room (later, latest).
18. My dog eats (more often, most often, more oftener, most oftenest) than my cat.

19. Which of the students in your class travels (farther, farthest) to school?

20. Of the six girls, which one arrived (earlier, earliest) for the interview?

Write the correct word from the choices in parentheses.

21. The crash between the car and the bicycle damaged the bicycle (bad, badly).

22. Corey (most, almost) always finishes his homework.

23. Are you (sure, surely) about that answer?

24. That fried chicken (sure, surely) smells (good, well).

25. Dionne finished her chores (quick, quickly).

26. How (good, well) do you swim half a mile?

27. Is that a (real, really) diamond?

28. (Most, Almost) children want a pet of some kind.

29. Do you feel (bad, badly) about the broken promise?

30. This new can opener works (real, really) (good, well).

Rewrite each sentence so it correctly expresses a negative idea.

31. There isn't nothing wrong with Monica's brother.

32. Maddie hadn't barely touched her food.

33. We didn't never expect the movie's sad ending.

34. There wasn't no one in the room.

35. I hadn't no knowledge of Kwanza until African American culture week.

36. Wasn't nobody listening to the weather reports?

37. Kevin couldn't take nobody with him to the audition.

38. Akiba wouldn't hardly do a thing like that.

39. The stray dog wasn't nowhere near the trash cans.

40. People in the space program won't never forget the tragedy of the space shuttle *Challenger.*

Prepositions, Conjunctions, and Interjections

PRETEST   Prepositions and Prepositional Phrases

*Write each prepositional phrase. Underline the preposition
and circle the object of the preposition. Then write the
word the prepositional phrase modifies. Finally, write*
adjective *or* adverb *to tell how the prepositional phrase is
used.*

1. The flowers along the fence look very pretty.
2. Just wait until tomorrow.
3. Emilio left the house without his jacket.
4. Have you read this letter from your cousin?
5. Are you busy for lunch?
6. During the last month, I have read ten books.
7. Have you read any books by S. E. Hinton?
8. Mitzi began her homework late in the afternoon.

9. Drive across the bridge and through the town.
10. Please put the clothes on your bureau into the washing machine.

PRETEST Pronouns as Objects of Prepositions

Write the correct word or phrase from the choices in parentheses.

11. Mr. Borelli made these costumes for Kiki and (she, her).
12. Give your money for the theater tickets to Mr. Corso or (they, them).
13. Please move your car around this van and (we, us).
14. To (who, whom) am I speaking?
15. Without Mudiwa and (he, him), we don't have a full team.
16. Except for Ms. Sandoval and (we, us), no one seems pleased by the announcement.
17. Cassy will sit between you and (I, me).
18. Across from (who, whom) did you sit?
19. Michael Jordan walked onto the court in front of Charlotte and (they, them).
20. Above (he and she, him and her, he and her, him and she) hung the family's portrait.

PRETEST Conjunctions

Write each conjunction. Then write compound subject, compound object, compound predicate, *or* compound sentence *to tell what parts the conjunction joins.*

21. The chemist or the geologist knows the answer.
22. My friend has a pager, but I don't want one.
23. Neither Michael Jordan nor Shaquille O'Neal is my favorite basketball player.
24. Mark handed my twin sister and me birthday cards.
25. Either a book or a game makes a good gift for John or Tonya.

26. In 1683 Anton van Leeuwenhoek first saw bacteria with a microscope, and in 1864 Louis Pasteur killed bacteria in milk.

27. I went to the library but forgot my library card.

28. Both Luke and Leah arrived late and left early.

29. We hiked or sat in the sun all day.

30. I admire both the suspension bridge and the covered bridge.

PRETEST Making Compound Subjects and Verbs Agree

Write the correct word from the choices in parentheses.

31. (Does, Do) men or women have more automobile accidents?

32. Andrea and Cliff (works, work) at the library.

33. Neither Hannah nor her sisters (has, have) met your cousin.

34. Either carrots or corn (accompanies, accompany) the pork chops on this menu.

35. (Is, Are) the Eiffel Tower or the Statue of Liberty taller than the Empire State Building?

36. Either the boat or the van (fits, fit) in the garage.

37. Both gas and electricity (provides, provide) fuel.

38. Neither the students nor the teacher (has, have) seen this film.

39. Neither the dog nor the cat (sleeps, sleep) outdoors.

40. Two uniformed guards and a fierce dog (guards, guard) the gate of the mansion.

PRETEST Conjunctive Adverbs

Write each sentence. Underline the conjunctive adverb. Add appropriate punctuation.

41. Grass cuttings contain nutrients for your lawn furthermore short clippings break down fast.

42. The Fukuyamas have a large garden consequently they eat many fresh vegetables.

43. You should stop now besides the report is not due until next week.

44. Put away all your sports equipment likewise put away your other toys.

45. France won the World Cup Brazil however was second.

7.1 PREPOSITIONS AND PREPOSITIONAL PHRASES

A **preposition** is a word that relates a noun or a pronoun to another word in a sentence.

EXAMPLE   The boy **near** the window is French.

The word *near* is a preposition. It shows the relationship between the noun *window* and the word *boy*.

COMMON PREPOSITIONS				
aboard	at	down	off	to
about	before	during	on	toward
above	behind	except	onto	under
across	below	for	opposite	underneath
after	beneath	from	out	until
against	beside	in	outside	up
along	besides	inside	over	upon
among	between	into	past	with
around	beyond	like	since	within
as	but (except)	near	through	without
	by	of	throughout	

A preposition may consist of more than one word.

EXAMPLE   Yasmin will visit Trinidad **instead of** Jamaica.

SOME PREPOSITIONS OF MORE THAN ONE WORD			
according to	aside from	in front of	instead of
across from	because of	in place of	on account of
along with	except for	in spite of	on top of

A **prepositional phrase** is a group of words that begins with a preposition and ends with a noun or a pronoun, which is called the **object of the preposition.**

EXAMPLE   Hang the painting **outside the new auditorium.**

A preposition may have a compound object.

EXAMPLE   Between the **chair** and the **table** was a window.

PRACTICE Identifying Prepositional Phrases

Write each prepositional phrase. Underline the preposition and draw a circle around the object of the preposition.

1. Under the books on the desk, you will find an envelope with your name on it.
2. The driver of the sleigh stopped in the woods near the lake for a few minutes.
3. Since last week, we have planted flowers along the fence and behind the house.
4. Until yesterday I had never been inside the museum without my parents.
5. Go down the street to the corner and turn left at the light.
6. After today Ms. Peters will arrive by bus at the stop across the street from the school.

7. The stranger walked past the post office and into the bank.

8. Will you sit beside me during the period before lunch?

9. The coach postponed the match between the Tigers and the Bears because of rain.

10. Today we go over the river and through the woods to Grandmother's house in a car instead of an old-fashioned buggy.

7.2 PRONOUNS AS OBJECTS OF PREPOSITIONS

When a pronoun is the object of a preposition, use an object pronoun, not a subject pronoun.

EXAMPLE Dan handed the tickets to Natalie.

EXAMPLE Dan handed the tickets to **her.**

In the example, the object pronoun *her* replaces *Natalie* as the object of the preposition *to.*

A preposition may have a compound object: two or more nouns, two or more pronouns, or a combination of nouns and pronouns. Use object pronouns in compound objects.

EXAMPLE I borrowed the suitcase from Ivan and Vera.

EXAMPLE I borrowed the suitcase from Ivan and **her.**

EXAMPLE I borrowed the suitcase from **him** and Vera.

EXAMPLE I borrowed the suitcase from **him** and **her.**

Object pronouns are used in the second, third, and fourth sentences. In the second sentence, *Ivan and her* is the compound object of the preposition *from.* In the third sentence, *him and Vera* is the compound object of the preposition *from.* In the fourth sentence, *him and her* is the compound object of the preposition *from.*

If you're not sure whether to use a subject pronoun or an object pronoun, read the sentence aloud with only the pronoun.

EXAMPLE   I borrowed the suitcase from **her.**

EXAMPLE   I borrowed the suitcase from **him.**

Who is a subject pronoun. *Whom* is an object pronoun.

EXAMPLE   **Who** lent you the suitcase?

EXAMPLE   From **whom** did you borrow the suitcase?

PRACTICE   **Using Pronouns as Objects of Prepositions**

Write the correct word or phrase from the choices in parentheses.

1. To (who, whom) did you give the message?
2. Sit between Tasha and (I, me).
3. Were you pointing to (they or we, they or us, them or us, them or we)?
4. The twins and their brother played against Keith and (we, us).
5. We will go to the movies without Kim and (she, her).
6. Did you buy that hot dog for (he or I, he or me, him or me, him or I)?
7. The principal hurried down the hall toward Mr. Corso and (we, us).
8. For Jerry and (she, her), math is easy.
9. Six cheerleaders were sitting near my mom and (I, me) at the restaurant.
10. We stood in line behind Miss O'Neill and (he, him) at the theater.

7.3 PREPOSITIONAL PHRASES AS ADJECTIVES AND ADVERBS

A prepositional phrase is an **adjective phrase** when it modifies, or describes, a noun or a pronoun.

EXAMPLE The servers **at the new restaurant** are courteous.

EXAMPLE The atmosphere includes photographs **from old movies.**

In the first sentence, the prepositional phrase *at the new restaurant* modifies the subject of the sentence, *servers.* In the second sentence, the prepositional phrase *from old movies* modifies the direct object, *photographs.*

Notice that, unlike most adjectives, an adjective phrase usually comes after the word it modifies.

A prepositional phrase is an **adverb phrase** when it modifies a verb, an adjective, or another adverb.

ADVERB PHRASES	
USE	**EXAMPLES**
Modifies a Verb	The servers *dress* **like movie characters.**
Modifies an Adjective	The restaurant is *popular* **with young people.**
Modifies an Adverb	The restaurant opens *early* **in the morning.**

Most adverb phrases tell *when, where,* or *how* an action takes place. More than one prepositional phrase may modify the same word.

HOW ADVERB PHRASES MODIFY VERBS	
WHEN?	Many people eat a light meal **during the lunch hour.**
WHERE?	Some eat lunch **on the covered patio.**
HOW?	Others eat their meals **in a hurry.**

Write each prepositional phrase. Then write the word it modifies. Finally, write adjective *or* adverb *to tell how it's used.*

1. How many countries lie on the equator?
2. I read a book about Martin Luther King Jr.
3. The patient sipped water through a straw.
4. The flowers along the fence are daffodils.
5. This game is perfect for a rainy day.
6. The day before yesterday was my birthday.
7. My great-grandparents came from Germany.
8. I like movies with action.
9. The luncheon will begin at noon.
10. The young man chose his career early in life.

7.4 TELLING PREPOSITIONS AND ADVERBS APART

Sometimes it can be difficult to tell whether a particular word is being used as a preposition or as an adverb. Both prepositions and adverbs can answer the questions *where?* and *when?* The chart below shows fifteen words that can be used as either prepositions or adverbs. Whether any one of these words is a preposition or an adverb depends on its use in a particular sentence.

SOME WORDS THAT CAN BE USED AS PREPOSITIONS OR ADVERBS		
about	below	out
above	down	outside
around	in	over
before	inside	through
behind	near	up

Chapter 7 Prepositions, Conjunctions, and Interjections **179**

If you have trouble deciding whether a word is being used as a preposition or as an adverb, look at the other words in the sentence. If the word is followed closely by a noun or a pronoun, the word is probably a preposition, and the noun or pronoun is the object of the preposition.

EXAMPLE   We ate our lunch **outside** the **library.**

EXAMPLE   We walked **around** the **park** for an hour.

In the first example, *outside* is followed closely by the noun *library. Outside* is a preposition, and *library* is the object of the preposition. In the second example, *around* is a preposition, and *park* is the object of the preposition.

If the word is not followed closely by a noun or a pronoun, the word is probably an adverb.

EXAMPLE   We ate our lunch **outside.**

EXAMPLE   We walked **around** for an hour.

In the first sentence, *outside* answers the question *where?* but is not followed by a noun or a pronoun. In this sentence, *outside* is an adverb. In the second sentence, *around* is an adverb. *For an hour* is a prepositional phrase.

PRACTICE   Identifying Prepositions and Adverbs

Write preposition *or* adverb *to identify each underlined word.*

1. A flock of geese flew <u>over</u>.
2. The cow jumped <u>over</u> the moon.
3. The boy hid <u>behind</u> a tree.
4. Zack fell <u>behind</u> in the race.
5. The detective entered the room and looked <u>around</u>.
6. He walked <u>around</u> the library several times.
7. From the top of the tower, we looked <u>down</u>.
8. Come <u>inside</u> and get warm.
9. Six impossible things happened <u>before</u> breakfast.
10. Don't stand <u>near</u> the door.

7.5 CONJUNCTIONS

A **coordinating conjunction** is a word used to connect compound parts of a sentence. *And, but, or, nor,* and *for* are coordinating conjunctions. *So* and *yet* are also sometimes used as coordinating conjunctions.

USING COORDINATING CONJUNCTIONS TO FORM COMPOUNDS	
COMPOUND SUBJECT	Allison **and** Rosita have lived in Mexico City.
COMPOUND OBJECTS	Give your suitcases **and** packages to Ben **or** Bill.
COMPOUND PREDICATE	Tourists shop **or** relax on the beaches.
COMPOUND SENTENCE	Tillie shopped every day, **but** we toured the city.

To make the relationship between words or groups of words especially strong, use correlative conjunctions.

Correlative conjunctions are pairs of words used to connect compound parts of a sentence. Correlative conjunctions include *both . . . and, either . . . or, neither . . . nor,* and *not only . . . but also.*

EXAMPLE   Examples of great architecture exist in **both** New York **and** Paris.

EXAMPLE   **Neither** Luis **nor** I have visited those cities.

When a compound subject is joined by *and,* the subject is usually plural. The verb must agree with the plural subject.

EXAMPLE   Winnie **and** Sumi **are** in Madrid this week.

When a compound subject is joined by *or* or *nor,* the verb must agree with the nearer subject.

EXAMPLE   **Neither** Rhondelle **nor** the twins **speak** Spanish.

EXAMPLE   **Neither** the twins **nor** Rhondelle **speaks** Spanish.

Write each conjunction. Then write compound subject, compound object, compound predicate, *or* compound sentence *to tell what parts the conjunction joins.*

1. Tom plays soccer, but his sister prefers softball.
2. Either Mrs. James or her husband will bring both the food and the flowers.
3. Neither the assistants nor the head coach teaches any classes.
4. I brought my raincoat but left my umbrella at home.
5. Midori will deliver the books or the old magazines to the hospital or the nursing center.
6. Give either Mrs. Rio or Ms. Stern my thanks for their help with the costumes and the scenery.
7. Enrique and Marisa told the twins and me a good joke.
8. Neither Stan nor his brothers have time for the job, and Ms. Hancock will not hire either Scott or Seth.
9. My sister will take her driver's test tomorrow or wait until next week.
10. Not only the mayor but also the council members will borrow a van or rent a car, but the students will walk to the parade site.

PRACTICE Making Compound Subjects and Verbs Agree

Write the correct word from the choices in parentheses.

1. Ted and his father (repairs, repair) motorcycles.
2. Neither the band nor sports (takes, take) all my extra time.
3. Either the teacher or her aide (prepares, prepare) the daily attendance report.
4. Neither potato chips nor candy (is, are) good for your health.

5. Either curtains or draperies (offers, offer) an attractive window treatment.

6. Neither Bubba nor Jethro (has, have) time for athletics in the summer.

7. Either my mom or my sisters (helps, help) me with my homework.

8. Either two chairs or a sofa (is, are) suitable for a small room.

9. Both biology and botany (is, are) life sciences.

10. Neither the Joneses nor the Hillmans (lives, live) on this street.

7.6 CONJUNCTIVE ADVERBS

You can use a special kind of adverb instead of a conjunction to join the simple sentences in a compound sentence. This special kind of adverb is called a **conjunctive adverb.**

EXAMPLE   Many people use forks, but some use chopsticks.

EXAMPLE   Many people use forks; **however,** some use chopsticks.

A conjunctive adverb, such as *however,* is usually stronger and more exact than a coordinating conjunction like *and* or *but.*

USING CONJUNCTIVE ADVERBS	
TO REPLACE *AND*	besides, furthermore, moreover
TO REPLACE *BUT*	however, nevertheless, still
TO STATE A RESULT	consequently, therefore, thus
TO STATE EQUALITY	equally, likewise, similarly

A **conjunctive adverb** may be used to join the simple sentences in a compound sentence.

Chapter 7 Prepositions, Conjunctions, and Interjections   **183**

When two simple sentences are joined with a conjunctive adverb, use a semicolon at the end of the first sentence. Place a comma after a conjunctive adverb that begins the second part of a compound sentence. If a conjunctive adverb is used in the middle of a simple sentence, set it off with commas.

EXAMPLE   The school cafeteria sometimes serves casseroles; **however,** these meals are not very tasty.

EXAMPLE   The school cafeteria sometimes serves casseroles; these meals, **however,** are not very tasty.

PRACTICE **Identifying Conjunctive Adverbs**

Write each sentence. Underline the conjunctive adverb. Add appropriate punctuation.

1. I forgot my lunch furthermore I have no money.
2. There is no train service from here to Biloxi a bus however leaves here at noon.
3. I have no talent for the piano still I do my best.
4. Harry is hoping for a career in the United States Marine Corps Michael likewise will join the armed forces.
5. Morgan gave the best campaign speech consequently she was elected.
6. Mr. Caruso is a great teacher besides he has a wonderful sense of humor.
7. The islands of the Caribbean have a tropical climate nevertheless pleasant ocean breezes cool the beaches of these islands.
8. Rick is a fine guitarist he has moreover written several original compositions.
9. The new restaurant had few customers thus it closed in a few months.
10. The crime was committed in a locked room the detective was therefore puzzled for a solution.

7.7 INTERJECTIONS

You can express emotions in short exclamations that aren't complete sentences. These exclamations are called interjections.

An **interjection** is a word or group of words that expresses emotion. It has no grammatical connection to other words in a sentence.

Interjections are used to express emotion, such as surprise or disbelief. They're also used to attract attention.

SOME COMMON INTERJECTIONS			
aha	great	my	ouch
alas	ha	no	well
gee	hey	oh	wow
good grief	hooray	oops	yes

An interjection that expresses strong emotion may stand alone. It begins with a capital letter and ends with an exclamation point.

EXAMPLE **Good grief!** My favorite restaurant has closed.

When an interjection expresses mild feeling, it is written as part of the sentence. In that case, the interjection is set off with commas.

EXAMPLE **Oh, well,** I'll just eat at home.

NOTE   Most words may be more than one part of speech. A word's part of speech depends on its use in a sentence.

EXAMPLE   A duck has soft **down** on its body. [noun]

EXAMPLE   The hungry boy **downed** the hamburger in three bites. [verb]

EXAMPLE   Libby felt **down** all day. [adjective]

EXAMPLE   The baby often falls **down.** [adverb]

EXAMPLE   A car drove **down** the street. [preposition]

EXAMPLE   **"Down!"** I shouted to the dog. [interjection]

PRACTICE **Writing Sentences with Interjections**

Write ten sentences, using a different interjection with each. Punctuate correctly.

PRACTICE **Proofreading**

Rewrite the following passage, correcting errors in spelling, capitalization, grammar, and usage. Add any missing punctuation. Write legibly to be sure one letter is not mistaken for another. There are ten errors.

Amy Tan

¹Amy Tan is the author of *The Joy Luck Club* and *The Kitchen God's Wife.* ²About who does she write? ³She writes about Chinese American women.

⁴Amy Tan was born on Febuary 19, 1952. ⁵At the age of fifteen, Tan moved to Europe. ⁶She attended high school in Switzerland; however she was unhappy there. ⁷She returned to the United States and studied English in college.

⁸Tan became a successful business writer nevertheless, she was dissatisfied with her career. ⁹For a change, she took jazz piano lessons; furthermore she joined a group of writers. ¹⁰She remembered stories about her mother. ¹¹Tan wrote about she and other women.

¹²Tan is a popular writer, and her husband is a tax attorney. ¹³Both she and her husband lives in California and New York.

¹⁴Tan is my favorite author. ¹⁵Her stories appeal to my cousin and I. ¹⁶Either Mom or my aunt discuss the stories with us. ¹⁷Maybe our teacher will assign more of Tan's stories. ¹⁸Great

Write each prepositional phrase. Underline the preposition and circle the object of the preposition. Then write the word the prepositional phrase modifies. Finally, write adjective *or* adverb *to tell how the prepositional phrase is used.*

1. Inside the dark and gloomy room, Lucy saw only the dim outlines of the bulky furniture.
2. Jacob kicked the ball down the field and between the goalposts.
3. Aboard the ship, many passengers without life jackets were frantic.
4. Our guests arrived late in the evening.
5. The library near the school will show an educational film on Sunday afternoon.
6. The park behind the library will be suitable for our picnic.
7. On account of rain, the umpire canceled the game.
8. The bakery across the street makes delicious sweet rolls.
9. I started this book about King Arthur at eight and finished it around midnight.
10. The cyclists rode past the barn, over the hill, through the trees, and along the stream.

Write the correct word from the choices in parentheses.

11. Did you eat lunch with Jorge and (they, them)?
12. The shiny black limousine drove slowly toward Kevin and (I, me).
13. Besides Hawa and (she, her), who screamed at the scary scene in the movie?
14. Mrs. Chang waved at the girls and (he, him).
15. Behind (who, whom) did you wait?
16. Did you hear the good news about Jeff and (they, them)?
17. Nothing stood between the barking dog and (we, us).
18. Against (who, whom) will you play in the tournament?

GRAMMAR / USAGE / MECHANICS

19. Mr. Alionzo hurried past Lorenzo and (I, me) on his way to the parking lot.

20. No one was in the room but (she, her) and her sister.

POSTTEST Conjunctions

Write each conjunction. Then write compound subject, compound object, compound predicate, *or* compound sentence *to tell what parts the conjunction joins.*

21. The doctor examined the patient, and the nurse took notes.

22. Neither Mom nor Dad enjoys television cartoons, but we children watch them faithfully.

23. Both Carla and Luisa dry flowers or press them between the pages of a book.

24. We wanted neither the spinach nor the zucchini, but our mother fed them to us.

25. Francis Scott Key wrote "The Star-Spangled Banner" in 1814, and the song became our national anthem in 1931.

26. Is the galaxy or the universe larger?

27. Did you find either the Nile River or the Amazon River on the map?

28. Muwanee will play the part of the judge or the mayor.

29. The students walk to school or take a bus.

30. Give either your aunt or your uncle those free passes.

POSTTEST Making Compound Subjects and Verbs Agree

Write the correct word from the choices in parentheses.

31. Neither a paper clip nor these postage stamps (weighs, weigh) much.

32. Neither these dimes nor this quarter (starts, start) the coin-operated washing machine.

33. Bill Nye and my science teacher (conducts, conduct) science experiments on television.

34. Either the captain or the sailors (helps, help) the passengers.

35. Either the spider exhibits or the snake house (gives, give) me a scare.

36. Both the turtle and the tortoise (has, have) shells of bony plates.

37. Either Amy or Ilom (rides, ride) the snowboard.

38. (Does, Do) a lion or a hyena hunt at night?

39. Neither Mark nor his father (wants, want) these old bicycle tires.

40. You or the twins (deserves, deserve) a merit badge.

POSTTEST **Conjunctive Adverbs**

Write each sentence. Underline the conjunctive adverb. Add appropriate punctuation.

41. Most farmers use machines at harvest time nevertheless some Amish farmers follow older traditions.

42. Fresh vegetables from your own garden taste delicious furthermore they're good for you.

43. Amelia Earhart flew successfully across the Atlantic in 1932 thus she won America's respect.

44. Niagara Falls touches New York likewise it touches Ontario, Canada.

45. Beavers dam waterways with their homes wolves however shelter in caves or dig dens.

Clauses and Complex Sentences

PRETEST   **Simple, Compound, and Complex Sentences**

Write simple, compound, *or* complex *to identify each sentence.*

1. The dollar is the basic unit of money in both the United States and Canada.
2. People in Jordan use the dinar when they buy things.
3. A Zambian buys goods with the kwacha, but a Brazilian buys them with the cruzeiro.
4. If you visit Mexico, convert your dollars into pesos.
5. A traveler visits a banker or a librarian for information on foreign money.
6. In 1700 B.C., people in the country of Lydia, which occupied the site of present-day Turkey, used the first coins as money.

7. A Dutch coin with the head of a lion traveled to the United States in 1620.

8. Did you know that George Washington began the first United States mint?

9. Silver was scarce, and Washington gave the mint some of his silver dishes.

10. Washington's portrait appears on a one-dollar bill; Abraham Lincoln appears on a penny and a five-dollar bill.

PRETEST   Adjective, Adverb, and Noun Clauses

Identify each italicized clause by writing adjective, adverb, *or* noun.

11. *How plants grow* will be our next topic of study.

12. Dad became angry *when he discovered the truth.*

13. Trains *that carry passengers* are becoming rare.

14. We promised *whoever found our dog* a reward.

15. The student *whose essay won first prize* is Beverly Ching.

16. *Before I had finished the assignment,* the bell rang.

17. The story "Basketball Blues," *which I read on Saturday,* is very funny.

18. Lurlene was hurrying *because she was late.*

19. No one knows *what the future will bring.*

20. The committee will award a silver trophy to *whoever designs the best plan.*

21. My brother, *who is captain of the football team,* will attend college in the fall.

22. Everyone rose *as the judge entered the courtroom.*

23. The counselor *whom I saw yesterday* gave me some good advice.

24. The truth is *that some people don't like sports.*

25. *If you submit your order by June 30,* you'll receive a free computer game.

8.1 SENTENCES AND CLAUSES CCSS L.7.1a, b, c

A **sentence** is a group of words that has a subject and a predicate and expresses a complete thought.

A **simple sentence** has one complete subject and one complete predicate.

The **complete subject** names whom or what the sentence is about. The **complete predicate** tells what the subject does or has. Sometimes the complete predicate tells what the subject is or is like. The complete subject or the complete predicate or both may be compound.

COMPLETE SUBJECT	COMPLETE PREDICATE
People	travel.
Neither automobiles nor airplanes	are completely safe.
Travelers	meet new people and see new sights.
Trains and buses	carry passengers and transport goods.

A **compound sentence** contains two or more simple sentences. Each simple sentence is called a main clause.

A **main clause** has a subject and a predicate and can stand alone as a sentence.

Main clauses can be connected by a comma and a conjunction, by a semicolon, or by a semicolon and a conjunctive adverb. The conjunctive adverb is followed by a comma. In the following examples, each main clause is in black. The connecting elements are in blue type.

EXAMPLE Many people live in cities, **but** others build houses in the suburbs. **[comma and coordinating conjunction]**

EXAMPLE Most people travel to their jobs**;** others work at home. **[semicolon]**

EXAMPLE Companies relocate to the suburbs**; therefore,** more people leave the city. **[semicolon and conjunctive adverb]**

Write each sentence. Underline each main clause. Add commas or semicolons where they're needed. Write simple *or* compound *to identify the sentence.*

1. The Falcons and the Red Hawks played yesterday and today both teams are exhausted.
2. The young boy survived alone in the wilderness.
3. Gordon joined the photography club but Marty and Manny had other plans.
4. The twins play in the band and sing in the chorus.
5. Mr. Jonquil planted tulips and daffodils his wife planted pumpkins and watermelons.
6. Dad and the girls washed the car and cleaned the garage.
7. The ideas in your composition are good however your handwriting is sloppy.
8. The house had a fresh coat of paint furthermore the yard looked clean and tidy.
9. Both Yoko and her mother enjoy nature walks in the fall.
10. Mrs. Gardenia washes her clothes by hand or her daughter takes them to a laundry.

8.2 COMPLEX SENTENCES   CCSS L.7.1a, b, c

A **main clause** has a subject and a predicate and can stand alone as a sentence. Some sentences have a main clause and a subordinate clause.

A **subordinate clause** is a group of words that has a subject and a predicate but does not express a complete thought and cannot stand alone as a sentence. A subordinate clause is always combined with a main clause in a sentence.

A **complex sentence** has one main clause and one or more subordinate clauses.

In each complex sentence that follows, the subordinate clause is in blue type.

EXAMPLE   Mariah, **who moved here from Montana,** is very popular.

EXAMPLE   **Since Mariah moved to Springfield,** she has made many new friends.

EXAMPLE   Everyone says **that Mariah is friendly.**

Subordinate clauses can function in three ways: as adjectives, as adverbs, or as nouns. In the examples, the first sentence has an adjective clause that modifies the noun *Mariah*. The second sentence has an adverb clause that modifies the verb *has made.* The third sentence has a noun clause that is the direct object of the verb *says.* Adjective, adverb, and noun clauses are used in the same ways one-word adjectives, adverbs, and nouns are used.

NOTE   A **compound-complex sentence** has two or more main clauses and one or more subordinate clauses.

PRACTICE Identifying Simple and Complex Sentences

Write each sentence. Underline each main clause once and each subordinate clause twice. Write simple *or* complex *to identify the sentence.*

1. I spoke before I thought.
2. After several weeks had passed, I wrote another letter to the mayor.
3. Mark and his best friend, Tony, work in the stables at Kingston Park.
4. We finished the job before noon.
5. Zeena dreamed that she was a colonist on Mars.
6. This book, which I read in a single evening, is hilarious.
7. After the movie, we stopped for a snack at Hamburger Heaven.

8. I like math because it's easy for me.

9. When we met, Connor pretended that he had never seen me before.

10. The baby, who has curly red hair, laughs if you tickle her.

8.3 ADJECTIVE CLAUSES CCSS L.7.1a, c

An **adjective clause** is a subordinate clause that modifies a noun or a pronoun in the main clause of a complex sentence.

EXAMPLE   The Aqua-Lung, **which divers strap on,** holds oxygen.

EXAMPLE   The divers breathe through a tube **that attaches to the tank.**

Each subordinate clause in blue type is an adjective clause that adds information about a noun in the main clause. An adjective clause is usually introduced by a relative pronoun. The relative pronoun *that* may refer to people or things. *Which* refers only to things.

RELATIVE PRONOUNS				
that	which	who	whom	whose

An adjective clause can also begin with *where* or *when*.

EXAMPLE   Divers search for reefs **where much sea life exists.**

EXAMPLE   Herb remembers the day **when he had his first diving experience.**

A relative pronoun that begins an adjective clause is often the subject of the clause.

EXAMPLE   Some divers prefer equipment **that is lightweight.**

EXAMPLE   Willa is a new diver **who is taking lessons.**

In the first sentence, *that* is the subject of the adjective clause. In the second sentence, *who* is the subject of the adjective clause.

Identifying Adjective Clauses

Write each adjective clause. Underline the subject of the adjective clause. Then write the word the adjective clause modifies.

1. I read a story that reminded me of you.
2. Tom Farmer, whose calf won a blue ribbon at the state fair, has been in 4-H for three years.
3. Is this the log cabin where Abraham Lincoln once lived?
4. The shoes that Carrie wants are somewhat expensive.
5. This computer, which is our newest model, has a reasonable price.
6. There are times when I don't like my brother.
7. We often visit my great-grandmother, who is eighty-six.
8. My cousin, whom you met yesterday, will move here permanently in June.
9. The boy who is standing beside Tammy is Nathan's brother.
10. The girls' basketball team, which has won the state championship five times, is the pride and joy of the school district.

8.4 ESSENTIAL AND NONESSENTIAL CLAUSES CCSS L.7.1a, c

Read the example sentence. Is the adjective clause in blue type needed to make the meaning of the sentence clear?

EXAMPLE   The girl **who is standing beside the coach** is our best swimmer.

The adjective clause in blue type is essential to the meaning of the sentence. The clause tells *which* girl is the best swimmer.

An **essential clause** is a clause that is necessary to make the meaning of a sentence clear. Don't use commas to set off essential clauses.

Now look at the adjective clause in this sentence.

EXAMPLE   Janice, **who is standing beside the coach,** is our best swimmer.

In the example, the adjective clause is set off with commas. The clause is nonessential, or not necessary to identify which swimmer the writer means. The clause simply gives additional information about the noun it modifies.

A **nonessential clause** is a clause that is not necessary to make the meaning of a sentence clear. Use commas to set off nonessential clauses.

In this book, adjective clauses that begin with *that* are always essential, and adjective clauses that begin with *which* are always nonessential.

EXAMPLE   Were you at the meet **that** our team won yesterday? **[essential]**

EXAMPLE   That meet, **which** began late, ended after dark. **[nonessential]**

GRAMMAR / USAGE / MECHANICS

Write each sentence. Underline the adjective clause. Add commas where they're needed. Write essential *or* non-essential *to identify each adjective clause.*

1. I like movies that have happy endings.
2. Jeff Brush whose sculpture was selected by the judges has won a scholarship to art camp.
3. This is the house where James Thurber lived as a child.
4. The ships that dock here are foreign vessels.
5. This photograph which I found in a trunk in the attic shows my great-grandmother as a girl.
6. That was the summer when I met my best friend.
7. Chris often discusses problems with her mother who is remarkably understanding.
8. Sada's aunt Carla whom I interviewed last week gave me some interesting information about Sacramento history.
9. The person who delivered the package was wearing a brown uniform and a baseball cap.
10. The White House which is located at 1600 Pennsylvania Avenue is the home of the president and his family.

8.5 ADVERB CLAUSES   CCSS L.7.1a, c

An **adverb clause** is a subordinate clause that often modifies the verb in the main clause of a complex sentence.

An adverb clause tells *how, when, where, why,* or *under what conditions* the action occurs.

EXAMPLE   **After we won the meet,** we shook hands with our opponents.

EXAMPLE   We won the meet **because we practiced hard.**

In the first sentence, the adverb clause *After we won the meet* modifies the verb *shook.* The adverb clause tells *when* we shook hands. In the second sentence, the adverb clause *because we practiced hard* modifies the verb *won*. The adverb clause tells *why* we won the meet.

An adverb clause is introduced by a subordinating conjunction. A subordinating conjunction signals that a clause is a subordinate clause and cannot stand alone.

SUBORDINATING CONJUNCTIONS			
after	because	though	whenever
although	before	till	where
as	if	unless	whereas
as if	since	until	wherever
as though	than	when	while

Use a comma after an adverb clause that begins a sentence. You usually don't use a comma before an adverb clause that comes at the end of a sentence.

NOTE   Adverb clauses can also modify adjectives and adverbs.

GRAMMAR / USAGE / MECHANICS

PRACTICE **Identifying Adverb Clauses**

Write each adverb clause. Underline the subordinating conjunction. Then write the verb the adverb clause modifies.

1. I will feel grateful if you will work with me on this project.
2. Although the detective had investigated the case for a year, he had found no other evidence.
3. I think of you whenever I hear that song.
4. As the sun sets over Honolulu, our plane departs for home.

5. When you're smiling, the whole world smiles with you.

6. Do nothing till you hear from me.

7. Since you went away, we have missed your happy disposition.

8. Three people called while you were sleeping.

9. Unless everyone cooperates, we will make no progress.

10. I failed the test because I did not study.

8.6 NOUN CLAUSES CCSS L.7.1a, c

A **noun clause** is a subordinate clause used as a noun.

Notice how the subject in blue type in the following sentence can be replaced by a clause.

EXAMPLE **A hockey player** wears protective equipment.

EXAMPLE **Whoever plays hockey** wears protective equipment.

The clause in blue type, like the words it replaces, is the subject of the sentence. Because this kind of clause acts as a noun, it's called a noun clause.

You can use a noun clause in the same ways you use a noun—as a subject, a direct object, an indirect object, an object of a preposition, and a predicate noun. In most sentences containing noun clauses, you can replace the noun clause with the word *it*, and the sentence will still make sense.

HOW NOUN CLAUSES ARE USED	
SUBJECT	**Whoever plays hockey** wears protective equipment.
DIRECT OBJECT	Suzi knows **that ice hockey is a rough game.**
INDIRECT OBJECT	She tells **whoever will listen** her opinions.
OBJECT OF A PREPOSITION	Victory goes to **whoever makes more goals.**
PREDICATE NOUN	This rink is **where the teams play.**

Here are some words that can introduce noun clauses.

WORDS THAT INTRODUCE NOUN CLAUSES		
how, however	when	who, whom
if	where	whoever, whomever
that	whether	whose
what, whatever	which, whichever	why

EXAMPLE **Whichever you choose** will look fine.

EXAMPLE **What I wonder** is **why she said that.**

EXAMPLE I don't know **who left this package here.**

EXAMPLE Ask the teacher **if this is the right answer.**

EXAMPLE Promise **whoever calls first** a special bonus.

EXAMPLE He worried about **what he had done.**

PRACTICE Identifying Noun Clauses

Write each noun clause. Then write subject, direct object, indirect object, object of a preposition, *or* predicate noun *to tell how the noun clause is used.*

1. The judges have promised whoever wins the essay contest a trip to Washington, D.C.
2. Tell us how you will achieve your goal.
3. What he said made no sense.
4. Pay attention to whatever the coach tells you.
5. This cave is where Johnson found the lost treasure of Timbaloo.
6. I don't know whether I passed the test.
7. The result of the argument was that the two women never spoke to each other again.
8. Give these free pamphlets to whomever you meet.
9. When they will return is still a mystery.
10. I understand why you did that.

Rewrite the following passage, correcting errors in spelling, capitalization, grammar, and usage. Add any missing punctuation. Write legibly to be sure one letter is not mistaken for another. There are ten errors.

Alice Walker

¹Alice Walker who was the youngest of eight children grew up in Eatonton, Georgia. ²When she was eight years old she injured her face. ³She was embarassed because her face was scarred. ⁴She spent much time alone. ⁵She read many novels and poems and she wrote poems. ⁶She was a clever student consequently, she finished first in her high school class. ⁷She attended Spelman College which is in Atlanta, Georgia. ⁸She also attended Sarah Lawrence College in New York. ⁹While she was a student she traveled to Africa.

¹⁰After she graduated from college Walker became a writer. ¹¹She wrote an essay that won *The American Scholar* essay contest. ¹²*The Color Purple* which won the Pulitzer Prize in 1983 and *The Temple of My Familiar* are two of her novels. ¹³Walker has written essays and reviews for *Ms.* magazine which contains articles about women's concerns.

POSTTEST Simple, Compound, and Complex Sentences

Write simple, compound, *or* complex *to identify each sentence.*

1. Ida Tarbell and Jacob Riis were two American writers who exposed social problems.
2. Ida Tarbell attacked John D. Rockefeller's control of the oil industry, and Jacob Riis criticized conditions in urban slums.

3. Although John D. Rockefeller was a heartless business-man, he gave away over 520 million dollars after his retirement.
4. Streets in cities were unbelievably dirty, and the street lighting was bad.
5. Many houses had no running water; tall buildings had no fire escapes.
6. Fire was a constant threat because most buildings were wooden and had little space between them.
7. Riis believed that such conditions were unhealthy and unsafe.
8. Jane Addams established a famous settlement house in Chicago in 1889.
9. Settlement houses provided neighborhood people with hot meals and educational and cultural activities.
10. Many people made suggestions for improvements in cities, but progress was slow.

POSTTEST Adjective, Adverb, and Noun Clauses

Identify each italicized clause by writing adjective, adverb, *or* noun.

11. Lashawnda takes the downtown bus *when she visits Betty.*
12. *After Owanah finished her homework,* she called her friend Jessica.
13. Brian worked on his English assignment *until the bell rang for lunch.*
14. Please tell me *how you did that trick.*
15. People *who live in the country* enjoy cleaner air.
16. Please sit *wherever you wish.*
17. Miguel's father shows Miguel's trophies to *whoever visits.*
18. A thesaurus, *which is a book of synonyms,* is a helpful tool for writers.
19. The problem is *that you won't cooperate.*

20. This is the spot *where the pirates found the buried treasure.*

21. *What you see before you* is my science project.

22. We're taking the flight *that leaves at 7:35 A.M.*

23. The doctor *whom Grandmother consulted* treated her kindly.

24. Amanda will give *whoever races from Milton Middle School* tough competition.

25. *Before we moved into this house,* we lived in an apartment.

Verbals

....

PRETEST **Verbal Phrases**

Identify each italicized phrase by writing participial, gerund, *or* infinitive.

1. The whole family enjoys *camping in the wilderness.*
2. Many people don't like *to speak before large groups.*
3. Are automobiles *made in Japan* better than American cars?
4. *To make a mistake* is human.
5. *Making craft items from seashells* is Miriam's hobby.
6. *Stepping onto the moon,* Neil Armstrong made his famous speech.
7. He was charged with *disturbing the peace.*
8. *To become a famous actor* is Marilyn's dream.
9. *Invented by Alexander Graham Bell in 1876,* the telephone revolutionized communication.
10. The team's mission was *to rescue the space travelers.*
11. *Pitching a perfect game* is a rare achievement.
12. The Gianellis increased the value of their home by *remodeling their kitchen.*
13. Jake offered *to help me.*
14. *To build a new stadium* will cost 55 million dollars.
15. The author's latest book, *written in just six weeks,* has become a best-seller.

16. The Underground Railroad assisted many African Americans *fleeing cruel masters in the South.*
17. I have finally stopped *worrying about the problem.*
18. Our job is *to build a better mousetrap.*
19. Wood *treated with chemicals* is suitable for decks and other outdoor structures.
20. Today I learned *to throw a curveball.*
21. *Lowering my voice,* I responded to Wendy's question.
22. I promise *to clean the garage on Saturday.*
23. *Designing computer programs* requires much technical knowledge.
24. The young woman *dancing with the prince* is Cinderella.
25. Jing-Mei thanked me for *helping her.*

9.1 PARTICIPLES AND PARTICIPIAL PHRASES
CCSS L.7.1a, c

A present participle is formed by adding *-ing* to a verb. A past participle is usually formed by adding *-d* or *-ed* to a verb. A participle can act as the main verb in a verb phrase or as an adjective to modify a noun or a pronoun.

EXAMPLE Erik is **taking** piano lessons. [present participle used as main verb in a verb phrase]

EXAMPLE His talent has **impressed** his teacher. [past participle used as main verb in a verb phrase]

EXAMPLE His **playing** skill improves daily. [present participle used as adjective modifying *skill*]

EXAMPLE He practices at home on a **rented** piano. [past participle used as adjective modifying *piano*]

A participle that is used as an adjective may be modified by a single adverb or by a prepositional phrase. It may also have a direct object.

EXAMPLE **Sitting quietly,** Erik loses himself in the music.

EXAMPLE **Sitting at the piano,** Erik loses himself in the music.

EXAMPLE **Playing the piano,** Erik loses himself in the music.

A **participial phrase** is a group of words that includes a participle and other words that complete its meaning.

A participial phrase that begins a sentence is always set off with a comma. Participial phrases in other places in a sentence may or may not need commas. If the phrase is necessary to identify the modified word, it is an essential phrase and should not be set off with commas. If the phrase simply gives additional information about the modified word, it is a nonessential phrase. Use commas to set off nonessential phrases.

EXAMPLE The musician **seated at the piano** is Erik. [essential]

EXAMPLE Erik, **dreaming of fame**, sits at the piano. [nonessential]

EXAMPLE **Dreaming of fame**, Erik sits at the piano. [nonessential]

An essential participial phrase must follow the noun it modifies. A nonessential participial phrase can appear before or after the word it modifies. Place the phrase as close as possible to the modified word to make the meaning of the sentence clear.

PRACTICE Identifying Participles

Write each participle. Then write main verb *or* adjective *to tell how the participle is used.*

1. Juan Escobeda has just moved to Taylorville from Puerto Rico.
2. Stay away from that deserted building.
3. Who is watching the baby?
4. Mr. and Mrs. Ford are shopping for a new car.
5. I am delivering meals to disabled shut-ins.
6. Mitsuko had entered the diving competition with high hopes.
7. The glaring lights of the bus station shone down on the stranded travelers.

8. Alicia's amazing writing skills have gained her many awards.
9. Mervin and Leroy were looking for you.
10. A battered old sprinkling can was standing on the porch.

PRACTICE Identifying Participial Phrases

Write each sentence. Underline the participial phrase once. Draw two lines under the word the participial phrase modifies. Add commas where they're needed.

1. The sculpture painted bright red gave the park a weird appearance.
2. Lingering at the door Bobbi Jo waited for her friend.
3. The price tag attached to the silk shirt read "$69.95."
4. Nurse Primrose opening the door to the examining room gave the patient a cheery smile.
5. Attacked by a wild boar the warrior bravely defended himself.
6. The boy peering through the window is my cousin Ned.
7. On the table were several packages wrapped in bright paper and tied with ribbons and bows.
8. Dressed in clown costumes the band marched onto the field.
9. Norm Spendall is the producer financing the movie.
10. Placing a comma after the participial phrase Jasmine finished the assignment.

9.2 GERUNDS AND GERUND PHRASES

CCSS L.7.1a, c

When a verb form ending in -*ing* is used as a noun, it's called a gerund.

EXAMPLE The **skating** rink is near my house. [adjective]

EXAMPLE **Skating** is a favorite winter pastime in my neighborhood. [noun, gerund]

A **gerund** is a verb form that ends in -*ing* and is used as a noun.

Like other nouns, a gerund may be used as a subject, a predicate noun, a direct object, or the object of a preposition.

EXAMPLE **Exercising** builds strength and endurance. [subject]

EXAMPLE My favorite activity is **exercising**. [predicate noun]

EXAMPLE Some people enjoy **exercising**. [direct object]

EXAMPLE What are the benefits of **exercising?** [object of a preposition]

A gerund may be modified by a single adverb or by a prepositional phrase. It may also have a direct object.

EXAMPLE **Exercising daily** is a good habit.

EXAMPLE Many people enjoy **exercising on a bike.**

EXAMPLE Tell me something about **exercising the body.**

A **gerund phrase** is a group of words that includes a gerund and other words that complete its meaning.

You can identify the three uses of -*ing* verb forms if you remember that a present participle can serve as part of a verb phrase, as an adjective, and as a noun.

EXAMPLE The young people are **bicycling** in the country. [main verb]

EXAMPLE The **bicycling** club travels long distances. [adjective]

EXAMPLE **Bicycling** is good exercise. [noun, gerund]

PRACTICE **Identifying Gerunds and Participles**

Write main verb, adjective, *or* gerund *to identify each underlined word.*

1. My favorite sport is <u>swimming</u>.
2. Everyone was <u>swimming</u> in the lake.
3. We all jumped into the <u>swimming</u> pool.
4. Few people enjoy <u>ironing</u>.

5. A <u>growing</u> child needs care, love, and attention.
6. John is <u>working</u> for his brother.
7. Those in the lifeboats helplessly watched the <u>sinking</u> ship.
8. Rosalind is <u>earning</u> money by <u>tutoring</u>.
9. I am <u>living</u> with my uncle Ralph and my aunt Susan.
10. <u>Studying</u> is a <u>learning</u> experience.

PRACTICE **Identifying Gerund Phrases**

Write each gerund phrase. Then write subject, predicate noun, direct object, *or* object of a preposition *to tell how it's used.*

1. I read a book about climbing Mount Everest.
2. Many people avoid speaking before large groups.
3. Her greatest talent was playing the flute.
4. After the first five minutes, I stopped listening to the speaker.
5. I exhausted myself by walking ten miles.
6. Becoming a medical doctor requires many years of education.
7. Poison ivy causes itching of the affected area.
8. Succeeding in school depends on hard work.
9. What are the advantages of living in Alaska?
10. Playing first base will be a real stretch for me.

9.3 INFINITIVES AND INFINITIVE PHRASES

CCSS L.7.1a, c

Another verb form that may be used as a noun is an infinitive.

EXAMPLE **To write** is Alice's ambition.

EXAMPLE Alice wants **to write.**

An **infinitive** is formed with the word *to* and the base form of a verb. Infinitives are often used as nouns in sentences.

How can you tell if the word *to* is a preposition or part of an infinitive? If the word *to* comes immediately before a verb, it's part of an infinitive.

EXAMPLE   Alice liked **to write.** [infinitive]

EXAMPLE   She sent a story **to a magazine.** [prepositional phrase]

In the first sentence, the words in blue type work together as a noun to name *what* Alice liked. In the second sentence, the words in blue type are a prepositional phrase used as an adverb to tell *where* she sent a story.

Because infinitives are used as nouns, they can be subjects, predicate nouns, and direct objects.

EXAMPLE   **To write** was Alice's ambition. [subject]

EXAMPLE   Alice's ambition was **to write.** [predicate noun]

EXAMPLE   Alice liked **to write.** [direct object]

An infinitive may be modified by a single adverb or by a prepositional phrase. It may also have a direct object.

EXAMPLE   **To write well** was Alice's ambition.

EXAMPLE   Alice's ambition was **to write for fame and money.**

EXAMPLE   Alice wanted **to write a great novel.**

An **infinitive phrase** is a group of words that includes an infinitive and other words that complete its meaning.

PRACTICE Identifying Infinitives and Prepositional Phrases

Write infinitive phrase *or* prepositional phrase *to identify each underlined group of words.*

1. Margo's goal was <u>to become a ballerina</u>.
2. I rode my bike <u>to the library</u>.
3. This shirt fits me <u>to perfection</u>.
4. <u>To criticize others</u> seems unkind.
5. I hate <u>to clean my room</u>.

6. James traveled <u>to Arizona</u> with his aunt Carla.
7. Please go <u>to the grocery</u> for a gallon of skim milk.
8. <u>To improve your grades</u> will take a great deal of work.
9. The cat likes <u>to look out the window</u>.
10. The road <u>to Mayberry</u> passes through Junebug.

Identifying Infinitive Phrases

Write each infinitive phrase. Then write subject, predicate noun, *or* direct object *to tell how it's used.*

1. Morton refused to help us.
2. Remember to brush your teeth.
3. To play the piano well requires practice.
4. Linda's decision was to sell her bicycle.
5. Robby learned to repair motorcycles.
6. My intention is to read one hundred books this year.
7. The baby began to cry loudly.
8. To sit in the sun on a spring day feels wonderful.
9. Don't forget to take out the garbage.
10. To blame others for your problems doesn't solve them.

Proofreading

Rewrite the following passage, correcting errors in spelling and adding missing punctuation. Write legibly to be sure one letter is not mistaken for another. There are ten errors.

Nikki Giovanni

[1]Growing up in Cincinnati Nikki Giovanni loved books. [2]She attended Fisk University. [3]Giovanni dissatisfied with the school was unhappy there. [4]Rebelling against the rules she ran home to her grandmother. [5]She later returned to Fisk and edited a school magazine. [6]Interested in civil rights she became politically active. [7]Taking

GRAMMAR / USAGE / MECHANICS

part in a writers' workshop she learned from a famous author. [8]Giovanni receiving honors graduated in 1967.

[9]After her graduation, Giovanni organized a black arts festival. [10]The festival held in Cincinnati celebrated African American arts and culture.

[11]Giovanni published *Spin a Soft Black Song* in 1971. [12]It was a book of childern's poems. [13]More poems for young people appeared in *Vacation Time: Poems for Children* published in 1980. [14]The book published in 1971 was her first book of children's poems.

[15]Many people recogized Giovanni's talent. [16]The album recorded in 1971 made her even more famous. [17]It is called *Truth Is on Its Way.* [18]Anyone having Giovanni's talent and ambition will always succeed.

POSTTEST Verbal Phrases

Identify each italicized phrase by writing participial, gerund, *or* infinitive.

1. *Eating strawberries* gives me hives.
2. *Waving to his family,* Charlie boarded the plane.
3. A soldier's duty is *to obey orders.*
4. I tried *to tell her the truth.*
5. The two women *playing tennis* are my mother and my aunt Virginia.
6. Meteorologists practice *forecasting the weather.*
7. Terri earned money by *walking her neighbor's dog.*
8. On one corner was a vacant lot *surrounded by a high fence.*
9. *To lose a friend* is painful.
10. My father likes *to sing in the shower.*
11. There lay the priceless vase, *shattered into a million pieces.*
12. Don't make any decision without *talking to your parents first.*
13. *Designed by James Hoban,* the White House has been the home of presidents since 1800.

14. *To walk to the nearest library* takes twenty minutes.
15. Jerry's suggestion for the class project was *to perform a musical show at the retirement home.*
16. Oscar, *winking at his brother,* slipped the rubber spider onto his sister's plate.
17. *Smoking cigarettes* is bad for your health.
18. Children *raised in poverty* are poor candidates for success in later life.
19. Harry and Sally refused *to join us for dinner.*
20. Who is the person *wearing the Superman costume*?
21. After *meeting with the counselor,* I decided *to take algebra next year.*
22. Aunt Cora has begun *studying art history.*
23. *To become an outstanding athlete* demands devotion and hard work.
24. My plan is *to join the Peace Corps.*
25. Chan enjoys *playing in the band.*

Chapter 10

Subject-Verb Agreement

PRETEST Subject-Verb Agreement

Write the correct verb from the choices in parentheses.

1. The class (wants, want) to enter their photographs in the contest.
2. The author and illustrator (is, are) Kwesi Malloum.
3. Meteorologists (studies, study) weather patterns.
4. *The Wind in the Willows* (is, are) my younger brother's favorite book.
5. Mathematics (is, are) difficult for me.
6. Those blue jays or that cardinal (eats, eat) the old bread.
7. In the alley behind the building (is, are) three dumpsters.
8. A brook (gurgles, gurgle) through the leafy forest.
9. Everyone (takes, take) an interest in the tournament.
10. The children (is, are) watching a cartoon.
11. Jamake (seems, seem) happy at his new school.
12. The farms of Nebraska (produces, produce) millions of bushels of grain.

13. Both Wayne Gretzky and Cammi Granato (deserves, deserve) respect for their playing ability.
14. Few (chooses, choose) spinach as their favorite vegetable.
15. These special scissors (cuts, cut) through metal.
16. They (listens, listen) to music in the evening.
17. A book of riddles (lies, lie) on the desk.
18. (Does, Do) robins migrate south for the winter?
19. Neither our congresswoman nor our two senators ever (votes, vote) for higher taxes.
20. Any of these sweaters (looks, look) good with jeans.
21. Here (is, are) three coins from ancient Rome.
22. Some of this clothing (is, are) going to the homeless shelter.
23. Three months (passes, pass) during summer vacation.
24. Some of the students (wants, want) more study time.
25. The Johnsons or their son (drives, drive) the car to the shop for repairs.

10.1 MAKING SUBJECTS AND VERBS AGREE

The basic idea of subject-verb agreement is a simple one: A singular subject requires a singular verb, and a plural subject requires a plural verb. The subject and its verb are said to *agree in number.*

Notice that in the present tense the singular form of the verb usually ends in *-s* or *-es.*

SUBJECT-VERB AGREEMENT WITH NOUNS AS SUBJECTS	
SINGULAR	**PLURAL**
A **botanist studies** plant life.	**Botanists study** plant life.
A **plant requires** care.	**Plants require** care.

A verb must also agree with a subject that is a pronoun. Look at the chart that follows. Notice how the verb changes. In the present tense, the *-s* ending is used with the subject pronouns *he, she,* and *it.*

SUBJECT-VERB AGREEMENT WITH PRONOUNS AS SUBJECTS

SINGULAR	PLURAL
I **work.**	We **work.**
You **work.**	You **work.**
He, she, or it **works.**	They **work.**

The irregular verbs *be, have,* and *do* can be main verbs or helping verbs. These verbs must agree with the subject whether they're main verbs or helping verbs.

EXAMPLES I **am** a botanist. He **is** a botanist. They **are** botanists. **[main verbs]**

EXAMPLES She **is** working. You **are** studying. **[helping verbs]**

EXAMPLES I **have** a job. She **has** a career. **[main verbs]**

EXAMPLES He **has** planted a tree. They **have** planted trees. **[helping verbs]**

EXAMPLES He **does** well. They **do** the job. **[main verbs]**

EXAMPLES It **does** sound good. We **do** work hard. **[helping verbs]**

PRACTICE Making Subjects and Verbs Agree I

Write the subject. Then write the correct verb from the choices in parentheses.

1. Forest fires (destroys, destroy) millions of trees each year.

2. He (is, are) reading about space travel.

3. The river (flows, flow) past the old cabin.

4. You (has, have) forgotten your homework again!

5. They (is, are) students at another school.

6. The children (shares, share) their toys.

7. I (does, do) my homework faithfully.

8. Janelle (does, do) play in the band.

9. Your idea (makes, make) sense to me.

10. She (has, have) a stamp collection.

10.2 PROBLEMS IN LOCATING THE SUBJECT

Making a verb agree with its subject is easy when the verb directly follows the subject. Sometimes, however, a prepositional phrase comes between the subject and the verb.

EXAMPLE   This **book** of Mark Twain's stories **appeals** to people of all ages.

EXAMPLE   **Stories** by Washington Irving **are** also popular.

In the first sentence, *of Mark Twain's stories* is a prepositional phrase. The singular verb *appeals* agrees with the singular subject, *book,* not with the plural noun *stories,* which is the object of the preposition *of.* In the second sentence, *by Washington Irving* is a prepositional phrase. The plural verb *are* agrees with the plural subject, *Stories,* not with the singular noun *Washington Irving,* which is the object of the preposition *by.*

An **inverted sentence** is a sentence in which the subject follows the verb.

Inverted sentences often begin with a prepositional phrase. Don't mistake the object of the preposition for the subject of the sentence.

EXAMPLE   Across the ocean **sail millions** of immigrants.

In inverted sentences beginning with *Here* or *There,* look for the subject after the verb. *Here* or *there* is never the subject of a sentence.

EXAMPLE Here **is a picture** of my grandparents.

EXAMPLE There **are** many **immigrants** among my ancestors.

By rearranging the sentence so the subject comes first, you can see the agreement between the subject and the verb.

EXAMPLE **Millions** of immigrants **sail** across the ocean.

EXAMPLE A **picture** of my grandparents **is** here.

EXAMPLE Many **immigrants are** there among my ancestors.

In some interrogative sentences, a helping verb comes before the subject. Look for the subject between the helping verb and the main verb.

EXAMPLE **Do** these **stories interest** you?

You can check the subject-verb agreement by making the sentence declarative.

EXAMPLE These **stories do interest** you.

PRACTICE Making Subjects and Verbs Agree II

Write the subject. Then write the correct verb from the choices in parentheses.

1. Among the shrubs (was, were) a tiny kitten.
2. (Has, Have) rabbits destroyed your garden this summer?
3. Here (is, are) the garden chairs for your party.
4. (Is, Are) the eighth-graders organizing the school picnic?
5. The fangs of a rattlesnake (carries, carry) poison to its prey.
6. (Does, Do) marigolds bloom in the spring?
7. There (is, are) your classmate across the street.
8. A nest of hornets (was, were) in the barn.

9. From the roof of the porch (hangs, hang) several baskets of geraniums.

10. Apartments in this neighborhood (is, are) inexpensive.

10.3 COLLECTIVE NOUNS AND OTHER SPECIAL SUBJECTS

A **collective noun** names a group.

Collective nouns follow special agreement rules. A collective noun has a singular meaning when it names a group that acts as a unit. A collective noun has a plural meaning when it refers to the members of the group acting as individuals. The meaning helps you decide whether to use the singular or plural form of the verb.

EXAMPLE   The **audience sits** in silence. [a unit, singular]

EXAMPLE   The **audience sit** on chairs and pillows. [individuals, plural]

Certain nouns, such as *news* and *mathematics,* end in *s* but require singular verbs. Other nouns that end in *s* and name one thing, such as *scissors* and *binoculars,* require plural verbs.

EXAMPLE   **News is** important to everyone. [singular]

EXAMPLE   The **scissors are** in the top drawer. [plural]

SPECIAL NOUNS THAT END IN *S*			
SINGULAR		**PLURAL**	
civics	physics	binoculars	scissors
Los Angeles	United Nations	jeans	sunglasses
mathematics	United States	pants	trousers
news		pliers	tweezers

A subject that refers to an amount as a single unit is singular. A subject that refers to a number of individual units is plural.

EXAMPLE **Ten years seems** a long time. [single unit]

EXAMPLE **Ten years pass** quickly. [individual units]

EXAMPLE **Three dollars is** the admission price. [single unit]

EXAMPLE **Three dollars are** on the table. [individual units]

The title of a book or a work of art is always singular, even if a noun in the title is plural.

EXAMPLE ***Snow White and the Seven Dwarfs* is** a good Disney movie.

EXAMPLE ***The Last of the Mohicans* was** written by James Fenimore Cooper.

PRACTICE Making Subjects and Verbs Agree III

Write the subject. Then write the correct verb from the choices in parentheses.

1. Ten minutes (is, are) a long time to a two-year-old.
2. Where (is, are) your sunglasses?
3. *Across Five Aprils* (tells, tell) the story of a family with sons on opposite sides in the Civil War.
4. The committee (is, are) studying the plan for the new lunchroom.
5. The orchestra (tunes, tune) their instruments.
6. *The Five Little Peppers* (was, were) once a popular series for young readers.
7. Ten dollars (was, were) scattered across the top of the bureau.
8. Every morning the family (goes, go) their separate ways to work or school.
9. Mathematics (is, are) fascinating to some students.
10. The jury (has, have) announced its verdict.

10.4 INDEFINITE PRONOUNS AS SUBJECTS

An **indefinite pronoun** is a pronoun that does not refer to a particular person, place, or thing.

Some indefinite pronouns are singular. Others are plural. When an indefinite pronoun is used as a subject, the verb must agree in number with the pronoun.

SOME INDEFINITE PRONOUNS			
SINGULAR			**PLURAL**
another	everybody	no one	both
anybody	everyone	nothing	few
anyone	everyone	one	many
anything	much	somebody	others
each	neither	someone	several
either	nobody	something	

The indefinite pronouns *all, any, most, none,* and *some* may be singular or plural, depending on the phrase that follows.

EXAMPLE **Most** of the forest **lies** to the east. **[singular]**

EXAMPLE **Most** of these scientists **study** forest growth. **[plural]**

Often a prepositional phrase follows an indefinite pronoun that can be either singular or plural. To decide whether the pronoun is singular or plural, look at the object of the preposition. In the first sentence, *most* refers to *forest.* Because *forest* is singular, *most* must be considered as a single unit. In the second sentence, *most* refers to *scientists.* Because *scientists* is plural, *most* should be considered as individual units.

Write the subject. Then write the correct verb from the choices in parentheses.

1. Everyone (shares, share) the work.
2. Some of the responsibility (was, were) yours.
3. Both (wishes, wish) to help with the scenery.
4. Most of the workers (has, have) left the building.
5. Neither of the girls (likes, like) chocolate pudding.
6. Few (has, have) time for other activities.
7. Any of this clothing (is, are) ready for the volunteers.
8. Something (is, are) wrong with the television set.
9. All of our supporters (was, were) cheering from the stands.
10. None of the weather report (has, have) changed since this morning.

10.5 AGREEMENT WITH COMPOUND SUBJECTS

A **compound subject** contains two or more simple subjects that have the same verb.

Compound subjects may require a singular or a plural verb, depending on how the subjects are joined. When two or more subjects are joined by *and* or by the correlative conjunction *both . . . and,* the plural form of the verb should be used.

EXAMPLE   New York, Denver, **and** London **have** smog.

EXAMPLE   **Both** automobiles **and** factories **contribute** to smog.

Sometimes *and* is used to join two words that are part of one unit or refer to a single person or thing. In these cases, the subject is singular. In the following example, *captain* and *leader* refer to the same person. Therefore, the singular form of the verb is used.

EXAMPLE   The captain **and** leader of the team **is** Ms. Cho.

When two or more subjects are joined by *or* or by the correlative conjunction *either . . . or* or *neither . . . nor*, the verb agrees with the subject that is closer to it.

EXAMPLE   The cities **or** the state **responds** to pollution complaints.

EXAMPLE   **Either** smoke **or** gases **cause** the smog.

In the first sentence, *responds* is singular because the closer subject, *state,* is singular. In the second sentence, *gases* is the closer subject. The verb is plural because the closer subject is plural.

PRACTICE **Making Subjects and Verbs Agree V**

Write the complete subject. Then write the correct verb from the choices in parentheses.

1. Ravi and his brother (is, are) participating in the science competition.
2. Neither Beth nor her sisters (has, have) studied Spanish.
3. Both the teachers and the principal (attends, attend) the school dances.
4. Either violins or a piano (plays, play) during dinner.
5. Washington, Jefferson, and Lincoln (is, are) three of our greatest presidents.
6. Our math teacher and softball coach (is, are) Ms. Fiorella.
7. Either the groom or his parents (provides, provide) the rehearsal dinner.
8. The suspect or his lawyer (answers, answer) questions.
9. Neither family responsibilities nor illness (has, have) kept Mrs. Portero from her job as a mail carrier.
10. Gloves and a hat (was, were) once important parts of a woman's costume.

PRACTICE Proofreading

Rewrite the following passage, correcting the errors in subject-verb agreement. Write legibly to be sure one letter is not mistaken for another. There are ten errors.

Mark Twain

¹Does Mark Twain's stories appeal to today's readers? ²Yes, books by Mark Twain is still popular today. ³There is two very famous books by Twain. ⁴They are called *The Adventures of Huckleberry Finn* and *The Adventures of Tom Sawyer.* ⁵The United States are the setting of these books. ⁶*The Adventures of Huckleberry Finn* are great. ⁷Both Huck and Jim is characters in the story. ⁸The main character and my favorite character are Huck. ⁹Down the Mississippi sails Huck and Jim.

¹⁰Each year, the school drama club choose a story. ¹¹Then students perform the story as a play. ¹²This year, the members chose *The Adventures of Huckleberry Finn.* ¹³There is an admittance charge. ¹⁴Five dollars are the price of the show.

GRAMMAR / USAGE / MECHANICS

POSTTEST Subject-Verb Agreement

Write the correct verb from the choices in parentheses.

1. Those jeans (is, are) too tight.
2. Everybody (donates, donate) something for the bake sale.
3. The news (is, are) good.
4. One of the girls usually (brings, bring) refreshments.
5. Two weeks (is, are) the length of the soccer camp.
6. Both the ostrich and the kangaroo (travels, travel) at high speeds.
7. The team (poses, pose) for its photograph.
8. The best trumpet player and soloist (is, are) Daniel.
9. Most appliances in your home (has, have) serial numbers.

10. I (finds, find) serial numbers on many of our appliances.
11. Trina, Soraya, and Kwami (is, are) playing a board game on the porch.
12. Either her grandparents or her father (stays, stay) with the children.
13. He (sees, see) something strange through the window.
14. There (is, are) thirteen stars, thirteen stripes, thirteen arrows, thirteen olive leaves, and thirteen levels to the pyramid on a dollar bill.
15. Most of the country (has, have) a temperate climate.
16. Most of the band members (has, have) their own instruments.
17. In the corner of the garden (grows, grow) tomatoes.
18. (Does, Do) those comedians seem funny to you?
19. Disney's *101 Dalmatians* (is, are) the children's favorite animated film.
20. Many (suffers, suffer) in hot weather.
21. How many people (has, have) visited the space exhibit?
22. The audience (scatters, scatter) toward the exits at the end of the show.
23. One mountain in the Cascades (is, are) Mount Shasta.
24. A cat or a dog (makes, make) a good pet.
25. Neither Lorna nor her sisters (plays, play) a musical instrument.

Diagraming Sentences

PRETEST   **Diagraming Sentences**

Diagram each sentence.

1. Máire smiled.
2. Joe is winning.
3. Did Rachel sing?
4. Stop!
5. Mail this letter.
6. Mr. Avila promised me a job.
7. Heidi sent Tim several postcards.
8. Outside the fierce wind howled viciously.
9. Your very delicious Irish stew disappeared so fast.

10. The door behind you leads to the kitchen.
11. My brother is growing taller.
12. That old bike looks a wreck.
13. Colds and the flu travel around school during winter.
14. These machines are slow but reliable.
15. The First Amendment protects freedom of speech, and the Thirteenth Amendment abolished slavery.
16. Jason wrote a letter to the president, but he received no reply.
17. Students who damage their books will pay a fine.
18. Before Ms. Sumi became a teacher, she was a flight attendant.
19. What I need is a new computer.
20. I do not know why Thai Tong missed the meeting.
21. Gabriel delivers hot meals to whoever needs them.
22. The wallet found in the victim's pocket contained no identification.
23. Smiling happily, Gina accepted the award.
24. Helping at the food drive took only two hours.
25. Mom likes to sing in the shower.

11.1 DIAGRAMING SIMPLE SUBJECTS AND SIMPLE PREDICATES CCSS L.7.1b

The basic parts of a sentence are the subject and the predicate. To diagram a sentence, first draw a horizontal line. Then draw a vertical line that crosses the horizontal line.

To the left of the vertical line, write the simple subject. To the right of the vertical line, write the simple predicate. Use capital letters as they appear in the sentence, but don't include punctuation.

EXAMPLE **People are working.**

| People | are working |

In a diagram, the positions of the subject and the predicate always remain the same.

EXAMPLE **Caravans rumbled** across the prairie.

$$\frac{\text{Caravans} \mid \text{rumbled}}{}$$

EXAMPLE Across the prairie **rumbled caravans.**

$$\frac{\text{caravans} \mid \text{rumbled}}{}$$

PRACTICE **Diagraming Simple Subjects and Simple Predicates**

Diagram the simple subject and the simple predicate.

1. Horns blare.
2. Overhead circled the vultures.
3. The boy seems nervous.
4. Jaleela will plan the party.
5. Several people were waiting patiently.
6. They have eaten the birthday cake.
7. Cody is writing his report.
8. I dozed restlessly.
9. The sailboat had sprung a leak.
10. You have finished the job.

11.2 DIAGRAMING THE FOUR KINDS OF SENTENCES CCSS L.7.1b

Study the diagrams of the simple subject and the simple predicate for the four kinds of sentences. Recall that in an interrogative sentence the subject often comes between the two parts of a verb phrase. In an imperative sentence, the simple subject is the understood *you.*

Notice that the positions of the simple subject and the simple predicate in a sentence diagram are always the same, regardless of the word order in the original sentence.

DECLARATIVE

EXAMPLE **People write** letters.

$$\begin{array}{c|c} \text{People} & \text{write} \end{array}$$

INTERROGATIVE

EXAMPLE **Do** many **people write** letters?

$$\begin{array}{c|c} \text{people} & \text{Do write} \end{array}$$

IMPERATIVE

EXAMPLE **Write** a letter.

$$\begin{array}{c|c} \text{(you)} & \text{Write} \end{array}$$

EXCLAMATORY

EXAMPLE What interesting letters **you write!**

$$\begin{array}{c|c} \text{you} & \text{write} \end{array}$$

PRACTICE **Diagraming the Four Kinds of Sentences**

Diagram the simple subject and the simple predicate.

1. Does the sun rise in the east?
2. Whales are mammals.
3. Send me a postcard.
4. The warm rain fell silently.
5. The detective has solved the mystery.
6. How happy I am today!
7. Is your mother's car blue?
8. Hand me that magazine.
9. Have you seen my camera?
10. How funny you look in that costume!

11.3 DIAGRAMING DIRECT AND INDIRECT OBJECTS

A direct object is part of the predicate. In a sentence diagram, write the direct object to the right of the verb. Draw a vertical line to separate the verb from the direct object. This vertical line, however, does *not* cross the horizontal line.

EXAMPLE **People invent machines.**

$$\text{People} \mid \text{invent} \mid \text{machines}$$

EXAMPLE **Students use computers.**

$$\text{Students} \mid \text{use} \mid \text{computers}$$

An indirect object is also part of the predicate. It usually tells to whom or for whom the action of a verb is done. An indirect object always comes before a direct object in a sentence. In a sentence diagram, write an indirect object on a horizontal line below and to the right of the verb. Join it to the verb with a slanted line.

EXAMPLE **Rosa gave the dog a bone.**

$$\text{Rosa} \mid \text{gave} \mid \text{bone}$$
$$\diagdown \text{dog}$$

PRACTICE Diagraming Direct and Indirect Objects

Diagram the simple subject, the simple predicate, and the direct object. Diagram the indirect object if the sentence has one.

1. Jamie brought his father the newspaper.
2. The mechanic fixed the truck.
3. Ms. Lawson teaches health.
4. She assigns the students special projects.
5. Carol played the class a tune on her harmonica.

6. The ship hit an iceberg.
7. Mr. Yamamoto is giving Lenora piano lessons.
8. The mayor has written Jonas a letter.
9. Each student will recite a poem.
10. This job will offer you many opportunities.

11.4 DIAGRAMING ADJECTIVES, ADVERBS, AND PREPOSITIONAL PHRASES

CCSS L.7.1a, c

In a diagram, write adjectives and adverbs on slanted lines beneath the words they modify.

EXAMPLE **Elena's strange** dream faded **quickly.**

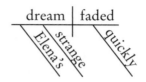

EXAMPLE **The very old** tree produced **incredibly delicious** apples **rather slowly.**

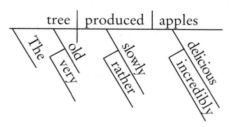

A prepositional phrase can be either an adjective phrase or an adverb phrase. Study the diagram for prepositional phrases.

EXAMPLE A woman **in a pink hat** was sitting **beside me.**

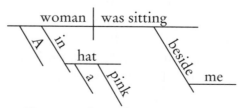

Diagram each sentence.

1. Several students were eating their lunch on the patio.
2. Petula's first performance in the play showed great talent.
3. This extremely expensive automobile has many extraordinary features.
4. A nasty storm attacked the coast of Florida yesterday.
5. Harry's mother was playing the old piano rather quietly.
6. Those very dark colors fade too quickly in the sun.
7. Now we shall see an unusually spectacular trapeze act.
8. The thoughtful girl bought her older brother an orange sweatshirt today.
9. These especially fragile Hawaiian flowers almost never grow outdoors here.
10. My grandma served the entire family a really delicious Thanksgiving dinner with pumpkin pie for dessert.

11.5 DIAGRAMING PREDICATE NOUNS AND PREDICATE ADJECTIVES

In a sentence diagram, a direct object follows the verb.

EXAMPLE   People use telephones.

$$\text{People} \mid \text{use} \mid \text{telephones}$$

To diagram a sentence with a predicate noun, write the predicate noun to the right of the linking verb. Draw a slanted line to separate the verb from the predicate noun.

EXAMPLE   Telephones are useful **instruments.**

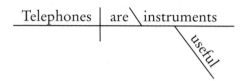

Diagram a predicate adjective in the same way.

EXAMPLE   Telephones are **useful.**

$$\text{Telephones} \mid \text{are} \diagdown \text{useful}$$

| PRACTICE | Diagraming Predicate Nouns and Predicate Adjectives |

Diagram each sentence.

1. You sound cheerful today.
2. The twins have become excellent pianists.
3. This soup tastes too salty.
4. Your room looks a mess.
5. The baby is growing fatter.
6. Everyone feels blue sometimes.
7. The attic was a marvelous hideaway.

8. Your meals always smell quite delicious.

9. Rover seems a gentle dog.

10. The swimmer's hair turned green.

11.6 DIAGRAMING COMPOUND SENTENCE PARTS CCSS L.7.1b

Coordinating conjunctions such as *and, but,* and *or* are used to join compound parts: words, phrases, or sentences. To diagram compound parts of a sentence, write the second part of the compound below the first. Write the coordinating conjunction on a dotted line connecting the two parts.

COMPOUND SUBJECT

EXAMPLE **Gas and oil** heat homes.

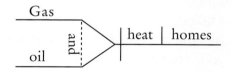

COMPOUND PREDICATE

EXAMPLE Babies **eat and sleep.**

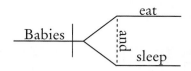

COMPOUND DIRECT OBJECT

EXAMPLE The bakery serves **sandwiches and beverages.**

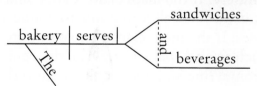

GRAMMAR / USAGE / MECHANICS

COMPOUND PREDICATE NOUN OR PREDICATE ADJECTIVE

EXAMPLE Dogs are **loyal and friendly.**

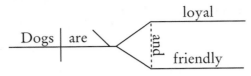

PRACTICE **Diagraming Compound Sentence Parts**

Diagram each sentence.

1. Shoes and socks littered the floor.
2. The engine coughed and sputtered.
3. Mr. Margolis grows tomatoes and cucumbers.
4. Tamako or Tyrone will be our representative.
5. These cars seem reliable but expensive.
6. Do you want peas or corn?
7. I tried but failed.
8. Ms. Diaz has been a coach and a teacher.
9. Give me your coat and your hat.
10. The big bad wolf huffed and puffed.

11.7 DIAGRAMING COMPOUND SENTENCES

CCSS L.7.1b

To diagram a compound sentence, diagram each main clause separately. If the main clauses are connected by a semicolon, use a vertical dotted line to connect the verbs of the clauses. If the main clauses are connected by a conjunction such as *and, but,* or *or,* write the conjunction on a solid horizontal line and connect it to the verb in each clause with a dotted line.

EXAMPLE James practices football after school, **and** on Saturdays he helps his parents at their restaurant.

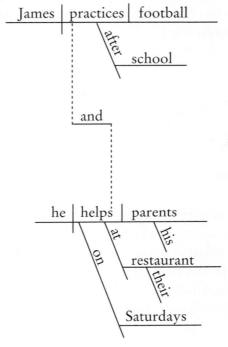

PRACTICE Diagraming Compound Sentences

Diagram each sentence.

1. Dad will grill hamburgers, or Mom will fry chicken.
2. Lori plays the saxophone, and Maggie plays the trombone.
3. I looked everywhere, but the letter had vanished.
4. Delaware was the first state; Hawaii was the fiftieth state.
5. Tami called the restaurant, but the line was busy.
6. Alaska is the largest state; Rhode Island is the smallest state.
7. The plane landed safely, and the passengers sighed with relief.
8. The band will play a few numbers, or the chorus will sing several songs.

9. The sun shone brightly; a gentle breeze stirred the leaves.
10. Johnson ran the ball into the end zone, and the fans poured onto the field.

11.8 DIAGRAMING COMPLEX SENTENCES WITH ADJECTIVE AND ADVERB CLAUSES CCSS L.7.1a, b, c

To diagram a sentence with an adjective clause, write the adjective clause below the main clause. Draw a dotted line between the relative pronoun in the adjective clause and the word the adjective clause modifies in the main clause. Position the relative pronoun according to its use in its own clause. In the first example, *who* is the subject of the verb *complete.* In the second example, *that* is the direct object of the verb *watched.*

ADJECTIVE CLAUSE

EXAMPLE Students **who complete their assignments** will surely succeed.

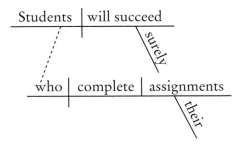

EXAMPLE The movie **that we watched** was very funny.

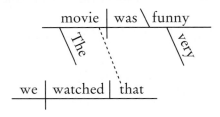

Diagram an adverb clause below the main clause. Draw a dotted line between the verb in the adverb clause and the word the adverb clause modifies in the main clause. Then write the subordinating conjunction on the dotted connecting line.

ADVERB CLAUSE

EXAMPLE   **If you complete your assignments,** you will surely succeed.

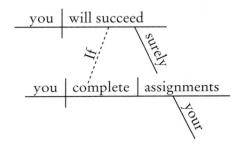

PRACTICE **Diagraming Complex Sentences with Adjective and Adverb Clauses**

Diagram each sentence.

1. A clause that modifies a noun is an adjective clause.
2. The bridge, which spans the river, carries heavy traffic.
3. Meet Ms. Rodriguez, who has just returned from Mexico.
4. My sister, whom you have met, is taking ballet lessons.
5. The person whose bicycle you are using is my cousin.
6. I read a magazine while I waited.
7. After the rain stopped, we played tennis.
8. I finished my homework before the show began.
9. When the package arrived, I put it in the kitchen.
10. I will pay you a dollar if you will help me.

11.9 DIAGRAMING NOUN CLAUSES   CCSS L.7.1a, c

Noun clauses can be used in sentences as subjects, direct objects, indirect objects, objects of prepositions, and predicate nouns. In the following example, the noun clause is the subject.

NOUN CLAUSE AS SUBJECT

EXAMPLE   **What she told us** was the simple truth.

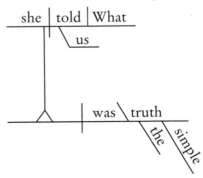

Notice that the clause is written on a "stilt" placed on the base line where the subject usually appears. The word that introduces a noun clause is diagramed according to its use within its own clause. In the noun clause in the example, the word *What* is the direct object. If the word that introduces the noun clause isn't really part of either the noun clause or the main clause, write the word on its own line.

NOUN CLAUSE AS DIRECT OBJECT

EXAMPLE   Terry knows **that good grades are important.**

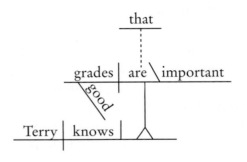

NOUN CLAUSE AS INDIRECT OBJECT

EXAMPLE   Tell **whomever you see** the news.

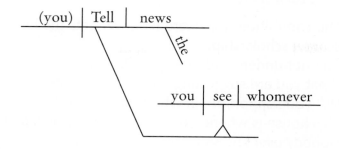

NOUN CLAUSE AS OBJECT OF A PREPOSITION

EXAMPLE   This is an example of **what I mean.**

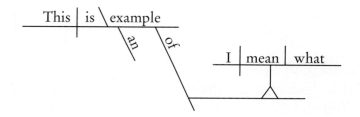

NOUN CLAUSE AS PREDICATE NOUN

EXAMPLE   The result was **that nobody believed me.**

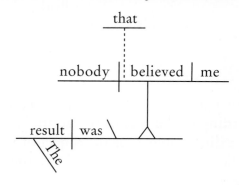

Diagram each sentence.

1. The committee will award whoever gets the highest score a scholarship.
2. I do not understand how you did that.
3. What you are suggesting makes perfect sense.
4. Will you support me in whatever I decide?
5. This house is where James Thurber lived as a boy.
6. Nobody ever knows when Sunny is blue.
7. The outcome of the vote was that the proposal was defeated.
8. Get the name of whomever you interview.
9. Who will provide the entertainment is a secret.
10. Tell me why Edgar Allan Poe is a great writer.

11.10 **DIAGRAMING VERBALS** CCSS L.7.1a, c

To diagram a participle or a participial phrase, draw a line that descends diagonally from the word the participle modifies and then extend it to the right horizontally. Write the participle along the angle, as shown.

EXAMPLE The birds, **singing merrily,** splashed in the birdbath.

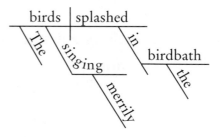

To diagram a gerund or a gerund phrase, make a "stilt," located according to the role of the gerund. (A gerund can be a subject, a direct object, or the object of a preposition.) Then write the gerund on a "step" above the stilt, as shown at the top of the next page.

EXAMPLE **Building new nests** is another job for the returning birds.

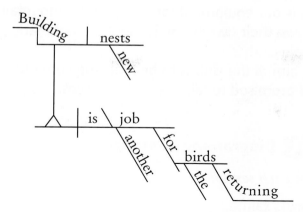

To diagram an infinitive or an infinitive phrase that is used as a noun, make a "stilt" in the appropriate position. Then diagram the phrase as you would a prepositional phrase.

EXAMPLE The purpose of a microscope is **to magnify objects.**

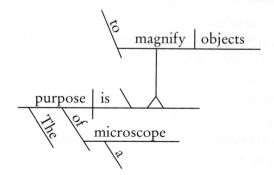

PRACTICE **Diagraming Verbals**

Diagram each sentence.

1. I replaced the broken vase.
2. Grabbing the baton, Tony sprinted down the track.
3. The twittering birds woke me at five.
4. I found a note written in code.

5. Building new roads improves the flow of traffic.
6. Stop giving the children candy.
7. This is our equipment for hiking in the mountains.
8. To own their own home is the dream of many young couples.
9. The aim of the club is to beautify the community.
10. Dad promised to take us to the movies.

POSTTEST Diagraming Sentences

Diagram each sentence.

1. Officers salute.
2. Children were playing.
3. Hide!
4. Does Theresa remember?
5. Accept my apology.
6. Lucinda gave us some advice.
7. The pitcher tossed the batter the ball.
8. The graceful antelope narrowly escaped the lion.
9. That rather silly movie contains several completely unbelievable scenes.
10. A table with a lace cover stood between the two windows.
11. This tea tastes very bitter.
12. The old wooden bridge is a tourist spot.
13. A dog or a cat makes a good pet.
14. Roberto is the coach and a great player.
15. Astronauts lose some muscle in a weightless atmosphere, and their hearts work less.
16. Fires in Yellowstone National Park destroy many trees, but new growth restores the forests.
17. The fire that killed the trees warmed the water in the streams.
18. When fire runs through Yellowstone again, nature will recover.
19. What you think is important to me.

20. Samantha is whom we chose.
21. Tell me how you make these delicious meatballs.
22. The kittens, born yesterday, have not yet opened their eyes.
23. The woman standing in the doorway is Ms. Benson.
24. Mr. Bernstein enjoys teaching science.
25. To find a new route to the East was Columbus's goal.

Capitalization

PRETEST Capitalization

Write each sentence. Use capital letters correctly.

1. we toured an oil tanker in the harbor.
2. "this oil tanker is so big," said Little Deer, the tour guide, "that three football fields could fit on its deck."
3. Harry asked, "how can i learn more about these ships?"
4. "pay attention," said Little Deer. "then try the Internet or your local library."
5. One of the girls said That she had seen underwater oil pipelines.
6. These salmon swim against the current of kenai river in alaska to return to the place they were born.
7. In 1853 a chef, george crum, invented the potato chip after a customer complained about his thick, soggy fried potatoes.
8. My cousin richard visited mammoth cave in kentucky during the summer.

9. The dentist, dr. truong, spoke with mrs. hampton about her toothache and recommended brite toothpaste.

10. I wonder if ducktown, tennessee, has a mallard avenue or a wood duck drive.

11. "Did we catch the illness in time, doctor?" asked the nurse.

12. Why did you send your cards to north pole, colorado, during december?

13. hector gonzalez jr. works at the gift shop in the statue of liberty on liberty island in new york.

14. my mother drinks a cup of french roast coffee every saturday morning.

15. At the airport, I helped mother and aunt fran with their luggage.

16. On memorial day, i spoke spanish with raul's many relatives.

17. If you move to north dakota, will you miss eastern tennessee?

18. The tacoma narrows bridge collapsed not long after it opened.

19. On sunday i read a story called "all for one" by a young canadian writer named monty preston.

20. On his tour, president clinton visited new england, the west coast, and the south in four days.

21. which groups were fighting in the war of 1812, world war II, and the american revolution?

22. This summer dr. wilson will read *roll of thunder, hear my cry* to his children and watch *my side of the mountain* with them.

23. In the autumn, we will travel from new mexico to maine with grandmother.

24. The librarian recommends the books of british author c. s. lewis, who wrote *the chronicles of narnia.*

25. Lauren buys computer games at a store called explosions and collisions.

12.1 CAPITALIZING SENTENCES, QUOTATIONS, AND LETTER PARTS

A capital letter marks the beginning of a sentence. A capital letter also marks the beginning of a direct quotation and the salutation and the closing of a letter.

RULE 1 Capitalize the first word of every sentence.

EXAMPLE **M**any people worked for the independence of the colonies.

RULE 2 Capitalize the first word of a direct quotation that is a complete sentence. A direct quotation gives a speaker's exact words.

EXAMPLE Travis said, "**O**ne of those people was Paul Revere."

RULE 3 When a direct quotation is interrupted by explanatory words, such as *she said,* don't begin the second part of the direct quotation with a capital letter.

EXAMPLE "I read a famous poem," said Kim, "**a**bout Paul Revere."

When the second part of a direct quotation is a new sentence, put a period after the explanatory words and begin the second part of the quotation with a capital letter.

EXAMPLE "I know that poem," said Sarah. "**M**y class read it last week."

RULE 4 Don't capitalize an indirect quotation. An indirect quotation does not repeat a person's exact words and should not be enclosed in quotation marks. An indirect quotation is often introduced by the word *that.*

EXAMPLE The teacher said **t**he poem was written by Longfellow.

EXAMPLE The teacher said **that t**he poem was written by Longfellow.

RULE 5 Capitalize the first word in the salutation and the closing of a letter. Capitalize the title and the name of the person addressed.

EXAMPLES   **D**ear **M**rs. **A**damson,   **S**incerely yours,

EXAMPLES   **M**y dear **A**bigail,   **W**ith love,

NOTE   Usually, the first word in each line of a poem is capitalized, but many modern poets don't follow this style. When you copy a poem, use the style of the original version.

PRACTICE   Capitalizing Sentences, Quotations, and Letter Parts

Write each sentence. Use capital letters correctly. If a sentence is already correct, write correct.

1. sombreros are hats with wide brims.
2. Lucy asked, "when does spring begin?"
3. "Spring begins," answered Suki, "About March 21."
4. "your reports are due tomorrow," said Ms. Perez. "there will be no other homework tonight."
5. Madison told me that He had tried out for the play.
6. Butter and cheese are made from milk.
7. Percy said, "my report will be about dairy farming."
8. "My parents are dairy farmers," said Ginny. "they could give you some information."
9. "I've never been to Germany," said Hildy, "but all my grandparents were born there."
10. *Rewrite each salutation or closing that is incorrect.*
    a. Dear Mom and Dad,   c. Best Wishes,
    b. my dear Ms. Murphy,   d. your Friend,

12.2 CAPITALIZING NAMES AND TITLES OF PEOPLE

RULE 1 Capitalize the names of people and the initials that stand for their names.

EXAMPLES   Clark Kent   Susan B. Anthony   E. C. Stanton

RULE 2 Capitalize a title or an abbreviation of a title when it comes before a person's name.

EXAMPLES   President Wilson   Dr. Martin Luther King   Ms. Ruiz

Capitalize a title when it's used instead of a name.

EXAMPLE   "Has the enemy surrendered, General?" asked the colonel.

Don't capitalize a title that follows a name or one that is used as a common noun.

EXAMPLE   Woodrow Wilson, president of the United States during World War I, supported cooperation among nations.

EXAMPLE   Who was Wilson's vice president?

RULE 3 Capitalize the names and abbreviations of academic degrees that follow a name. Capitalize *Jr.* and *Sr.*

EXAMPLES   M. Katayama, M.D.   Janis Stein, Ph.D.   Otis Ames Jr.

RULE 4 Capitalize words that show family relationships when they're used as titles or as substitutes for names.

EXAMPLE   Last year Father and Aunt Beth traveled to several western states.

Don't capitalize words that show family relationships when they follow possessive nouns or pronouns.

EXAMPLE   Jo's uncle took photographs. My aunt Mary framed them.

RULE 5 Always capitalize the pronoun *I*.

EXAMPLE American history is the subject **I** like best.

PRACTICE Capitalizing Names and Titles of People

Write each sentence. Use capital letters correctly. If a sentence is already correct, write correct.

 1. A favorite author for young people is robert louis stevenson.
 2. My father's boss is j. d. bailey.
 3. Do you know who dr. jonas salk is?
 4. "Will i be all right, doctor?" asked lynn.
 5. "The doctor will see you now," said the nurse.
 6. The guest speaker was alma prado, ph.d.
 7. My mom and sid's aunt suzi are good friends.
 8. Last week grandpa meyer and aunt rachel opened their own restaurant.
 9. Sometimes i'm not sure if i should speak up or keep quiet.
10. Do you know the story of captain john smith and pocahontas?

12.3 CAPITALIZING NAMES OF PLACES

The names of specific places are proper nouns and should be capitalized. Don't capitalize articles and short prepositions that are part of geographical names.

RULE 1 Capitalize the names of cities, counties, states, countries, and continents.

EXAMPLES

| San Diego | Cook County | North Carolina |
| Japan | Mexico | Europe |

RULE 2 Capitalize the names of bodies of water and other geographical features.

EXAMPLES   Lake Michigan   Gulf of Mexico   Pacific Ocean

                Mojave Desert   Napa Valley   Rocky Mountains

RULE 3 Capitalize the names of sections of a country.

EXAMPLES   the Sun Belt   New England   the Great Plains

RULE 4 Capitalize direction words when they name a particular section of a country.

EXAMPLES   the South   the West Coast   the Northeast

     Don't capitalize direction words used in other ways.

EXAMPLES   southern California   northerly winds
                Kansas is west of Missouri.

RULE 5 Capitalize the names of streets and highways.

EXAMPLES   Main Street   Route 66   Pennsylvania Turnpike

RULE 6 Capitalize the names of particular buildings, bridges, monuments, and other structures.

EXAMPLES   the White House   Golden Gate Bridge
                Lincoln Memorial   the Rose Bowl

PRACTICE   Capitalizing Names of Places

Write each sentence. Use capital letters correctly.

1. Is mount mckinley the highest mountain in north america?
2. Is mexico south of the united states of america?
3. Is helena the capital of montana?
4. Is kansas city located in the great plains?
5. Is seattle the largest city in the northwest?
6. Does route 40 cross southern ohio?

7. Are the empire state building and the brooklyn bridge in new york city?
8. Which is smaller, lake erie or lake ontario?
9. Did pioneers travel west to reach the pacific ocean?
10. Is the cotton bowl in the south?

12.4 CAPITALIZING OTHER PROPER NOUNS AND ADJECTIVES

Many nouns besides the names of people and places are proper nouns and should be capitalized. Adjectives formed from proper nouns are called proper adjectives and should also be capitalized.

RULE 1 Capitalize all important words in the names of clubs, organizations, businesses, institutions, and political parties.

EXAMPLES	Girl Scouts of America	American Red Cross
	Microsoft Corporation	Smithsonian Institution
	University of Nebraska	Republican Party

RULE 2 Capitalize brand names but not the nouns following them.

EXAMPLES   Downhome soup   Lull-a-bye diapers   Kruncho crackers

RULE 3 Capitalize all important words in the names of particular historical events, time periods, and documents.

EXAMPLES   Revolutionary War   Iron Age   Gettysburg Address

RULE 4 Capitalize the names of days of the week, months of the year, and holidays. Don't capitalize the names of the seasons.

EXAMPLES   Sunday   April   Thanksgiving Day   spring

RULE 5 Capitalize the first word and the last word in the titles of books, chapters, plays, short stories, poems, essays, articles, movies, television series and programs, songs, magazines, and newspapers. Capitalize all other words except articles, coordinating conjunctions, and prepositions of fewer than five letters. Don't capitalize the word *the* before the title of a magazine or newspaper.

EXAMPLES   *A Wrinkle in Time*   "Mammals and Their Young"
            "The Lady or the Tiger?" "The Truth About Dragons"
            "Over the Rainbow"   *Seventeen*

RULE 6 Capitalize the names of languages, nationalities, and ethnic groups.

EXAMPLES   English   Japanese   Native Americans

RULE 7 Capitalize proper adjectives. A proper adjective is an adjective formed from a proper noun.

EXAMPLES   African American voters   Mexican art
            a Broadway musical   Appalachian families

NOTE   Capitalize the names of religions and the people who practice them. Capitalize the names of holy days, sacred writings, and deities.

EXAMPLES   Islam   Muslims   Easter   the Bible   Allah

NOTE   Capitalize the names of trains, ships, airplanes, and spacecraft.

EXAMPLES   the Orient Express   *Titanic*
            Spirit of St. Louis   *Voyager 2*

NOTE   Don't capitalize the names of school subjects, except for proper nouns and adjectives and course names followed by a number.

EXAMPLES   language arts   geography   earth science
            American history   French   Algebra 1

Capitalizing Other Proper Nouns and Adjectives

Write each sentence. Use capital letters correctly.

1. Several republican candidates will speak at yale university in october.
2. Many american automobile manufacturers once felt threatened by japanese carmakers like honda.
3. My dad uses gleemo car wax on his ford truck every saturday.
4. Did Thomas Jefferson write the declaration of independence or the gettysburg address?
5. Do you know anyone who served in world war II?
6. Every thanksgiving day, we sing "over the river and through the woods" on our way to Grandma's.
7. I plan to study french in the fall.
8. A famous work of american literature is *the last of the mohicans.*
9. The united nations had 184 members as of august 1994.
10. My favorite movie about aliens is *e.t.*

Proofreading

Rewrite the following letter, correcting errors in capitalization and spelling. Write legibly to be sure one letter is not mistaken for another. There are ten errors.

¹dear Ms. Simpson,
  ²I highly reccomend a book. ³It is called *the call of the wild.* ⁴The author of the book is named Jack london.
  ⁵Have you heard of Jack London? ⁶He was born in san francisco. ⁷Flora Wellman was his Mother. ⁸His stepfather, John London, had fought in the civil war.

⁹At the age of twenty-one, London spent one Winter in the Klondike. ¹⁰He found many story ideas there.

¹¹London wrote novels, short stories, and essays. ¹²Sometimes he wrote for fifteen hours each day. ¹³He said, "at times, I forgot to eat."

¹⁴Best wishes,

¹⁵Fred Ramírez jr.

POSTTEST Capitalization

Write each sentence. Use capital letters correctly.

1. does miss america use reel kleen soap?
2. Kyosha asked, "when does winter begin?"
3. "Winter begins," answered Benny, "About december 21."
4. "meet in the band room at three o'clock," said the band director. "we will practice for an hour."
5. "do you support the bill, congresswoman?" asked the reporter for *people's news and views of washington*.
6. She presented the trophy to harriet klein, president of national motors company, for her design of the new zephyr automobile.
7. Pioneers settled the west, but they took the land from such tribes as the sioux, the cherokee, and the comanche.
8. Every saturday I mow the grass for grandpa.
9. Celia told me that She is looking for a summer job.
10. How do you celebrate new year's day?
11. On friday night, i sang "on top of old smoky" in the school play.
12. Is the phone call for neil sindato jr. or neil sindato sr.?
13. In the spring, aunt mary and uncle ken visited the appalachian mountains to gather wildflowers.
14. Head east on kettering avenue, turn right onto odette drive, and stop at 3692.
15. The outlaw jesse w. james fought for the south during the civil war.

16. We ate at a chinese restaurant with dr. montez.

17. To cross the east river in new york, drive along the brooklyn bridge, which opened in may 1883 and is still in use.

18. The speaker, d. c. madison, ph.d., talked to our history class about the declaration of independence.

19. Does your mother or your uncle fred vote for the republican candidates?

20. During the winter, i use sofskin hand cream.

21. troops from the girl scouts and the boy scouts visited mammoth site museum in hot springs, south dakota, where they examined the bones of mammoths from the ice age.

22. the bostonian architecture reminds me of the buildings i saw in providence, rhode island.

23. How many presidents have come from the midwest?

24. We must choose between *the eagle of the ninth,* by rosemary sutcliff, and *the cry of the crow,* by jean craighead george.

25. Please tell me which sports these teams play: the miami dolphins, the baltimore orioles, and the houston comets.

Punctuation

PRETEST **Commas, Semicolons, Colons, and End Punctuation**

Write each sentence. Add commas, semicolons, colons, and end punctuation where needed.

1. Hey Where are you going in such a hurry
2. Yes Ted I *do* like green vegetables
3. "The post office is down the street around the corner and past the library" said Felicia.
4. After a month in the country we felt happy and content
5. The dog was barking and the baby was crying
6. On the side opposite the stands were full
7. Do you listen to music while you do your homework
8. Whenever I mow the lawn my allergies bother me

9. Ms. Workman said "Potato chips too have a high fat content."
10. Send your application to Lydia Chekhov Ph.D. 1212 Patterson Drive Yakima WA 98901
11. Leaving the others behind Suzy and Jaime headed down the trail that led to the lake
12. Bring the following a jar with a lid a rubber band a pencil and a notebook
13. Mrs. Lawson our band director has been ill however Mr. Ito has done a fine job in her place
14. The Murphys lived in Flagstaff Arizona from June 1 1998 to May 1999
15. My aunt Morgan who has just arrived for a visit brought her luggage her dog and her cat we were not expecting the dog and the cat

PRETEST Quotation Marks, Italics, and Apostrophes

Write each sentence. Add quotation marks, underlining (for italics), apostrophes, and other punctuation marks where they're needed. If the sentence is already correct, write correct.

16. Today said Mr. Papaleonardos we will talk about seven amazing things that people built before 1700
17. Its anybodys guess how long it took to build the Great Wall of China he added.
18. Who built the wall asked Tsuruji. Its important for me to know
19. Many students reports will tell more about the walls construction replied the teacher.
20. Theres some information from Time magazine in Chriss report.
21. If youre interested in U.S. history, read the article Recollecting the Presidents in the magazine Smithsonian.

22. Are these books and papers yours or hers?

23. Did you say I cant wait for school to begin

24. The boys basketball team won only half its games.

25. Did you ask me if these dolls and trucks are the children drens toys said Susan.

PRETEST **Hyphens, Dashes, Parentheses, and Numbers**

Write each sentence. Add hyphens, dashes, and parentheses where they're needed. Use the correct form for each number. If the sentence is already correct, write correct.

26. The leaves of poison ivy *Toxicodendron radicans* in Latin grow in clusters of 3.

27. This fast food restaurant serves thirty three kinds of well done hamburgers.

28. Two thirds of the information in this report is not up to date; search the Internet for up to date information.

29. My great aunt, an ex salesperson, said that one hundred sixty million people bought the cheaper jacket.

30. The baby was born on the first day of the month about four o'clock in the morning; he weighed seven pounds and was twenty-one inches long.

31. Only sixty people have read this book, but 111 people have read that one.

32. On May 16th at four forty five P.M., I tried to return the sweater to the store located at One Two Two Newbury Drive.

33. Mary Ann and Josh they're our neighbors' children often visit my parents.

34. 245 people attended the free performance on 5th Avenue.

35. In the survey of students, forty-nine percent were against wearing school uniforms, and fifty-one percent favored wearing uniforms.

13.1 USING END PUNCTUATION

RULE 1 Use a period at the end of a declarative sentence. A declarative sentence makes a statement.

EXAMPLE Tractors perform many jobs on a farm.

EXAMPLE I worked on a farm during the summer.

RULE 2 Use a period at the end of an imperative sentence. An imperative sentence gives a command or makes a request.

EXAMPLE Turn the key. **[command]**

EXAMPLE Please start the motor. **[request]**

RULE 3 Use a question mark at the end of an interrogative sentence. An interrogative sentence asks a question.

EXAMPLE Who built the first tractor?

EXAMPLE Did you know that?

RULE 4 Use an exclamation point at the end of an exclamatory sentence. An exclamatory sentence expresses strong feeling.

EXAMPLE How powerful your tractor is!

EXAMPLE What a loud noise it makes!

RULE 5 Use an exclamation point after a strong interjection. An interjection is a word or group of words that expresses emotion.

EXAMPLES
Wow!	Whew!	My goodness!	Ouch!
Yippee!	Hi!	Hey!	Oops!

Write each sentence. Add the correct end punctuation.
Then write declarative, imperative, interrogative, exclamatory, *or* interjection *to show the reason for the end mark*
you chose.

1. The announcement was a surprise to the entire class
2. Wow Did you see that elephant in the middle of Main Street
3. Show me a sample of your very best handwriting
4. My goodness How smart you are
5. Have you cleaned your room yet
6. What a funny story that was
7. The president asked his fellow citizens for their support
8. Turn off the lights and put out the cat
9. A pale moon shone down on the silent castle
10. Who will be on your volleyball team

13.2 USING COMMAS I

When you use commas to *separate* items, you place a
comma between items. When you use commas to *set off* an
item, you place a comma before and after the item. Of
course, you never place a comma at the beginning or the
end of a sentence.

RULE 1 Separate three or more words, phrases, or clauses in a
series.

EXAMPLE Cars, buses, and trucks clog city streets. **[words]**

EXAMPLE Beside the fence, on the porch, or outside the back door
is a good place for that potted plant. **[phrases]**

EXAMPLE Call me before you leave town, while you're in Florida,
or after you return home. **[clauses]**

RULE 2 Set off an introductory word such as *yes, no,* or *well.*

EXAMPLE   Yes, we enjoyed your performance in the play.

EXAMPLE   No, you didn't sing off key.

RULE 3 Set off names used in direct address.

EXAMPLE   Claire, have you ever traveled on a ship?

EXAMPLE   I traveled to Alaska, Mr. Hess, on a cruise ship.

EXAMPLE   Did you enjoy your trip down the Ohio River, Dale?

RULE 4 Set off two or more prepositional phrases at the beginning of a sentence. Set off a single long prepositional phrase at the beginning of a sentence.

EXAMPLE   In the fall of 1998, Frank Jordan ran for mayor. **[two prepositional phrases—*In the fall* and *of 1998*]**

EXAMPLE   Beneath a dozen fluttering red and blue banners, he made his campaign speech. **[one long prepositional phrase— *Beneath a dozen fluttering red and blue banners*]**

You need not set off a single short prepositional phrase, but it's not wrong to do so.

EXAMPLE   In 1998 Frank Jordan ran for mayor. **[one short prepositional phrase—*In 1998*]**

RULE 5 Set off participles and participial phrases at the beginning of a sentence.

EXAMPLE   Talking, we lost track of the time.

EXAMPLE   Talking on the telephone, we lost track of the time.

Set off a participial phrase that is not essential to the meaning of a sentence.

EXAMPLE   The band, marching in formation, moves down the field.

EXAMPLE   Independence Day, celebrated on July 4, is a national holiday.

RULE 6 Set off words that interrupt the flow of thought in a sentence.

EXAMPLE   Politicians, of course, sometimes forget their campaign promises after the election.

RULE 7 Use a comma after a conjunctive adverb, such as *however, moreover, furthermore, nevertheless,* or *therefore.*

EXAMPLE   The school district is growing; therefore, taxes will rise.

RULE 8 Set off an appositive that is not essential to the meaning of a sentence.

EXAMPLE   The *Titanic,* a luxury liner, sank on its first voyage.
[The appositive, *a luxury liner,* is not essential.]

PRACTICE   Using Commas I

Write the following sentences. Add commas where they're needed.

1. Strolling through the mall Amy spotted her aunt Marge outside the bookstore.
2. Jim Wong our best pitcher has injured his arm; furthermore Rocky Solo our best hitter has the flu.
3. In the heat of the moment Mother I lost my temper.
4. That home run by the way was Rocky's twenty-fifth of the season.
5. The children ran out the door across the lawn and into the woods behind the house.
6. The puppy wrapped in an old blue bath towel shivered in my arms.
7. Are you going to the Toads concert Ali?
8. Yes Dad I will do my homework clean my room and wash the dishes while you're gone.

9. For many years after the war there was bad feeling between the two nations; nevertheless they maintained courteous public relations.

10. Among the green blue and yellow lawn chairs the baby sat in her stroller.

13.3 USING COMMAS II

RULE 9 Use a comma before a coordinating conjunction (*and, but, or, nor,* or *for*) that connects the two parts of a compound sentence.

EXAMPLE   Steve opened the door, and the dog ran out.

EXAMPLE   Mari called her best friend, but no one answered.

EXAMPLE   They will raise money, or they will donate their time.

RULE 10 Set off an adverb clause at the beginning of a sentence. An adverb clause begins with a subordinating conjunction, such as *after, although, as, because, before, if, since, though, unless, until, when, whenever, where, wherever,* or *while.*

EXAMPLE   Whenever I feel afraid, I whistle a happy tune.

Usually, an adverb clause that falls at the end of a sentence is not set off.

EXAMPLE   I whistle a happy tune whenever I feel afraid.

RULE 11 Set off a nonessential adjective clause. A nonessential adjective clause simply gives additional information and is not necessary to the meaning of a sentence. An adjective clause usually begins with a relative pronoun, such as *who, whom, whose, which,* or *that.*

EXAMPLE   My house, which has green shutters, is at the corner of Elm and Maple.

Don't set off an essential adjective clause. An essential adjective clause is necessary to the meaning of a sentence.

EXAMPLE   The house that has green shutters is at the corner of Elm and Maple.

Write each sentence. Add commas where they're needed. If a sentence needs no commas, write correct.

1. Will your dad drive us to the museum or shall we take a bus?
2. After I had scraped the mud from my shoes I went indoors.
3. The principal entered the room and the students became silent.
4. Jamaica Hightower who will be sixteen soon is learning to drive.
5. I have already read the book that you chose for your report.
6. Please don't leave until I'm ready.
7. Although the sun was shining the air was cold.
8. I took my umbrella with me for it was raining hard.
9. Margarine has less animal fat but butter tastes better.
10. The dingo which is a wild dog is a native of Australia.

13.4 USING COMMAS III

RULE 12 In a date, set off the year when it's used with both the month and the day. Don't use a comma if only the month and the year are given.

EXAMPLE   The ship struck an iceberg on April 14, 1912, and sank early the next morning.

EXAMPLE   The ship sank in April 1912 on its first voyage.

RULE 13 Set off the name of a state or a country when it's used after the name of a city. Set off the name of a city when it's used after a street address. Don't use a comma after the state if it's followed by a ZIP code.

EXAMPLE   The ship was sailing from Southampton, England, to New York City.

EXAMPLE   You can write to Leeza at 15 College Court, Stanford, CA 94305.

RULE 14 Set off an abbreviated title or degree following a person's name.

EXAMPLE   Michelle Nakamura, Ph.D., will be the graduation speaker.

EXAMPLE   Letisha Davis, M.D., is our family physician.

RULE 15 Set off *too* when it's used in the middle of a sentence and means "also." Don't set off *too* at the end of a sentence.

EXAMPLE   Parents, too, will attend the ceremony.

EXAMPLE   Parents will attend the ceremony too.

RULE 16 Set off a direct quotation.

EXAMPLE   Mom asked, "Have you finished your homework?"

EXAMPLE   "I did it," I replied, "in study hall."

EXAMPLE   "Tell me what you learned," said Mom.

RULE 17 Use a comma after the salutation of a friendly letter and after the closing of both a friendly letter and a business letter.

EXAMPLES   Dear Dad,   Your loving daughter,   Yours truly,

RULE 18 Use a comma to prevent misreading.

EXAMPLE   Instead of two, five teachers made the trip.

EXAMPLE   In the field below, the brook gurgled merrily.

PRACTICE Using Commas III

Write each sentence. Add commas where they're needed.

1. "Mrs. Roberts" I told Mom "is moving to Atlanta Georgia in June."
2. Sweet potatoes too are high in vitamin C.
3. An assassination in Sarajevo Bosnia-Herzegovina in June 1914 set the stage for World War I.
4. "Gettysburg Pennsylvania was the scene of a major battle of the Civil War" said Serena.

5. The Carters left Los Angeles California on Thursday and arrived in Orlando Florida a week later.
6. Sam Lee Ph.D. has written a book on the environment of the Everglades.
7. John commented "Robert E. Lee surrendered at Appomattox Virginia on April 9 1865 to Ulysses S. Grant."
8. The address on the envelope was 1234 Oak Street Houston TX 77032.
9. Soon after they immigrated to the United States.
10. *Write the following message, adding commas where needed.*

Dear Aunt Julia

   Thanks for the book. Camp is great. Scott too is enjoying himself.

Your nephew
David

13.5 USING SEMICOLONS AND COLONS

RULE 1 Use a semicolon to join the main clauses of a compound sentence if they're not joined by a conjunction such as *and, but, or, nor,* or *for.*

EXAMPLE The electric car was once the most popular car in the United States; people liked electric cars because they were clean and quiet.

RULE 2 Use a semicolon to join the main clauses of a compound sentence if they're long and if they already contain commas. Use a semicolon even if the clauses are joined by a coordinating conjunction such as *and, but, or, nor,* or *for.*

EXAMPLE Before the invention of the automobile, people rode horses, bicycles, or streetcars for short distances; and they used horse-drawn carriages, trains, or boats for longer trips.

RULE 3 Use a semicolon to separate main clauses joined by a conjunctive adverb, such as *consequently, furthermore, however, moreover, nevertheless,* or *therefore.*

EXAMPLE   I started my homework immediately after school; consequently, I finished before dinner.

RULE 4 Use a colon to introduce a list of items that ends a sentence. Use a word or a phrase such as *these, the following,* or *as follows* before the list.

EXAMPLE   I'll need **these** supplies for my project: newspapers, flour, water, string, and paint.

EXAMPLE   I participate in **the following** sports: softball, tennis, basketball, and swimming.

Don't use a colon immediately after a verb or a preposition.

EXAMPLE   My subjects **include** reading, math, home economics, and language arts.

EXAMPLE   I sent messages **to** Grandma, Aunt Rita, and Julie.

RULE 5 Use a colon to separate the hour and the minutes when you use numerals to write the time of day.

EXAMPLE   The train left the station at 10:17 A.M. and arrived in the city at 12:33 P.M.

RULE 6 Use a colon after the salutation of a business letter.

EXAMPLES   Dear Professor Sanchez: Dear Editor in Chief:

PRACTICE Using Semicolons and Colons

Write each sentence. Add semicolons and colons where they're needed. If a sentence is already correct, write correct.

1. Night fell the moon rose.
2. Please do not bring any of these items to the test site radios, pagers, food, beverages.

3. The three travelers looked at the object in amazement they had never seen anything like it.
4. It was 3 12 P.M. when I looked at the clock.
5. I have received pamphlets from Camp Lookout, Camp Dawn, and the Camp in the Pines however, I have not yet made my selection.
6. During the last two years, our family has traveled to Oregon, Washington, Idaho, and Montana and in the next three months, we will see California, Arizona, and New Mexico.
7. The departure time for our flight is 1117 A.M. the plane will land in Houston at 104 P.M.
8. My favorite teams are the Bulls, the Cubs, and the Bears.
9. In the nineteenth century, Henry Wadsworth Longfellow was a popular poet, a professor at Harvard University, and a loving husband and his works include *Evangeline, The Courtship of Miles Standish, The Song of Hiawatha,* and "Paul Revere's Ride."
10. *Write the following business letter, adding necessary punctuation.*

Dear Mr. Barnes

Please send me information about the following computer programs Games for Brains, Computer Construction, and Explorers in Space.

Yours truly,
Shana O'Neill

13.6 USING QUOTATION MARKS AND ITALICS

RULE 1 Use quotation marks to enclose a direct quotation.

EXAMPLE "Please return these books to the library," said Ms. Chu.

RULE 2 Use quotation marks to enclose each part of an interrupted quotation.

EXAMPLE "Spiders," explained Sean, "have eight legs."

RULE 3 Use commas to set off an explanatory phrase, such as *he said,* from the quotation itself. Place commas inside closing quotation marks.

EXAMPLE   "Spiders," explained Sean, "have eight legs."

RULE 4 Place a period inside closing quotation marks.

EXAMPLE   Toby said, "My aunt Susan received her degree in June."

RULE 5 Place a question mark or an exclamation point inside closing quotation marks if it's part of the quotation.

EXAMPLE   Yoko asked, "Have you ever visited Florida?"

Place a question mark or an exclamation point outside closing quotation marks if it's part of the entire sentence but not part of the quotation.

EXAMPLE   Did Jerry say, "Spiders have ten legs"?

When both a sentence and the direct quotation at the end of the sentence are questions (or exclamations), use only one question mark (or exclamation point). Place the mark inside the closing quotation marks.

EXAMPLE   Did Yoko ask, "Have you ever visited Florida?"

NOTE   When you're writing conversation, begin a new paragraph each time the speaker changes.

EXAMPLE

"You're kidding!" I exclaimed. "That sounds unbeliev-able. Did she really say that?"

"Indeed she did," Kara insisted.

RULE 6 Enclose in quotation marks titles of short stories, essays, poems, songs, articles, book chapters, and single television shows that are part of a series.

EXAMPLES   "Charles" [short story]   "Jingle Bells" [song]

RULE 7 Use italics or underlining for titles of books, plays, movies, television series, magazines, newspapers, works of art, music albums, and long musical compositions. Also use italics or underlining for the names of ships, airplanes, and spacecraft. Don't italicize or underline the word *the* before the title of a magazine or newspaper.

EXAMPLE	*The Adventures of Tom Sawyer* [book]
EXAMPLE	<u>The Monsters Are Due on Maple Street</u> [play]
EXAMPLE	*The Hunchback of Notre Dame* [movie]
EXAMPLE	<u>Sesame Street</u> [television series]
EXAMPLE	*Cricket* [magazine]
EXAMPLE	the <u>New York Times</u> [newspaper]
EXAMPLE	the *Mona Lisa* [painting]
EXAMPLE	<u>The Best of Reba McEntire</u> [music album]
EXAMPLE	*Rhapsody in Blue* [long musical composition]
EXAMPLE	<u>Titanic</u> [ship]
EXAMPLE	the *Spirit of St. Louis* [airplane]
EXAMPLE	<u>Friendship 7</u> [spacecraft]

GRAMMAR / USAGE / MECHANICS

Using Quotation Marks, Italics, and Other Punctuation

Write each sentence. Add quotation marks, underlining (for italics), and other punctuation marks where they're needed.

1. For my book report said Samantha I will read Treasure Island, by Robert Louis Stevenson
2. Then Jeff played Deep in the Heart of Texas on the piano.
3. What a hilarious story that was exclaimed Trixie.
4. Doesn't the magazine National Geographic have some fine nature photographs asked Dean.
5. I am writing in my journal Zelda told her brother.
6. That movie said Susan was very funny
7. I have never seen it Todd replied.
8. Did Angel say I have never heard of that movie
9. Running Deer said This is the place of the high waters
10. Rita called her essay The Perfect Sandwich

GRAMMAR / USAGE / MECHANICS

13.7 USING APOSTROPHES

RULE 1 Use an apostrophe and *s* (*'s*) to form the possessive of a singular noun.

EXAMPLES   girl + **'s** = girl**'s**   James + **'s** = James**'s**

RULE 2 Use an apostrophe and *s* (*'s*) to form the possessive of a plural noun that does not end in *s*.

EXAMPLES   men + **'s** = men**'s**   geese + **'s** = geese**'s**

RULE 3 Use an apostrophe alone to form the possessive of a plural noun that ends in *s*.

EXAMPLES   boys + **'** = boys**'**   judges + **'** = judges**'**

RULE 4 Use an apostrophe and *s ('s)* to form the possessive of an indefinite pronoun, such as *everyone, everybody, anyone, no one,* or *nobody.*

EXAMPLES   anybody + **'s** = anybody**'s**   someone + **'s** = someone**'s**

Don't use an apostrophe in the possessive personal pronouns *ours, yours, his, hers, its,* and *theirs.*

EXAMPLES   That car is **ours.**   Is that cat **yours**?

The bird flapped **its** wings.   These skates are **hers.**

RULE 5 Use an apostrophe to replace letters that are omitted in a contraction.

EXAMPLES   it is = it's   you are = you're
             I will = I'll   is not = isn't

PRACTICE **Using Apostrophes**

Write each sentence. Add apostrophes where they're needed. If the sentence is already correct, write correct.

1. The girls chorus and the boys glee club will sing at the nursing center on Saturday.
2. Ill tell Debbies father the news.
3. Someones history book is in the teachers workroom.
4. The dog put its head on my knee.
5. The childrens party will begin at one at our house.
6. Shell put everyones reports on the bulletin board.
7. The cars engine sputtered, and its frame shook.
8. That bicycle isnt yours.
9. Its a quarter to three, and nobodys parents have arrived to collect their children.
10. Youre in charge of the luncheon for the womens political club.

13.8 USING HYPHENS, DASHES, AND PARENTHESES

RULE 1 Use a hyphen to divide a word at the end of a line. Divide words only between syllables.

EXAMPLE   With her husband, Pierre, Marie Sklodowska Curie discovered radium and polonium.

RULE 2 Use a hyphen in compound numbers.

EXAMPLES   **thirty-two** pianos   **sixty-five** experiments

RULE 3 Use a hyphen in fractions expressed in words.

EXAMPLE   Add **one-half** cup of butter or margarine.

EXAMPLE   **Three-fourths** of the students sing in the chorus.

RULE 4 Use a hyphen or hyphens in certain compound nouns. Check a dictionary for the correct way to write a compound noun.

EXAMPLES   great-aunt   brother-in-law   attorney-at-law

editor in chief   vice president

RULE 5 Use a hyphen in a compound modifier when it comes before the word it modifies.

EXAMPLES   Fido is a **well-trained** dog.   The dog is **well trained.**

RULE 6 Use a hyphen after the prefixes *all-*, *ex-*, and *self-*. Use a hyphen to separate any prefix from a word that begins with a capital letter.

EXAMPLES   all-powerful   ex-president

self-educated   trans-Atlantic

RULE 7 Use dashes to set off a sudden break or change in thought or speech.

EXAMPLE   Billy Adams—he lives next door—is our team manager.

RULE 8 Use parentheses to set off words that define or explain a word.

EXAMPLE Simulators (devices that produce the conditions of space flight) are used in flight training for the space program.

PRACTICE **Using Hyphens, Dashes, and Parentheses**

Write each sentence. Add hyphens, dashes, and parentheses where they're needed.

1. I have collected twenty seven glass bottles and fifty three plastic ones.
2. Two tenths is the same as one fifth.
3. One of the twins I forget which one has won the citizenship award for self improvement.
4. Their property consists of one half acre 21,780 square feet.
5. Susie's brother in law he's our next door neighbor is my science teacher.
6. The Joneses have well behaved children.
7. Use three fourths cup of sugar and one fourth cup of butter.
8. Those seventh grade students are really well liked.
9. Arachnids spiders, scorpions, mites, and ticks are frightening to some people.
10. Kyle's great grandfather was born in Ireland eighty one years ago; he was an all American football player in college.

13.9 USING ABBREVIATIONS

RULE 1 Use the abbreviations *Mr., Mrs., Ms.,* and *Dr.* before a person's name. Abbreviate professional or academic degrees that follow a person's name. Abbreviate *Junior* as *Jr.* and *Senior* as *Sr.* when they follow a person's name.

EXAMPLES   **Mr.** Ed Hall   **Dr.** Ann Chu   Juan Diaz, **Ph.D.**

Ava Danko, **D.D.S.**   Amos Finley **Jr.**

RULE 2 Use capital letters and no periods for abbreviations that are pronounced letter by letter or as words. Exceptions are *U.S.* and Washington, *D.C.,* which should have periods.

EXAMPLES   **MVP** most valuable player   **EST** eastern standard time

NASA National Aeronautics and Space Administration

RULE 3 Use the abbreviations *A.M.* (*ante meridiem,* "before noon") and *P.M.* (*post meridiem,* "after noon") with times. For dates use *B.C.* (before Christ) and, sometimes, *A.D.* (*anno Domini,* "in the year of the Lord," after Christ).

EXAMPLES   6:22 A.M.   4:12 P.M.   33 B.C.   A.D. 476

RULE 4 Abbreviate days and months only in charts and lists.

EXAMPLES   **Mon.   Wed.   Thur.   Jan.   Apr.   Aug.   Nov.**

RULE 5 In scientific writing, abbreviate units of measure. Use periods with abbreviations of U.S. units but not with abbreviations of metric units.

EXAMPLES   inch(es) **in.**   foot (feet) **ft.**   gram(s) **g**   liter(s) **l**

RULE 6 In addressing envelopes, abbreviate words that refer to streets. Spell out these words everywhere else.

EXAMPLES   **St.** (Street)   **Ave.** (Avenue)   **Rd.** (Road)

I live at the corner of Elm **Street** and Maple **Road.**

RULE 7 In addressing envelopes, use the two-letter postal abbreviations for states. Spell out state names everywhere else.

EXAMPLES   Texas **TX**   Florida **FL**   California **CA**

My cousin lives in Chicago, **Illinois.**

RULE 8 When an abbreviation with a period falls at the end of a sentence, don't add another period. Add a question mark if the sentence is interrogative; add an exclamation point if the sentence is exclamatory.

EXAMPLE   I just met Francis X. Colavito Jr.

EXAMPLE   Have you met Francis X. Colavito Jr.?

For more information about abbreviations, see pages 56–61 in Part One, Ready Reference.

PRACTICE **Using Abbreviations**

Write the abbreviation for each item described.

1. the day after Tuesday
2. fourteen minutes after two in the afternoon
3. the title used with the name of an unmarried woman
4. United States
5. Scott Avenue
6. the state of Florida in an address on an envelope
7. the title used before the name of a person who has a medical degree
8. the month before May
9. inches
10. the phrase *before Christ* when it is used with a date

13.10 WRITING NUMBERS

In charts and tables, always write numbers as figures. In ordinary sentences, you sometimes spell out numbers and sometimes write them as numerals.

RULE 1 Spell out numbers you can write in one or two words. If the number is greater than 999,999, see Rule 4.

EXAMPLE   There are **twenty-six** students in the class.

EXAMPLE   The arena holds **fifty-five hundred** people.

RULE 2 Use numerals for numbers of more than two words.

EXAMPLE   The distance between the two cities is **150** miles.

RULE 3 Spell out any number that begins a sentence or reword the sentence so it doesn't begin with a number.

EXAMPLE   **Four thousand two hundred eighty-three** fans attended the game.

EXAMPLE   Attendance at the game was **4,283.**

RULE 4 Use figures for numbers greater than 999,999, followed by the word *million, billion*, and so on, even if the number could be written in two words.

EXAMPLES   **1 million**   **280 billion**   **3.2 trillion**

RULE 5 Numbers of the same kind should be written in the same way. If one number must be written as a numeral, write all the numbers as numerals.

EXAMPLE   On September 8, **383** students voted for the new rule, and **50** students voted against it.

RULE 6 Spell out ordinal numbers (*first, second, third*, and so on) under one hundred.

EXAMPLE   The **ninth** of June will be the couple's **twenty-fourth** wedding anniversary.

RULE 7 Use words to write the time of day unless you are using *A.M.* or *P.M.*

EXAMPLE   I usually go for a walk at **four o'clock** in the afternoon. I return home at **a quarter to five.**

EXAMPLE   The first bell rang at **8:42** A.M., and the last one rang at **3:12** P.M.

RULE 8 Use numerals to write dates, house numbers, street numbers above ninety-nine, apartment and room numbers, telephone numbers, page numbers, amounts of money of more than two words, and percentages. Write out the word *percent.*

EXAMPLE On June **10, 1999,** I met Jan at **41** East **329th** Street in Apartment **3G.** Her telephone number is **555-2121.**

EXAMPLE Our class meets in Room **12; 55 percent** of the students are girls.

EXAMPLE I found **two dollars** between page **250** and page **251** in this book. The book's original price was **$12.95.**

PRACTICE Writing Numbers

Write each sentence. Use the correct form for each number. If the sentence is already correct, write correct.

1. I have read 75 books this year.

2. From 1920 to 1930, the population of the United States grew from one hundred six million to one hundred twenty-three million, an increase of sixteen percent.

3. In this ballpark, the distance from home plate to the fence in center field is 410 feet.

4. I'll need $20 for fees and supplies by Monday, September thirtieth.

5. We picked ten bushels of apples and 12 bushels of peaches.

6. Only thirty-three % of the voters turned out for the election on November second, 1999.

7. I called nine one one when I saw the accident at the corner of West 150th Street and Madison Avenue.

8. Josh has collected twenty-seven hundred baseball cards.

9. 423 students were in my sister's graduating class; my sister ranked 10th in the class.

10. Please arrive between half past 7 and 8 o'clock.

PRACTICE Proofreading

Rewrite the following passage, adding missing punctuation. Write legibly to be sure one letter is not mistaken for another. There are ten errors.

Robert Frost

[1]Robert Frost was a well loved poet. [2]He was born on March 26 1874. [3]He spent his first ten years in San Francisco California. [4]His father William Frost died when Frost was ten. [5]After his father's death, Frost moved east to Massachusetts with his mother. [6]At the age of twenty one, Frost attended Harvard.

[7]After several years as a teacher, Frost moved to England he wrote many poems there and lived on a farm. [8]He published his first book of poems, A Boy's Will, at the age of forty. [9]Readers loved his poems. [10]He won the Pulitzer Prize four times; furthermore twenty-eight universities gave him honorary degrees.

[11]Frost once talked to a friend about poetry. [12]He said "It begins as a lump in the throat." [13]These are some of Frost's poems "Stopping by Woods on a Snowy Evening," "The Telephone," and "To Earthward."

POSTTEST Commas, Semicolons, Colons, and End Punctuation

Write each sentence. Add commas, semicolons, colons, and end punctuation where needed.

1. Wow Can you imagine rowing a galley in the Spanish Armada

2. Rowers grow hot tired sweaty and unhappy after several hours of rowing

3. When the Spanish ships met the English ships in 1588 what happened

4. "The English ships were faster" said Joyce "and no Spaniards boarded them."

5. "Yes I too heard that" said Heather. "The captains of the Spanish Armada gave up went home and repaired their ships."

6. Dawn Moffa Ph.D. has studied the American Revolution consequently she will talk with our class about the war

7. "Does anyone know what happened on March 5 1770 in Boston?" she asked.

8. Choose one of the following events the Boston Tea Party the Battle of Bunker Hill or the Boston Massacre

9. "Dr. Moffa was it the Boston Massacre?" asked Al who moved here from Boston.

10. Yes that's right. Will you tell me how many people died what started the fight and how the Americans reacted

11. The event that interests me most is the writing of the Declaration of Independence I wish I could hear more about the person who wrote it

12. Visit Philadelphia Pennsylvania which was the home of the Continental Congress

13. Freezing at Valley Forge some soldiers died before the winter ended

14. By the end of the summer Jane had read *Treasure Island Robinson Crusoe The Wind in the Willows* and *Bridge to Terabithia* and her friend Tom had read *Tom Sawyer Huckleberry Finn* and *Kon-Tiki*

15. The night before the storm had destroyed most of Xenia a small town in central Ohio

POSTTEST Quotation Marks, Italics, and Apostrophes

Write each sentence. Add quotation marks, underlining (for italics), apostrophes, and other punctuation marks where they're needed. If the sentence is already correct, write correct.

16. For every rule said our guest speaker there is someone or something that doesnt fit it

17. Consider the idea that cats hate water he said.

18. Did you know that one cat loves water he asked.

19. Did you say Cats love water

20. The fishing cat earns its name by fishing for its food.

21. A scientists videotape shows a fishing cat swimming in the water added the speaker.

22. Youre teasing us said Jessica.

23. Why dont you ask for some zookeepers opinions he said.

24. Ill read this article Little Cats in the Wild or look at the March 1998 issue of the magazine Zoobooks.

25. Well store everyones equipment in the mens locker room.

POSTTEST Hyphens, Dashes, Parentheses, and Numbers

Write each sentence. Add hyphens, dashes, and parentheses where they're needed. Use the correct form for each number.

26. The crowd of 32,000 fans booed when the umpire threw 1/5 of the players out of the game in the 7th inning.

27. The part time secretary asked the 6 job applicants to wait in Room 32.

28. 2 days into the trip, the all terrain vehicle broke down in the middle of a stream.

29. Sherry's brother in law, who is 27, broke his ankle on July 16, 1998, at Sixty One East Two Hundred Twenty Second Street.

30. Is 120 12% of 1,000?

31. The game begins at seven thirty five P.M.; it will end about nine o'clock.

32. Turn to page 58 to read about four endangered animals; then answer the questions on page sixty.

33. Mrs. Mandrake she's our school librarian has collected thirty seven dollars and ninety five cents in fines.

34. A one gallon container holds one gallon 4 quarts.

35. More than 267,000,000 people live in the United States.

Chapter 14

Sentence Combining

PRETEST **Compound Elements**

Combine the sentences in each numbered item by using a coordinating conjunction. Add commas where they're needed. (Hint: Combine the elements listed in brackets at the end of each pair of sentences.)

1. a. Rosalia has a new computer game.
   b. Norman has a new computer game. [subjects]
2. a. Virginia Hamilton wrote *M. C. Higgins, the Great.*
   b. She also wrote *Zeely.* [direct objects]
3. a. Sandra went to the mall with Carlotta.
   b. Sandra went to the mall with An-Mei. [objects of preposition]
4. a. Geraldo fixed a sandwich.
   b. Geraldo poured a glass of milk. [predicates]
5. a. Zack gave the dog a bath.
   b. Zack gave the cat a bath. [indirect objects]
6. a. It was a holiday weekend.
   b. Traffic was heavy. [sentences]

7. a. Lana will grill hamburgers.
b. Seth will order a pizza. [sentences]
8. a. Melissa sings in the chorus.
b. Nikki plays in the band. [sentences]
9. a. Shawna wanted to call her friend.
b. She had too much homework. [sentences]
10. a. I could write a letter to Grandma.
b. I could watch a movie. [sentences]

PRETEST **Prepositional Phrases and Appositive Phrases**

Combine the sentences in each numbered item by adding the new information in the second sentence to the first sentence in the form of a prepositional phrase or an appositive phrase.

11. a. I found my boots.
b. They were in the closet.
12. a. Shannon Miller won seven Olympic medals.
b. She is a gymnast.
13. a. Edmund Hillary reached the top of Mount Everest in May 1953.
b. Hillary was an adventurer from New Zealand.
14. a. I read a good book last week.
b. It was about volcanoes.
15. a. Mount Etna is located in southern Italy.
b. Etna is the most active volcano in Europe.
16. a. The committee will meet tomorrow.
b. It will meet at three o'clock.
17. a. The principal presented an award to Mr. Scott.
b. Mr. Scott is a science teacher.
18. a. I baked a chocolate cake.
b. The cake is for Theo's birthday.

19. a. We collected several autographs.
    b. We collected them from the players.

20. a. The heads of four presidents are carved into Mount Rushmore.
    b. The presidents are Washington, Jefferson, Lincoln, and Theodore Roosevelt.

PRETEST Adjective and Adverb Clauses

Combine the sentences in items 21–25 by changing the new information in the second sentence to an adjective clause and adding it to the first sentence. Begin your clause with the word in brackets. Add commas if they're needed.

Combine the sentences in items 26–30 by changing the information in one sentence to an adverb clause and adding it to the other sentence. Begin your clause with the word in brackets. Add a comma if it's needed.

21. a. Dr. Hershfield will remove my tonsils.
    b. My parents respect her. [whom]

22. a. Kelly Starr tutors me after school.
    b. Kelly is very good in math. [who]

23. a. The snacks contained no sugar.
    b. They tasted great. [which]

24. a. Mother has a beautiful old quilt.
    b. The quilt has been in her family for generations. [that]

25. a. Shel Silverstein writes for both children and adults.
    b. His poems are humorous. [whose]

26. a. Juan spent more time on his studies. [When]
    b. His grades improved.

27. a. I finish my homework.
    b. I play computer games. [before]

28. a. I wash the dishes. [After]
    b. I play outdoors.

29. a. You were tired. [Because]
    b. You fell asleep.
30. a. The general raised the flag.
    b. The trumpets played a song. [as]

14.1 COMPOUND SENTENCES CCSS L.7.1b

When you have written a few simple sentences that are closely related in meaning, try combining them to form compound sentences. A compound sentence often states your meaning more clearly than a group of simple sentences. By using some compound sentences, you can also vary the length of your sentences.

EXAMPLE   **a.** Sam had three sisters.

       b. Matt had only one. **[but]**

       Sam had three sisters, **but** Matt had only one.

In this example, simple sentence *a* is joined to simple sentence *b* with the coordinating conjunction *but*. Note that a comma is used before the conjunction.

A **compound sentence** is made up of two or more simple sentences. You can combine two or more simple sentences in a compound sentence by using the conjunction *and, but,* or *or.*

PRACTICE **Combining Simple Sentences**

Combine the sentences in each numbered item by using a comma and a coordinating conjunction. For the first three items, use the coordinating conjunction shown in brackets at the end of the first sentence.

1. a. John may work for his uncle this summer. [or]
    b. His parents may send him to camp.
2. a. Sharon has a bad cold. [and]
    b. Her sister has the flu.

3. a. Mrs. Malone had many problems. [but]

  b. She was happy in spite of them.

4. a. Mom prepares dinner.

  b. Dad cleans up afterward.

5. a. Jacob smiled at the other boy.

  b. He did not trust him.

6. a. The sun was shining brightly.

  b. The birds were singing in the trees.

7. a. For her week of community service, Tessa might volunteer at a hospital.

  b. She might help the patients at a nursing center.

8. a. Maria made the first team.

  b. Nicole made the second team.

9. a. Mr. McCall could not afford a new car.

  b. He bought one anyway.

10. a. This afternoon I could clean the garage.

  b. I could lie on the couch and read a book.

14.2 COMPOUND ELEMENTS CCSS L.7.1b

Sometimes several sentences share information—for example, the same subject or verb. By combining such sentences and using compound elements, you can avoid repeating words. Sentences with compound elements also add variety to your writing.

EXAMPLE   **a.** Helen wore a purple dress.

  b. She **carried a red handbag. [and]**

  Helen wore a purple dress **and carried a red handbag.**

Sentences *a* and *b* share information about Helen. The combined version takes the new information from sentence *b, carried a red handbag,* and joins it to sentence *a,* using the coordinating conjunction *and.*

You can avoid repeating information by using **compound elements.** Join compound elements with the conjunctions *and, but,* or *or.*

Combine the sentences in each numbered item by using a coordinating conjunction to form a compound element. Add the new information from the second sentence to the first sentence. For the first three items, the new information is in italics, and the conjunction you should use is shown in brackets at the end of the first sentence.

1. a. We planted flowers in the garden. [and]
   b. We also planted *vegetables* in the garden.
2. a. Mr. Gonzales owns a bicycle. [but]
   b. He does *not* own *a car.*
3. a. Carmelita might become a chemist. [or]
   b. She might become *a writer.*
4. a. The designer decorated the hat with buttons.
   b. He also decorated it with bows.
5. a. The newlyweds may buy a house.
   b. They may rent an apartment.
6. a. We paid Carla in cash.
   b. We also paid Carlos in cash.
7. a. Mrs. Ito speaks Japanese.
   b. She does not speak English.
8. a. The day was cold.
   b. It was windy.
9. a. You could wear a blue tie with that suit.
   b. You could wear a red tie with that suit.
10. a. Melinda helped us with the children.
   b. Stephanie also helped us with the children.

14.3 PREPOSITIONAL PHRASES   CCSS L.7.1a, c

Prepositional phrases are useful in sentence combining. Like adjectives and adverbs, they present more information about nouns and verbs. Because prepositional phrases show relationships, they can often express complicated ideas effectively.

a. The family took a trip.

b. It was a **hot summer day.** [on]

c. They went **to the beach.**

On a hot summer day, the family took a trip **to the beach.**

The new information in sentence *b* is added to sentence *a* as a prepositional phrase, and the new information in sentence *c* is moved to sentence *a*. In the new sentence, the prepositional phrase *On a hot summer day* modifies the verb, *took.* The phrase *to the beach* modifies the noun *trip.* Notice that a prepositional phrase that modifies a noun follows the noun it modifies. Prepositional phrases that modify verbs can occupy different positions in a sentence. (For a list of common prepositions, see page 174.)

A **prepositional phrase** is a group of words that begins with a preposition and ends with a noun or a pronoun. Prepositional phrases most often modify nouns and verbs.

PRACTICE **Combining Sentences with Prepositional Phrases**

Combine the sentences in each numbered item by adding the prepositional phrase from the second sentence to the first sentence. For the first three items, the prepositional phrase in the second sentence is shown in italics. In the last item, you will need to combine three sentences.

1. a. The store was full of customers.
   b. The store was *opposite the barber shop.*
2. a. We stood in line.
   b. We were *with several other people.*
3. a. Our dog, Lottie, was swimming.
   b. She was *in the pool.*
4. a. Mrs. Morgenstern planted daffodils.
   b. She planted them along the fence.

5. a. The team plays its next game on Saturday.
   b. The game is against the Bulldogs.
6. a. The horses trotted.
   b. They trotted around the track.
7. a. The party finally ended.
   b. It was after midnight.
8. a. The Tylers moved here last month.
   b. They came from St. Louis.
9. a. The mail carrier delivered a package.
   b. It was for Tanya.
10. a. My report is due.
   b. It's about racehorses.
   c. It's due by tomorrow.

14.4 APPOSITIVES   CCSS L.7.1a, c

You can use appositives to combine sentences in a compact and informative way. Appositives and appositive phrases identify or rename nouns.

EXAMPLE   **a.** Maya Lin designed the Vietnam Veterans Memorial.

b. She was **an architecture student.**

Maya Lin, **an architecture student,** designed the Vietnam Veterans Memorial.

The appositive phrase *an architecture student* identifies the noun *Maya Lin.* Note that the appositive phrase is set off with commas because it gives nonessential information about Maya Lin. If an appositive or an appositive phrase gives information that is essential for identifying a noun, it's not set off with commas. (For more information about appositives, see pages 89–90.)

An **appositive** is a noun placed next to another noun to identify it or give additional information about it. An **appositive phrase** includes an appositive and other words that modify it.

PRACTICE Combining Sentences with Appositives

Combine the sentences in each numbered item by changing the new information in the second sentence to an appositive or an appositive phrase and adding it to the first sentence. For the first three items, the appositive or appositive phrase in the second sentence is shown in italics. Add commas where they're needed.

1. a. The first man on the moon was born in Wapakoneta, Ohio.
   b. He was *Neil Armstrong.*
2. a. Mr. and Mrs. Kelly have bought a new car.
   b. They're *our neighbors.*
3. a. Meteors are often called shooting stars.
   b. Meteors are *chunks of metal or stone.*
4. a. Graceland is in Memphis, Tennessee.
   b. Graceland is the home of Elvis Presley.
5. a. Suzy loves to go for walks in the woods.
   b. Suzy is my pet terrier.
6. a. The house stood on a bare hill.
   b. The house was a mansion with thirty-five rooms.
7. a. The students traveled to Lexington, Kentucky.
   b. They were all band members.
8. a. My mother lost her favorite earrings.
   b. They were a gift from my father.
9. a. The Missouri River flows from southwestern Montana to St. Louis, Missouri.
   b. It is the longest river in the United States.
10. a. Jalitza is six feet two inches tall.
   b. She is our star basketball player.

14.5 ADJECTIVE AND ADVERB CLAUSES CCSS L.7.2a, c

When two sentences share information, one of the sentences can often be made into an adjective clause modifying a word in the other sentence.

EXAMPLE **a.** Carla and Darla entered the dance contest.

b. Carla and Darla **are identical twins. [, who . . . ,]**

Carla and Darla, **who are identical twins,** entered the dance contest.

The new information (in blue type) in sentence *b* becomes an adjective clause modifying *Carla and Darla. Who* now connects the clauses. Notice the commas in the new sentence. Adjective clauses that add nonessential information are set off with commas. Those that add essential information are not. (For more information about adjective clauses, see page 195.)

An **adjective clause** is a subordinate clause that modifies a noun or a pronoun in the main clause. A relative pronoun, such as *who, whom, whose, which,* or *that,* is used to tie the adjective clause to the main clause. The words *where* and *when* can also be used as connectors.

You can also use adverb clauses to combine sentences. Adverb clauses are especially effective in showing relationships between actions. For example, an adverb clause can show when one action takes place in relation to another.

EXAMPLE **a.** Lee read a great deal as a boy.

b. He was recovering from an accident. **[while]**

Lee read a great deal as a boy **while he was recovering from an accident.**

In the new sentence, the adverb clause *while he was recovering from an accident* modifies the verb *read.* The adverb clause tells when Lee read a great deal. Note that the subordinating conjunction *while* makes the relationship between the two actions clear. An adverb clause may occupy different positions within a sentence. If it begins the sentence, it's followed by a comma. (For more information about adverb clauses, see pages 198–199.)

An **adverb clause** is a subordinate clause that often modifies the verb in the main clause. Adverb clauses are introduced by subordinating conjunctions, such as *after, although, as, because, before, if, since, unless, until, when, whenever, where, wherever,* and *while.*

PRACTICE Combining Sentences with Adjective and Adverb Clauses

Combine the sentences in items 1–5 by changing the new information in the second sentence to an adjective clause and adding it to the first sentence. For items 1–3, the new information in the second sentence is shown in italics. Begin your clause with the word in brackets. Add commas if they're needed.

Combine the sentences in items 6–10 by changing the information in one sentence to an adverb clause and adding it to the other sentence. Begin your clause with the word in brackets. Add a comma if it's needed.

1. a. Pietro made sculptures of marble.
   b. The marble *came from Italy.* [that]
2. a. My sewing scissors are missing.
   b. They *were in this drawer.* [which]
3. a. The Petersons have gone on a cruise.
   b. Their *child is staying with us.* [whose]
4. a. The boys earned ten dollars.
   b. They fixed my bicycle. [who]
5. a. Felicia will accompany us.
   b. You have already met her. [whom]
6. a. Delia made an outline.
   b. She wrote her report. [before]
7. a. Dante works hard.
   b. He wants to be a success. [because]
8. a. We lost the game. [Although]
   b. We played our best.

9. a. The driver approached the stop sign. [As]
    b. She slowed down.
10. a. There was a phone call for you.
    b. You were sleeping. [while]

PRACTICE Proofreading

Rewrite each of the following passages, combining sentences that are closely related in meaning. Write legibly to be sure one letter is not mistaken for another.

Robert Browning

On his fourteenth birthday, Robert Browning received a book. It was a book of poems. It was by Percy Bysshe Shelley. Browning loved these poems. The poems inspired his own poem *Pauline*.

Browning married Elizabeth Barrett. She was also a poet. She is famous for her love poems. Browning is famous for his dramatic monologues. Browning was one of the great poets of the Victorian era. He was buried in the Poets' Corner of Westminster Abbey.

T. S. Eliot

Thomas Stearns Eliot was born in the United States. He spent most of his life in England. Eliot wrote poems in his spare time. He was working as a bank clerk.

Eliot wrote about modern problems. He was a famous poet. He wrote "The Waste Land." He also wrote "The Love Song of J. Alfred Prufrock" and "The Hollow Men." Eliot won the Nobel Prize. He won the prize in 1948.

Combine the sentences in each numbered item by using a coordinating conjunction. Add commas where they're needed. (Hint: Combine the elements listed in brackets at the end of each pair of sentences.)

1. a. Shelly is taking trombone lessons.
   b. Ricardo is taking trombone lessons. [subjects]
2. a. Mr. Estevez grows tomatoes in his garden.
   b. Mr. Estevez grows carrots in his garden. [direct objects]
3. a. Meg Ryan starred in *Sleepless in Seattle.*
   b. She also starred in *You've Got Mail.* [objects of preposition]
4. a. Maria plays the piano.
   b. Maria sings in the choir. [predicates]
5. a. Grandma knitted Su-Lin socks and mittens.
   b. Grandma knitted Maya socks and mittens. [indirect objects]
6. a. Dad likes a thick, juicy steak occasionally.
   b. Mom refuses to eat meat. [sentences]
7. a. Buddy will play Romeo.
   b. Cissy will play Juliet. [sentences]
8. a. Sidney may enlist in the army.
   b. She may attend a community college. [sentences]
9. a. Cinderella had no gown for the ball.
   b. She did have a fairy godmother. [sentences]
10. a. Samuel Taylor Coleridge was a poet.
    b. Samuel Coleridge Taylor was a composer. [sentences]

Combine the sentences in each numbered item by adding the new information in the second sentence to the first sentence in the form of a prepositional phrase or an appositive phrase.

11. a. Jim, Natalie, and Singh received awards.
    b. They received the awards for perfect attendance.
12. a. Confucius lived from 551 to 479 B.C.
    b. He was a famous Chinese philosopher.
13. a. Shanda hid the present.
    b. She hid it under her bed.
14. a. Eddie plays the drums.
    b. He plays them with enthusiasm.
15. a. The monument stood on the steps of the capitol.
    b. The monument was a statue of Christopher Columbus.
16. a. This story takes place during the Civil War.
    b. The story is by Irene Hunt.
17. a. A hundred students participated in the production of the play.
    b. The play was a musical comedy.
18. a. My drawing won a prize in the competition.
    b. The drawing was a sketch of the river.
19. a. My grandparents' portrait hangs in the living room.
    b. It hangs over the fireplace.
20. a. On Sunday mornings, my parents enjoy a cup of mocha.
    b. Mocha is a mixture of chocolate and coffee.

GRAMMAR / USAGE / MECHANICS

Combine the sentences in items 21–25 by changing the new information in the second sentence to an adjective clause and adding it to the first sentence. Begin your clause with the word in brackets. Add commas if they're needed.

Combine the sentences in items 26–30 by changing the information in one sentence to an adverb clause and adding it to the other sentence. Begin your clause with the word in brackets. Add a comma if it's needed.

21. a. The park ranger was kind.
b. She helped me find my family. [who]

22. a. My cast comes off soon.
b. It has been on my leg for five weeks. [which]

23. a. The city will build a new stadium.
b. The new stadium will seat twice as many people as the old one. [that]

24. a. My brother has been accepted at Northwestern University.
b. His grades are excellent. [whose]

25. a. Mayor Roberts is improving the city's parks.
b. The voters elected him two years ago. [whom]

26. a. The skunk smells terrible to people. [Although]
b. The stinkbug smells terrible to other insects.

27. a. We hiked to the lake.
b. The sun was rising. [as]

28. a. Yoko takes out the trash. [While]
b. Her brother sweeps the floor.

29. a. Harriet missed her ballet class.
b. She overslept. [because]

30. a. Mrs. Cuentres gave the baby a bath.
b. She put him to bed. [before]

Chapter 15

Spelling and Vocabulary

15.1 SPELLING RULES   CCSS L.7.2b

English spelling often seems to make no sense. Usually there are historical reasons for the spellings we use today, but you don't need to study the history of the English language to spell correctly. The rules in this section work most of the time, but there are exceptions to every rule. When you're not sure how to spell a word, the best thing to do is check a dictionary.

Spelling *ie* and *ei*

An easy way to learn when to use *ie* and when to use *ei* is to memorize a simple rhyming rule. Then learn the common exceptions to the rule.

RULE	EXAMPLES
WRITE *I* BEFORE *E*	achieve, believe, brief, chief, die, field, friend grief, lie, niece, piece, pier, quiet, retrieve, tie, yield
EXCEPT AFTER *C*	ceiling, conceit, conceive, deceit, deceive, receipt, receive
OR WHEN SOUNDED LIKE *A*, AS IN *NEIGHBOR* AND *WEIGH*.	eight, eighty, freight, neigh, reign, sleigh, veil, vein, weigh, weight

Some exceptions: caffeine, either, foreign, forfeit, height, heir, leisure, neither, protein, seize, species, their, weird; words ending in *cient (ancient)* and *cience (conscience);* plurals of nouns ending in *cy (democracies);* the third-person singular form of verbs ending in *cy (fancies);* words in which *i* and *e* follow *c* but represent separate sounds *(science, society)*

Words Ending in *cede, ceed,* and *sede*

The only English word ending in *sede* is *supersede.* Three words end in *ceed: proceed, exceed,* and *succeed.* You can remember these three words by thinking of the following sentence.

EXAMPLE   If you **proceed** to **exceed** the speed limit, you will **succeed** in getting a ticket.

All other words ending with the "seed" sound are spelled with *cede: precede, recede, secede.*

Adding Prefixes

Adding prefixes is easy. Keep the spelling of the root word and add the prefix. If the last letter of the prefix is the same as the first letter of the word, keep both letters.

un- + happy = unhappy	co- + operate = cooperate
dis- + appear = disappear	il- + legal = illegal
re- + enlist = reenlist	un- + natural = unnatural
mis- + spell = misspell	im- + migrate = immigrate

Adding Suffixes

When you add a suffix beginning with a vowel, double the final consonant if the word ends in a **single consonant following a single vowel** *and*

- the word has one syllable

mud + -y = muddy	sad + -er = sadder
put + -ing = putting	stop + -ed = stopped

- the word is stressed on the last syllable and the stress remains on the same syllable after the suffix is added

occur + -ence = occurrence	repel + -ent = repellent
regret + -able = regrettable	commit + -ed = committed
begin + -ing = beginning	refer + -al = referral

Don't double the final letter if the word ends in *s, w, x,* or *y: buses, rowing, waxy, employer.*

Don't double the final consonant before the suffix *-ist* if the word has more than one syllable: *druggist* but *violinist, guitarist.*

Adding suffixes to words that end in *y* can cause spelling problems. Study these rules and note the exceptions.

When a word ends in a **vowel and *y*,** keep the *y*.

play + -s = plays	joy + -ous = joyous
obey + -ed = obeyed	annoy + -ance = annoyance
buy + -ing = buying	enjoy + -ment = enjoyment
employ + -er = employer	enjoy + -able = enjoyable
joy + -ful = joyful	boy + -ish = boyish
joy + -less = joyless	coy + -ly = coyly

SOME EXCEPTIONS: gay + -ly = gaily, day + -ly = daily, pay + -d = paid, lay + -d = laid, say + -d = said

When a word ends in a **consonant and *y*,** change the *y* to *i* before any suffix that doesn't begin with *i*. Keep the *y* before suffixes that begin with *i*.

carry + -es = carries	deny + -al = denial
dry + -ed = dried	rely + -able = reliable
easy + -er = easier	mercy + -less = merciless
merry + -ly = merrily	likely + -hood = likelihood
happy + -ness = happiness	accompany + -ment =
beauty + -ful = beautiful	accompaniment
fury + -ous = furious	carry + -ing = carrying
defy + -ant = defiant	baby + -ish = babyish
vary + -ation = variation	lobby + -ist = lobbyist

SOME EXCEPTIONS: shy + -ly = shyly, dry + -ly = dryly, shy + -ness = shyness, dry + -ness = dryness, biology + -ist = biologist, economy + -ist = economist, baby + -hood = babyhood

Usually a **final silent *e*** is dropped before a suffix, but sometimes it's kept. The following chart shows the basic rules for adding suffixes to words that end in silent *e*.

ADDING SUFFIXES TO WORDS THAT END IN SILENT *E*

RULE	EXAMPLES
Drop the *e* before suffixes that begin with a vowel.	care + -ed = cared dine + -ing = dining move + -er = mover type + -ist = typist blue + -ish = bluish arrive + -al = arrival desire + -able = desirable accuse + -ation = accusation noise + -y = noisy
Some exceptions	mile + -age = mileage dye + -ing = dyeing
Drop the *e* and change *i* to *y* before the suffix *-ing* if the word ends in *ie*.	die + -ing = dying lie + -ing = lying tie + -ing = tying
Keep the *e* before suffixes that begin with *a* and *o* if the word ends in *ce* or *ge*.	dance + -able = danceable change + -able = changeable courage + -ous = courageous
Keep the *e* before suffixes that begin with a vowel if the word ends in *ee* or *oe*.	see + -ing = seeing agree + -able = agreeable canoe + -ing = canoeing hoe + -ing = hoeing
Some exceptions	free + -er = freer free + -est = freest
Keep the *e* before suffixes that begin with a consonant.	grace + -ful = graceful state + -hood = statehood like + -ness = likeness encourage + -ment = encouragement care + -less = careless sincere + -ly = sincerely

GRAMMAR / USAGE / MECHANICS

RULE	EXAMPLES
Some exceptions	awe + -ful = awful
	judge + -ment = judgment
	argue + -ment = argument
	true + -ly = truly
	due + -ly = duly
	whole + -ly = wholly
Drop *le* before the suffix *-ly* when the word ends with a consonant and *le*.	possible + -ly = possibly
	sniffle + -ly = sniffly
	sparkle + -ly = sparkly
	gentle + -ly = gently

When a word ends in *ll*, drop one *l* when you add the suffix *-ly*.

dull + -ly = dully   full + -ly = fully

chill + -ly = chilly   hill + -ly = hilly

Compound Words

Keep the original spelling of both parts of a compound word.

Remember that some compounds are one word, some are two words, and some are hyphenated. Check a dictionary when in doubt.

foot + lights = footlights   fish + hook = fishhook

busy + body = busybody   with + hold = withhold

book + case = bookcase   book + keeper = bookkeeper

light + house = lighthouse   heart + throb = heartthrob

Spelling Plurals

A singular noun names one person, place, thing, or idea. A plural noun names more than one. To form the plural of most nouns, you simply add *-s*. The following chart shows other basic rules.

GRAMMAR / USAGE / MECHANICS

GENERAL RULES FOR FORMING PLURALS

NOUNS ENDING IN	TO FORM PLURAL	EXAMPLES
ch, s, sh, x, z	Add -*es.*	lunch → lunches bus → buses dish → dishes box → boxes buzz → buzzes
a vowel and *y*	Add -*s.*	boy → boys turkey → turkeys
a consonant and *y*	Change *y* to *i* and add -*es.*	baby → babies penny → pennies
a vowel and *o*	Add -*s.*	radio → radios rodeo → rodeos
a consonant and *o*	Usually add -*es.*	potato → potatoes tomato → tomatoes hero → heroes echo → echoes
	Sometimes add -*s.*	zero → zeros photo → photos piano → pianos
f or *fe*	Usually change *f* to *v* and add -*s* or -*es.*	wife → wives knife → knives life → lives leaf → leaves half → halves shelf → shelves wolf → wolves thief → thieves
	Sometimes add -*s.*	roof → roofs chief → chiefs cliff → cliffs giraffe → giraffes

GRAMMAR / USAGE / MECHANICS

The plurals of **proper names** are formed by adding -*es* to names that end in *ch, s, sh, x,* or *z.*

EXAMPLE   The **Woodriches** live on Elm Street.

EXAMPLE   There are two **Jonases** in our class.

EXAMPLE   Have you met your new neighbors, the **Gomezes?**

Just add -*s* to form the plural of all other proper names, including those that end in *y.*

EXAMPLE   The **Kennedys** are a famous American family.

EXAMPLE   I know three **Marys.**

EXAMPLE   The last two **Januarys** have been especially cold.

To form the plural of a **compound noun written as one word,** follow the general rules for plurals. To form the plural of **hyphenated compound nouns or compound nouns of more than one word,** usually make the most important word plural.

EXAMPLE   A dozen **mailboxes** stood in a row at the entrance to the housing development.

EXAMPLE   The two women's **fathers-in-law** have never met.

EXAMPLE   The three **post offices** are made of brick.

Some nouns have **irregular plural forms** that don't follow any rules.

man → men

woman → women

child → children

foot → feet

tooth → teeth

mouse → mice

goose → geese

ox → oxen

Some nouns have the same singular and plural forms. Most of these are the names of animals, and some of the plural forms may be spelled in more than one way.

deer → deer

sheep → sheep

head (cattle) → head

Sioux → Sioux

series → series

species → species

fish → fish *or* fishes

antelope → antelope *or* antelopes

buffalo → buffalo *or* buffaloes *or* buffalos

PRACTICE **Spelling Rules**

Find the misspelled word in each group and write it correctly.

1. recieve, believe, their
2. reelect, imature, unnecessary
3. reference, taxable, occasionnal
4. payed, merriment, hurrying
5. loving, probably, noticable
6. nightime, knickknack, taillight
7. potatoes, monkies, foxes
8. womens, mice, geese
9. succeed, secede, procede
10. livelihood, fryed, pitiful

15.2 IMPROVING YOUR SPELLING CCSS L.7.2b

You can improve your spelling by improving your study method. You can also improve your spelling by thoroughly learning certain common but frequently misspelled words.

HOW TO STUDY A WORD

By following a few simple steps, you can learn to spell new words. Pay attention to unfamiliar or hard-to-spell words in your reading. As you write, note words that you have trouble spelling. Then use the steps below to learn to spell those difficult words.

1. Say It
Look at the word and say it aloud. Say it again, pronouncing each syllable clearly.

2. See It
Close your eyes. Picture the word in your mind. Visualize the word letter by letter.

3. Write It
Look at the word again and write it two or three times. Then write the word without looking at the printed spelling.

4. Check It
Check your spelling. Did you spell the word correctly? If not, repeat each step until you can spell the word easily.

Get into the habit of using a dictionary to find the correct spelling of a word. How do you find a word if you can't spell it? Write down letters and letter combinations that could stand for the sound you hear at the beginning of the word. Try these possible spellings as you look for the word in a dictionary.

SPELLING PROBLEM WORDS

The following words are often misspelled. Look for your problem words in the list. What words would you add to the list?

Often Misspelled Words

absence	definite	laboratory
accidentally	descend	leisure
accommodate	develop	library
achievement	discipline	license
adviser	disease	maintenance
alcohol	dissatisfied	medicine
all right	eligible	mischievous
analyze	embarrass	misspell
answer	envelope	modern
athlete	environment	molasses
attendant	essential	muscle
ballet	familiar	necessary
beautiful	February	neighborhood
beginning	foreign	niece
believe	forty	ninety
beneficial	fulfill	noticeable
blaze	funeral	nuisance
business	genius	occasion
cafeteria	government	original
canceled	grammar	pageant
canoe	guarantee	parallel
cemetery	height	permanent
changeable	humorous	physical
choir	hygiene	physician
college	imaginary	picnic
colonel	immediate	pneumonia
commercial	incidentally	privilege
convenient	incredibly	probably
courageous	jewelry	pronunciation
curiosity	judgment	receipt

receive	separate	traffic
recognize	similar	truly
recommend	sincerely	unanimous
restaurant	souvenir	usually
rhythm	succeed	vacuum
ridiculous	technology	variety
schedule	theory	various
sense	tomorrow	Wednesday

PRACTICE **Spelling Problem Words**

Find each misspelled word and write it correctly.

1. That child is a notisable newsence.
2. What is the occassion for the pajent?
3. Would you recomend that resterant?
4. Should I close this letter with *Yours sinserely* or *Yours truely?*
5. Do you beleive the reason for his absense?
6. He said his father's busness was in a blase.
7. Do you have an anser for the problems in the cafateria?
8. I have a definate curiousity about that cemetary.
9. Don't embarras yourself at the funral.
10. Is absolute quiet neccesary in the liberry?

15.3 USING CONTEXT CLUES

The surest way to learn the meaning of a new word is to use a dictionary. However, you won't always have a dictionary handy. You can often figure out the meaning of an unfamiliar word by looking for clues in the words and sentences around it. These surrounding words and sentences are called the context.

USING SPECIFIC CONTEXT CLUES

Writers often give clues to the meaning of unfamiliar words. Sometimes they even tell you exactly what a word means. The following chart shows five types of specific context clues. It also gives examples of words that help you identify the type of context clue.

INTERPRETING CLUE WORDS IN CONTEXT		
TYPE OF CONTEXT CLUE	CLUE WORDS	EXAMPLES
Definition The meaning of the unfamiliar word is given in the sentence.	in other words or that is which is which means	Jamake *inscribed* his name; **that is,** he wrote his name on the card. Jaleesa put the wet clay pot in the *kiln,* **or** oven, to harden.
Example The meaning of the unfamiliar word is explained through familiar examples.	for example for instance including like such as	Some people are afraid of *arachnids,* **such as** spiders and ticks. The new program has been *beneficial* for the school; **for example,** test scores are up, and absences are down.

chart continued on next page

TYPE OF CONTEXT CLUE	CLUE WORDS	EXAMPLES
Comparison The unfamiliar word is compared to a familiar word or phrase.	also identical like likewise resembling same similarly too	Maria thought the dress was *gaudy.* Lisa, **too,** thought it was flashy. A *rampant* growth of weeds and vines surrounded the old house. The barn was **likewise** covered with uncontrolled and wild growth.
Contrast The unfamiliar word is contrasted to a familiar word or phrase.	but however on the contrary on the other hand unlike	Robins are *migratory* birds, **unlike** sparrows, which live in the same region all year round. Martin didn't *bungle* the arrangements for the party; **on the contrary,** he handled everything smoothly and efficiently.
Cause and effect The unfamiliar word is explained as part of a cause-and-effect relationship.	as a result because consequently therefore thus	**Because** this rubber raft is so *buoyant,* it will float easily. Kevin is very *credulous;* **consequently,** he'll believe almost anything.

USING GENERAL CONTEXT

Sometimes there are no special clue words to help you understand an unfamiliar word. However, you can still use the general context. That is, you can use the details in the words or sentences around the unfamiliar word. Read the following sentences:

Joel was chosen student **liaison** to the faculty. Everyone hoped his appointment would improve communication between the students and the teachers.

The first sentence tells you that Joel is serving as a kind of connection between the students and the faculty. The word *communication* helps you figure out that being a liaison means acting as a line of communication between two groups.

PRACTICE Using Context Clues

Use context clues to figure out the meaning of the italicized word. Write the meaning. Then write definition, example, comparison, contrast, cause and effect, *or* general *to tell what type of context clue you used to define the word.*

1. Dr. Patel specializes in *oncology,* which is the study of tumors.
2. The *susurration* of voices from the next room was like the whisper of the breeze in the trees.
3. Cyril is the most *pusillanimous* person I've ever known; Raji, on the other hand, is as brave as a lion.
4. My *olfactory* senses became irritated as a result of the foul-smelling smoke.
5. The author takes an *omniscient* point of view; she reports what all her characters are thinking and feeling.
6. *Bovines,* including domestic cattle and the American bison, are an important source of food for many cultures.
7. How I hate these *ubiquitous* commercial advertisements! They're in your mailbox, on television, on the radio, on billboards, even on the Internet!
8. *Indolence* is not a characteristic of successful people. In other words, lazy people don't succeed.
9. His handwriting is *illegible.* It resembles chicken scratchings in a barnyard.
10. Kareem does his chores *conscientiously,* but his sister, Rani, must be reminded constantly.

15.4 ROOTS, PREFIXES, AND SUFFIXES

You can often figure out the meaning of an unfamiliar word by dividing it into parts. The main part of the word is called the root, and it carries the word's basic meaning. A root is often a word by itself. For example, *read* is a word. When a prefix or a suffix is added to it, *read* becomes a root, as in *unreadable.*

Prefixes and suffixes can be added to a root to change its meaning. A prefix is added to the beginning of a root. A suffix is added to the end of a root. A word can have both a prefix and a suffix: *un + read + able = unreadable.*

ROOTS

The root of a word carries the main meaning. Some roots, like *read,* can stand alone. Other roots may have parts added to make a complete word. For example, the root *port* ("carry") by itself is a place to which ships carry goods. Combined with a prefix, it can become *report, deport,* or *transport.* Add a suffix and you can get *reporter, deportment,* or *transportation.*

Learning the meanings of common roots can help you figure out the meanings of many unfamiliar words. The chart on the following pages shows some common roots.

GRAMMAR / USAGE / MECHANICS

ROOTS

ROOTS	WORDS	MEANINGS
bio means "life"	biography	a written story of a person's life
	biosphere	the part of the atmosphere where living things exist
dec or *deca* means "ten"	decade	ten years
	decathlon	an athletic contest consisting of ten events
dent means "tooth"	dentist	a doctor who treats the teeth
	trident	a spear with three prongs, or teeth
dict means "to say"	dictionary	a book of words
	dictator	one who rules absolutely
	predict	to say before (something happens)
duc or *duct* means "to lead"	conductor	one who leads or directs
	produce	to bring into existence
flect or *flex* means "to bend"	flexible	able to bend
	reflect	to bend back (light)
graph means "to write" or "writing"	autograph	one's own signature
	biography	a written story of a person's life
lect means "speech"	lecture	a speech
	dialect	the speech of a certain region
miss or *mit* means "to send"	omit	to fail to send or include
	missile	something sent through the air or by mail
phon means "sound" or "voice"	phonograph	an instrument for playing sounds
	telephone	a device for transmitting voices over a distance
port means "to carry"	transport	to carry across a distance
	porter	one who carries baggage

GRAMMAR / USAGE / MECHANICS

ROOTS	WORDS	MEANINGS
script means "writing"	prescription	a written order for medicine
	postscript	a message added at the end of a letter
spec or *spect* means "to look" or "to watch"	spectator	one who watches
	inspect	to look closely
	prospect	to look for (mineral deposits)
tele means "distant"	telephone	a device for transmitting voices over a distance
	television	a device for transmitting pictures over a distance
tri means "three"	triathlon	an athletic contest consisting of three events
	tricycle	a three-wheeled vehicle
vid or *vis* means "to see"	vision	the ability to see
	videotape	a recording of visual images
voc or *vok* means "to call"	vocation	an inclination, or call, to a certain pursuit
	revoke	to recall or take back

PREFIXES

The following chart shows some prefixes and their meanings. Notice that some prefixes, such as *dis-*, *in-*, *non-*, and *un-*, have the same or nearly the same meaning. A single prefix may have more than one meaning. The prefix *in-*, for example, can mean "into," as in *inject*, as well as "not," as in *indirect*. The prefix *re-* can mean "again" or "back."

Note that *il-*, *im-*, *in-*, and *ir-* are variations of the same prefix. *Il-* is used before roots that begin with *l (illegal)*; *im-* is used before roots that begin with *m (immature)*; and *ir-* is used before roots that begin with *r (irregular)*. *In-* is used before all other letters.

CATEGORIES	PREFIXES	WORDS	MEANINGS
Prefixes that reverse meanings	*de-* means "remove from" or "reduce"	defrost devalue	to remove frost to reduce the value of
	dis- means "not" or "do the opposite of"	disagreeable disappear	not agreeable to do the opposite of appear
	in-, il-, im-, and *ir-* mean "not"	incomplete illegal immature irregular	not complete not legal not mature not regular
	mis- means "bad," "badly," "wrong," or "wrongly"	misfortune misbehave misdeed misjudge	bad fortune to behave badly a wrong deed to judge wrongly
	non- means "not" or "without"	nonathletic nonfat	not athletic without fat
	un- means "not" or "do the opposite of"	unhappy untie	not happy to do the opposite of tie
Prefixes that show relationship	*co-* means "with," "together," or "partner"	coworker coexist coauthor	one who works with another to exist together an author who writes as a partner with another
	inter- means "between"	interscholastic	between schools
	post- means "after"	postseason	after the regular season
	pre- means "before"	preseason	before the regular season

GRAMMAR / USAGE / MECHANICS

CATEGORIES	PREFIXES	WORDS	MEANINGS
	re- means "back" or "again"	repay recheck	to pay back to check again
	sub- means "under" or "below"	submarine substandard	under the sea below standard
	super- means "more than"	superabundant	more than abundant
	trans- means "across"	transport	to carry across a distance
Prefixes that show judgment	*anti-* means "against"	antiwar	against war
	pro- means "in favor of"	progovernment	in favor of the government
Prefixes that show number	*bi-* means "two"	bicycle	a two-wheeled vehicle
	semi- means "half" or "partly"	semicircle semisweet	half a circle partly sweet
	uni- means "one"	unicycle	a one-wheeled vehicle

SUFFIXES

A suffix added to a word can change the word's part of speech as well as its meaning. For example, adding the suffix *-er* to *read* (a verb) makes *reader* (a noun). Adding *-less* to *faith* (a noun) makes *faithless* (an adjective).

The following chart shows some common suffixes and their meanings. Notice that some suffixes, such as *-er, -or,* and *-ist,* have the same or nearly the same meaning. A single suffix may have more than one meaning. The suffix *-er,* for example, can also mean "more," as in *bigger.*

GRAMMAR / USAGE / MECHANICS

SUFFIXES

CATEGORIES	SUFFIXES	WORDS	MEANINGS
Suffixes that mean "one who" or "that which"	*-ee, -eer*	employee	one who is employed
		charioteer	one who drives a chariot
	-er, -or	worker	one who works
		sailor	one who sails
	-ian	physician	one who practices medicine (once called physic)
		musician	one who plays or studies music
	-ist	pianist	one who plays the piano
		chemist	one who works in chemistry
Suffixes that mean "full of" or "having"	*-ful*	joyful	full of joy
		suspenseful	full of suspense
		beautiful	having beauty
	-ous	furious	full of fury
		famous	having fame
		courageous	having courage
Suffixes that show a state, a condition, or a quality	*-hood*	falsehood	quality of being false
	-ness	happiness	state of being happy
	-ship	friendship	condition of being friends
Suffixes that show an action or process or its result	*-ance, -ence*	performance	action of performing
		conference	process of conferring
	-ation, -ion	flirtation	action of flirting
		invention	result of inventing
	-ment	argument	result of arguing
		arrangement	result of arranging
		enjoyment	process of enjoying

CATEGORIES	SUFFIXES	WORDS	MEANINGS
Suffixes that mean "relating to," "characterized by," or "like"	*-al*	musical comical	relating to music relating to comedy
	-ish	childish foolish	like a child like a fool
	-y	witty hairy	characterized by wit characterized by hair
Other common suffixes	*-able* and *-ible* mean "capable of," "fit for," or "likely to"	breakable collectible agreeable	capable of being broken fit for collecting likely to agree
	-ize means "to cause to be" or "to become"	visualize familiarize	to cause to be made visual to become familiar
	-less means "without"	hopeless careless	without hope done without care
	-ly means "in a (certain) manner"	easily sadly	in an easy manner in a sad manner

Notice that sometimes the spelling of a word changes when a suffix is added. For example, when *-ous* is added to *fury,* the *y* in *fury* changes to *i.* See pages 301–304 to learn more about spelling words with suffixes.

More than one suffix can be added to a single word. The following examples show how suffixes can change a single root word.

peace **[noun]**

peace + ful = peaceful **[adjective]**

peace + ful + ly = peacefully **[adverb]**

peace + ful + ness = peacefulness **[noun]**

Divide the following words. Write their parts in three columns headed prefix, root, *and* suffix. *In a fourth column, write another word that has the same prefix or the same suffix or both. Then write a definition for each word.*

1. semitropical
2. prediction
3. disadvantageous
4. deductible
5. mismanagement
6. reflector
7. invisible
8. transmitter
9. unmercifully
10. immeasureableness

GRAMMAR / USAGE / MECHANICS

Part Three

Composition

The time to begin writing an article is when you have finished it to your satisfaction. By that time you begin to clearly and logically perceive what it is you really want to say.

—Mark Twain

Persuasive Essay

Look around you. Magazines, newspapers, books, posters, letters, e-mails, blogs, radio and television programs—almost anything you read, see, or hear can include persuasion. One purpose of persuasive writing is to make readers, listeners, or viewers think or feel a certain way about an idea or a product. Another purpose is to make people take action. When you write to persuade, you try to convince your audience to think or act in a particular way. In order to persuade, you must catch and hold the attention of your audience.

Often persuasive writing begins by stating the writer's goal or position. Then evidence—information to support that position—follows. Some supporting evidence will make you think, and some will make you feel a certain way. Near the end, there is usually a reminder of what the writer wants you to do or think.

The instruction on the pages that follow will guide you through the process of writing a persuasive essay and meeting the Common Core State Standards for persuasive, or argumentative, writing. For a list of the writing and grammar Common Core State Standards, see pages 439–447.

16.1 PLAN

Graphic Organizers

During the Plan stage, you will gather and organize writing ideas. You may wish to use a graphic organizer, such as the Persuasive Essay Chart on page 382.

Identify Your Thesis

Write the topic of your persuasive essay. The **topic** is the general subject you wish to write about. Then write your **thesis**, or the main idea of your essay. A thesis is usually one or two sentences. In a persuasive essay, your thesis is your **claim**, or a statement of your position on the topic or issue.

Your thesis is related to your purpose and audience. Remember that your **purpose** is your reason for writing, and your **audience** includes the people who will be reading your essay.

To identify your thesis, consider

- what you want your audience to think about the topic
- which actions you want your audience to take after reading your essay CCSS W.7.1a

Gather Reasons and Evidence

Before you begin drafting, gather reasons and relevant evidence to support your thesis, or claim. **Reasons** explain why someone should accept the claim. **Relevant evidence** consists of examples, facts, and expert opinions that are directly related to your argument.

Be sure to **differentiate**, or distinguish between, fact and opinion. A **fact** is a statement that can be proved to be true. An **opinion** is what someone believes, based on his or her personal viewpoint.

COMPOSITION

Write evidence you know from background knowledge. Then gather information from

- newspaper and magazine articles
- neighborhood newsletters
- reliable Web sites
- interviews with experts

Make sure each source you use is accurate and credible. An **accurate** source provides factual, true information. A **credible** source provides trustworthy information by authors who are experts or who know a lot about the topic.

List your evidence. Take notes about how your evidence supports your thesis. Then identify whether each piece of evidence is a fact or an opinion. CCSS W.7.1a, b

Analyze Your Audience

In order to create strong arguments, writers of persuasive essays must think about opinions other than their own. Think about your topic, thesis, and audience. Consider and anticipate the **views**, **concerns**, and **counter-arguments** that others might have about your topic and thesis.

TERM	DEFINITION
View	a belief
Concern	a worry
Counter-argument, or opposing claim	a statement that opposes another argument

Take notes about how you would respond to other views and answer readers' concerns and counter-arguments. CCSS W.7.1a

COMPOSITION

16.2 DRAFT

Write the Introduction
Write your introductory paragraph. Your introduction should

- grab your readers' attention
- state your topic
- introduce your thesis, or claim
- briefly explain why your audience should care about the issue CCSS W.7.1a

Write the Body: Organization
Organize your reasons and evidence in a logical structure. You might organize reasons and evidence using the following strategies:

STRATEGY	DEFINITION
Order of importance	to put the most important information first or last
Cause and effect	to describe an event or action and what results from it
Comparison and contrast	to describe similarities and differences among things or ideas

Focus each paragraph around one main idea. Then include reasons and evidence that support that idea. Make sure your reasons and evidence directly relate to your thesis, or claim. Clearly identify facts and opinions. The organization of your essay should help your readers clearly identify your claim, your reasons and evidence, and any opposing ideas. As you develop your essay, build on your ideas to create a focused, organized, and coherent draft. CCSS W.7.1a, b

COMPOSITION

Write the Body: Analyze Audience

As you write, show your readers that you understand your topic and issue. Include views, concerns, and counter-arguments that your readers might have about your topic and thesis. Then respond to these views, concerns, and counter-arguments using logical reasons and relevant evidence. CCSS W.7.1a, b

Write the Body: Word Choice

As you continue to write your main paragraphs, use transitions to clarify the relationships among your claim, counter-claims, reasons, and evidence. **Transitions** are words and phrases that show the relationship between ideas or events. Use some of the transitions in the following chart to clarify the ideas in your essay. CCSS W.7.1c

RELATIONSHIP	EXAMPLES OF TRANSITIONS
Addition	*also, and, besides, both . . . and, furthermore, in addition*
Contrast	*but, however, instead, nevertheless, on the contrary, on the other hand, still, yet*
Importance	*first, last, mainly, most important, most of all*
Cause and effect	*as a result, consequently, for, so, so that, then, therefore, thus*
Sequence	*after, as, before, next, since, then, until, when, while*

COMPOSITION

Writing Tip

As you write, be sure to use and maintain a formal style. In formal writing, you usually write from the third-person point of view and avoid using slang, contractions, and conversational language.
CCSS W.7.1d

Write the Conclusion

Write an effective conclusion to your essay. Your conclusion should follow from and support the argument you present. Make sure your conclusion

- restates your thesis
- briefly summarizes your key ideas
- encourages readers to agree with your position
- encourages readers to take action CCSS W.7.1e

16.3 REVISE

Introduction to Revision

To revise your essay, you will focus on the content or the message of your writing. You will apply one or more of these four revision strategies:

- **Add** details and information to make the message clearer.
- **Delete** unnecessary words or ideas.
- **Substitute** more exact or stronger words for dull or overused language.
- **Rearrange** phrases and sentences to be sure readers can understand the message.

COMPOSITION

The questions that follow will show you how to use these revision strategies. The questions will also help you rethink how well you've addressed purpose, audience, and genre.

- Your **purpose** is your reason for writing. Your purpose might be to describe, explain, narrate, amuse, or persuade.
- The **audience** includes the people who will be reading your writing.
- The **genre** is the writing mode, such as story, poem, play, or essay. CCSS W.7.4, W.7.5

Focus and Coherence
Ask yourself:
✓ Does my essay have a clear focus?
✓ Do all parts work together so that my argument is clear and persuasive for readers?

Organization
Ask yourself:
✓ Does the beginning introduce the thesis?
✓ Does the middle follow a logical order?
✓ Does the conclusion support the argument? CCSS W.7.1a, b, e

Development of Ideas
Ask yourself:
✓ Are my claim and ideas fully developed and supported by relevant reasons and evidence? CCSS W.7.1b

Voice–Word Choice
Ask yourself:
✓ Does my essay include precise, formal language?
✓ Does my essay include effective transitions that link sentences and paragraphs? CCSS W.7.1c, d

Voice–Sentence Fluency

Ask yourself:

✓ Do sentences vary in length and structure?

✓ Does the writing flow smoothly?

 Revising Tip

As you revise, make sure you express ideas precisely and concisely. Use a thesaurus to find exactly the right words to communicate your ideas. Vary your words and sentences to eliminate wordiness and redundancy, or the use of too many words. CCSS L.7.3a

16.4 EDIT

Correct Errors in Grammar

Editing involves correcting errors in grammar, usage, mechanics, and spelling.

Begin the editing stage by taking a careful look at your sentences. Make sure that each sentence expresses a complete thought in a way that is grammatically correct. Use the checklist below to edit your sentences. CCSS W.7.5, L.7.1

Sentence-Editing Checklist

✓ Have I avoided sentence fragments?

✓ Have I avoided run-on sentences?

✓ Do verbs agree with their subjects?

✓ Have I used verb tenses and forms correctly?

✓ Have I used pronouns and adjectives correctly?

✓ Are my sentences parallel?

COMPOSITION

Grammar Link: Misplaced and Dangling Modifiers

Phrases and clauses can be used within a sentence to **modify,** or tell more about, other parts of the sentence. A modifying phrase or clause that is not near enough to the word it is intended to modify is called a **misplaced modifier.**

Incorrect: We talked about which sports team won the game **in study hall. [The game was not in study hall.]**

Correct: We talked **in study hall** about which sports team won the game. **[The people referred to as "we" talked in study hall.]**

Another problem exists when there is no word in the sentence that the modifier refers to. This is called a **dangling modifier.**

Incorrect: Having arrived late to school, a written excuse was needed. **[The written excuse did not arrive late to school.]**

Correct: Having arrived late to school, **the student** needed a written excuse. **[The student arrived late to school.]**

✎ Check your persuasive essay for misplaced and dangling modifiers. Correct any errors that you find.
CCSS L.7.1c

Correct Errors in Mechanics and Spelling

Next check for and correct any errors in mechanics (punctuation and capitalization) and spelling.

Use the Proofreading Checklist on the next page to edit your essay. Use a dictionary to check and confirm spellings.
CCSS L.7.2, b

Proofreading Checklist

✓ Have I used correct punctuation?

✓ Have I written possessives correctly?

✓ Have I spelled all words correctly?

✓ Have I used capital letters as needed?

Peer and Teacher Review

In addition to revising and editing your own essay, you will revise your work through peer review and teacher review. During **peer review**, you will share your writing with a partner or classmates in a writing group. You will discuss how you can each improve your writing. During **teacher review**, you will submit your essay to your teacher. Your teacher will read it and make suggestions on how to improve your essay.

Use the **Peer Review Guide** on page 390 to respond to your classmate's writing.

16.5 PUBLISH

After you have written, revised, and edited your essay, you will publish and present it. You may wish to consider the following publishing and presenting options. Some of these options require you to collaborate with your classmates and use technology.

- Submit your essay to your school newspaper.
- Send your essay as a letter to an appropriate Web site or online newspaper.
- Share your essay in a small group.
- Create a blog and use your essay to start an online class debate. CCSS W.7.6

Reflecting on your own writing can help you improve your writing skills. Use the **Reflection Guide** on page 391 to think about the writing you did in this workshop.

COMPOSITION

Chapter 17

Response Essay

The goal of expository writing is to explain or inform. There are many types of expository writing, from letters to essays to research reports. A response essay is one type of expository writing. In a response essay, you examine and interpret a literary or expository text. You might summarize the text by explaining your interpretation of the text, give your opinion by explaining why you agree or disagree with the text, or share whether you can connect ideas in the text with personal experience. You might also discuss the strengths and weaknesses of the text or analyze the author's craft and style. In any response essay, you use text evidence to support your ideas.

Writing a response essay involves careful thought, planning, and organization. The instruction on the pages that follow will guide you through the process of writing a response essay and meeting the Common Core State Standards for informative and explanatory writing. For a list of the writing and grammar Common Core State Standards, see pages 439–447.

17.1 PLAN

Graphic Organizers

During the Plan stage, you will gather and organize writing ideas. You may wish to use a graphic organizer, such as the Evidence Chart on page 383.

Identify Your Controlling Idea

Write down the literary or expository text to which you want to respond. Then write a controlling idea. The **controlling idea,** or **thesis,** is the focus of your response essay. Your controlling idea should sum up your response. As you draft, you will give details and examples that support your controlling idea. CCSS W.7.2a

Writing Tip

Don't worry about finalizing your controlling idea in the Plan stage. As you gather evidence and draft your paper, you can narrow or broaden your controlling idea. CCSS W.7.2a

Gather Evidence

Identify passages in the text that support your controlling idea. For example, if you are analyzing the author's style, you might look for sentences that help create a specific tone. **Style** is a writer's personal way of using language. The **tone** expresses the writer's feelings and attitude toward the topic or theme.

With your controlling idea in mind, write evidence from the text that you will include in your response. **Evidence** is something that provides proof. Include details and quotations from the text. Make sure the evidence supports your controlling idea. CCSS W.7.2b; W.7.9a, b

COMPOSITION

Synthesize Ideas

When you **synthesize** ideas, you combine ideas to create a new idea or reach a new understanding. You may synthesize ideas from several sources in order to support your controlling idea and main points. Sources may include

- personal experience
- books, stories, essays, and articles
- Web sites

Continue recording evidence. Take notes about the related ideas from your sources. Then synthesize these ideas with details from the text. After you synthesize, you may need to revise your controlling idea. CCSS W.7.2b; W.7.9a, b

17.2 DRAFT

Write the Introduction

An effective introduction grabs readers' interest and gives a brief explanation of what your paper is about. It also states your controlling idea.

In order to engage readers, use language that catches their attention. You might begin your response essay with a **rhetorical element,** or a technique that hooks readers and makes them think and care about your topic. As you draft your introduction, use some of the rhetorical elements from the chart on the next page.

ELEMENT	DEFINITION
Quotation	well-chosen words from the selection
Description	words that describe a setting, person, or event and appeal to the senses
Rhetorical question	a question to which no answer is expected
Anecdote	a brief story based on an interesting or amusing event from a person's life
Analogy	a comparison between two things that may not be similar
Parallelism	the use of a series of words, phrases, or sentences that have similar grammatical structure
Repetition	the repeated use of a word, phrase, sound, or other part of a text

Write the introduction to your response essay. Include two of these rhetorical elements, and be sure to state your controlling idea. You might freewrite several introductions before deciding on the best one. CCSS W.7.2a

 Writing Tip

Don't worry about details of punctuation, spelling, or grammar as you draft your essay. You can fix those later. The important thing is to get your ideas on paper.

Write the Body Paragraphs

Use a logical structure to organize your main points and supporting details. A clear organization will help readers see the connections among the parts of your essay. You may organize ideas using the strategies in the following chart. Then write the body of your essay. CCSS W.7.2a, b

STRATEGY	DEFINITION
Order of importance	to explain the most important ideas first or last
Comparison and contrast	to describe similarities and differences among things and ideas
Cause and effect	to describe an event and what results from it
Sequence of events	to discuss events in the order that they happened

 Writing Tip

Make sure the facts and details you include are not **extraneous**, or unnecessary. The facts and details should relate to your controlling idea. CCSS W.7.2b; W.7.9a, b

Maintain a Formal Style

Throughout your essay, use precise language and vocabulary that is specific to your topic. Be sure to use and maintain a formal style. In formal writing, you usually write from the third-person point of view and avoid using slang, contractions, and conversational language. CCSS W.7.2d, e

COMPOSITION

Use Transitions

To make your writing flow smoothly, use transitions to link sentences and paragraphs. **Transitions** are words and phrases that show the relationship between ideas or events. Use some of the transitions from the following chart to clarify the ideas in your response essay. CCSS W.7.2c

RELATIONSHIP	EXAMPLES OF TRANSITIONS
Addition	*also, and, besides, both . . . and, furthermore, in addition*
Contrast	*but, however, instead, nevertheless, on the contrary, on the other hand, still, yet*
Importance	*first, last, mainly, most important, most of all*
Cause and effect	*as a result, consequently, for, so, so that, then, therefore, thus*
Sequence	*after, as, before, next, since, then, until, when, while*

Write the Conclusion

Write an effective conclusion to your response essay. An effective conclusion will support the information you presented and tie up your essay. Your conclusion should

- restate your controlling idea
- summarize your main points
- give your readers something further to think about CCSS W.7.2f

17.3 REVISE

Introduction to Revision

To revise your response essay, you will focus on the content or the message of your writing. You will apply one or more of these four revision strategies:

- **Add** details and information to make the message clearer.
- **Delete** unnecessary words or ideas.
- **Substitute** more exact or stronger words for confusing or overused language.
- **Rearrange** phrases and sentences to be sure readers can understand the message.

The questions that follow will show you how to use these revision strategies. The questions will also help you rethink how well you've addressed purpose, audience, and genre.

- Your **purpose** is your reason for writing. Your purpose might be to describe, explain, narrate, amuse, or persuade.
- The **audience** includes the people who will be reading your writing.
- The **genre** is the writing mode, such as story, poem, play, or essay. CCSS W.7.4, W.7.5

Focus and Coherence

Ask yourself:

✓ Does the essay have a clear focus?

✓ Do all the parts work together so that readers understand my purpose and ideas? CCSS W.7.2a

Organization

Ask yourself:

✓ Does the introduction state the controlling idea?

✓ Does the body explain my ideas?

✓ Does the conclusion summarize my essay? CCSS W.7.2a, f

Development of Ideas

Ask yourself:

✓ Are my points supported by appropriate evidence?
CCSS W.7.2b; W.7.9a, b

Voice–Word Choice

Ask yourself:

✓ Does my essay include precise words and vocabulary that are specific to my topic?

✓ Does my essay include transitions that link sentences and paragraphs? CCSS W.7.2c, d; L.7.3a

Voice–Sentence Fluency

Ask yourself:

✓ Do the sentences vary in length and structure?

✓ Does the writing flow smoothly?

17.4 EDIT

Correct Errors in Grammar

Editing involves correcting errors in grammar, usage, mechanics, and spelling.

Begin the editing stage by taking a careful look at your sentences. Make sure that each sentence expresses a complete thought and is grammatically correct. Use the Sentence-Editing Checklist on the following page to edit your sentences. CCSS W.7.5, L.7.1

COMPOSITION

Sentence-Editing Checklist

✓ Have I avoided sentence fragments?

✓ Have I avoided run-on sentences?

✓ Do verbs agree with their subjects?

✓ Have I used verb tenses and forms correctly?

✓ Have I used pronouns and adjectives correctly?

✓ Are my sentences parallel?

Correct Errors in Mechanics and Spelling

Next check for and correct any errors in mechanics (punctuation and capitalization) and spelling.

Use the Proofreading Checklist below to edit your essay. You should use a dictionary to check spellings. CCSS L.7.2, b

Proofreading Checklist

✓ Have I used correct punctuation?

✓ Have I written possessives correctly?

✓ Have I spelled all words correctly?

✓ Have I used capital letters as needed?

Peer and Teacher Review

In addition to revising and editing your own essay, you will revise your work through peer review and teacher review. During **peer review**, you will share your writing with a partner or classmates in a writing group. You will discuss how you can each improve your writing. During **teacher review**, you will submit your essay to your teacher. Your teacher will read it and make suggestions on how to improve your response essay.

Use the **Peer Review Guide** on page 390 to respond to your classmate's writing. CCSS W.7.5

17.5 PUBLISH

After you have written, revised, and edited your essay, you will publish and present it. You may wish to consider the following publishing and presenting options. Some of these options require you to collaborate with your class-mates and use technology.

- Create a class collection of response essays.
- Enter your essay into a writing contest.
- Share your essay in a small group.
- Post your essay on your school or class Web site.
- Publish your essay as a blog entry and invite other students to comment on it. CCSS W.7.6

Reflecting on your own writing can help you improve your writing skills. Use the **Reflection Guide** on page 391 to think about the writing you did in this workshop.

Multi-Paragraph Essay

The goal of expository writing is to explain or inform. In expository writing, the text is organized around one topic and developed with facts, statistics, examples, reasons, and specific details. There are many types of expository writing, including essays, research reports, and magazine articles.

The instruction on the pages that follow will guide you through the process of writing a multi-paragraph essay while meeting the Common Core State Standards for informative and explanatory writing. For a list of the writing and grammar Common Core State Standards, see pages 439–447.

18.1 PLAN

Graphic Organizers

During the Plan stage, you will gather and organize writing ideas. To do this, you may wish to use a graphic organizer, such as the Evidence Chart on page 383.

Identify Your Controlling Idea

Write down the topic of your essay. The **topic** is the general subject you wish to write about. Then write a controlling idea. The **controlling idea**, or **thesis**, is the main idea of an essay or report. The controlling idea is usually stated in one or two sentences.

As you draft, you will give details and examples that support your controlling idea. You can revise your controlling idea throughout the Plan and Draft stages. CCSS W.7.2a

Gather Facts and Details

Write down facts and details from your background knowledge that relate to your topic. These facts and details should support your controlling idea. Then conduct research to find more evidence. **Evidence** is something that provides proof. You may look for information in

- reference books, such as encyclopedias
- magazine or newspaper articles
- trustworthy Web sites

Analyze your research findings. Which evidence is the strongest? Which evidence is the weakest? Take notes about how the facts and details support your controlling idea. CCSS W.7.2b

Writing Tip

Do not plagiarize information from any of your research sources. When you **plagiarize**, you take ideas from someone else and present them as your own. Plagiarizing is against the law. CCSS W.7.8

Synthesize Ideas

When you **synthesize** ideas, you combine ideas to create a new idea or reach a new understanding. A writer may synthesize ideas from several sources in order to support his or her controlling idea and main points. A writer may combine ideas from

- personal experience
- background knowledge
- books, essays, and articles
- Web sites

Continue recording evidence. Take notes about the related ideas from your sources. Then synthesize the ideas. After you synthesize, you may need to revise your controlling idea. CCSS W.7.2b

18.2 DRAFT

Write the Introduction

An effective introduction grabs readers' interest and introduces the topic. It also states the controlling idea.

In order to engage readers, use language that catches their attention. You might begin your essay with a **rhetorical element,** or a technique that hooks readers and makes them think and care about your topic.

Write your introduction. Include two or more of the rhetorical elements from the chart on the following page.

ELEMENT	DEFINITION
Quotation	well-chosen words from an author about your topic
Interesting fact	a statement that can be proven as true
Rhetorical question	a question to which no answer is expected
Anecdote	a brief story based on an interesting or amusing event from a person's life
Analogy	a comparison between two things that may not be similar
Parallelism	the use of a series of words, phrases, or sentences that have similar grammatical structure
Repetition	the repeated use of a word, phrase, sound, or other part of a text

 Writing Tip

If you are stuck, just start writing. Your first attempt does not have to be perfect. You might freewrite more than one introduction before deciding on the best one. CCSS W.7.2a

COMPOSITION

Write the Body Paragraphs

Use a logical structure to organize your ideas. You may organize ideas using the following strategies:

STRATEGY	DEFINITION
Definition	to explain technical or specialized vocabulary and terms related to specific areas of study or work
Classification	to group information by type
Comparison and contrast	to describe similarities and differences among things or ideas
Process	to explain the order of an action or an event
Cause and effect	to describe an event and what results from it
Sequence of events	to discuss events in the order that they happened

Write the body of your essay. Make sure the facts and details you include are not **extraneous,** or unnecessary. The facts and details should relate to your controlling idea. CCSS W.7.2a, b

Maintain a Formal Style

Throughout your essay, use precise language and vocabulary that is specific to your topic. Be sure to use and maintain a formal style. In formal writing, you usually write from the third-person point of view and avoid using slang, contractions, and conversational language. CCSS W.7.2d, e

Use Transitions

To make your writing flow smoothly, use transitions to link sentences and paragraphs. **Transitions** are words and phrases that show the relationship between ideas or events. Use some of the transitions in the chart below to clarify the ideas in your essay. CCSS W.7.2c

RELATIONSHIP	EXAMPLES OF TRANSITIONS
Addition	*also, and, besides, both . . . and, furthermore, in addition*
Contrast	*but, however, instead, nevertheless, on the contrary, on the other hand, still, yet*
Importance	*first, last, mainly, most important, most of all*
Cause and effect	*as a result, consequently, for, so, so that, then, therefore, thus*
Sequence	*after, as, before, next, since, then, until, when, while*

Incorporate Visual Elements

To help readers better understand the ideas in your essay, you may wish to include

- graphics, such as images, maps, and charts
- formatting, such as heads and subheads
- multimedia elements, such as links to video clips
  CCSS W.7.2a

Write the Conclusion

Write an effective conclusion that follows from and supports the information in your essay. Your conclusion should

- restate your controlling idea
- summarize your main points
- give your readers something further to think about CCSS W.7.2f

18.3 REVISE

Introduction to Revision

To revise your essay, you will focus on the content or the message of your writing. You will apply one or more of these four revision strategies:

- **Add** details and information to make the message clearer.
- **Delete** unnecessary words or ideas.
- **Substitute** more exact or stronger words for confusing or overused language.
- **Rearrange** phrases and sentences to be sure readers can understand the message.

The questions that follow will show you how to use these revision strategies. The questions will also help you rethink how well you've addressed purpose, audience, and genre.

- Your **purpose** is your reason for writing. Your purpose might be to describe, explain, narrate, amuse, or persuade.
- The **audience** includes the people who will be reading your writing.
- The **genre** is the writing mode, such as story, poem, play, or essay. CCSS W.7.4, W.7.5

Focus and Coherence

Ask yourself:

✓ Does the essay have a clear focus?

✓ Do all the parts work together so that readers understand my purpose and ideas? CCSS W.7.2a

Organization

Ask yourself:

✓ Does the introduction state the controlling idea?

✓ Does the body explain my ideas?

✓ Does the conclusion summarize my essay? CCSS W.7.2a, f

Development of Ideas

Ask yourself:

✓ Are my ideas supported by relevant facts, details, and examples? CCSS W.7.2b

Voice–Word Choice

Ask yourself:

✓ Does my essay include precise words and vocabulary that are specific to my topic?

✓ Does my essay include transitions that clarify the relationships among my ideas? CCSS W.7.2c, d; L.7.3a

Voice–Sentence Fluency

Ask yourself:

✓ Do the sentences vary in length and structure?

✓ Does the writing flow smoothly?

 Revising Tip

As you revise, make sure you express ideas precisely and concisely. Use a thesaurus to find exactly the right words to communicate your ideas. Vary your words and sentences to eliminate wordiness and redundancy, or the use of too many words. CCSS L.7.3a

COMPOSITION

18.4 EDIT

Correct Errors in Grammar

Editing involves correcting errors in grammar, usage, mechanics, and spelling.

Begin the editing stage by taking a careful look at your sentences. Make sure that each sentence expresses a complete thought and is grammatically correct. Use the Sentence-Editing Checklist to edit your sentences. CCSS W.7.5, L.7.1

Sentence-Editing Checklist

✓ Have I avoided sentence fragments?

✓ Have I avoided run-on sentences?

✓ Do verbs agree with their subjects?

✓ Have I used verb tenses and forms correctly?

✓ Have I used pronouns and adjectives correctly?

✓ Are my sentences parallel?

Correct Errors in Mechanics and Spelling

Next check for and correct any errors in mechanics (punctuation and capitalization) and spelling.

Use the Proofreading Checklist to edit your essay. You should use a dictionary to check spellings. CCSS L.7.2, b

Proofreading Checklist

✓ Have I used correct punctuation?

✓ Have I written possessives correctly?

✓ Have I spelled all words correctly?

✓ Have I used capital letters as needed?

Peer and Teacher Review

In addition to revising and editing your own essay, you will revise your work through peer review and teacher review. During **peer review**, you will share your writing with a partner or classmates in a writing group. You will discuss how you can each improve your writing. During **teacher review**, you will submit your essay to your teacher. Your teacher will read it and make suggestions on how to improve your essay.

Use the **Peer Review Guide** on page 390 to respond to your classmate's writing. CCSS W.7.5

18.5 PUBLISH

After you have written and revised your essay, you will publish and present your essay. You may wish to consider the following publishing and presenting options. Some of these options require you to collaborate with your class-mates and use technology.

- Create a class collection of essays.
- Enter your essay into a writing contest.
- Share your essay in a small group.
- Post your essay on your school or class Web site.
- Use publishing software to create a newsletter that features your essay. CCSS W.7.6

Reflecting on your own writing can help you improve your writing skills. Use the **Reflection Guide** on page 391 to think about the writing you did in this workshop.

COMPOSITION

Chapter 19

Research Report

When you write a research report, you investigate a topic and present information about the topic to your readers. You've probably seen reports in newspapers and magazines. Journalists write these reports to investigate such topics as politics, environmental issues, and business concerns. They use a variety of sources to find information, and then they present this information to their readers.

To write a research report, you should

- choose a topic that interests you
- decide on a purpose for your report
- gather information from sources
- take notes, organize your notes, and write an outline
- write about your purpose and main idea in a thesis statement
- present the information about your topic to your readers in your own words
- prepare a list of your sources

The instruction on the pages that follow will guide you through the process of writing a research report and meeting the Common Core State Standards for informative and explanatory writing. For a list of the writing and grammar Common Core State Standards, see pages 439–447.

19.1 PLAN

Graphic Organizers

During the Plan stage, you will gather and organize writing ideas. You may wish to use graphic organizers, such as the Main Idea Map, Source Card, and Note Card on pages 384–386.

Do Preliminary Research

Choose a topic. A **topic** is the general subject of a piece of writing. Then do some preliminary research. Look up your topic in a reference work, such as an encyclopedia, to find general information. Then find additional information by conducting text searches in a search engine. CCSS W.7.7

Formulate a Major Research Question

Write questions about your topic that you would like to answer in your research report. You might find it helpful to write questions that begin with *who, what, when, where, why,* and *how.*

From your list of questions, choose one question to be your major research question. You may also combine related questions to come up with a major research question. The answer to your major research question will be your thesis. The **thesis** is the main idea of an essay or a report. The thesis is usually one or two sentences. CCSS W.7.7

COMPOSITION

Write a Research Plan

Now that you have done preliminary research and formulated your major research question, write a research plan. Your plan should list

- what other information you need
- which types of sources you will use
- what questions you want to answer through further research and investigation

Remember to include both print and digital sources.
CCSS W.7.7

Gather Sources

Follow your research plan. Gather information from the Internet and from your school media center or local library. Remember to use a wide variety of print and digital sources. In order to find exactly what you are looking for, use effective search terms and advanced search options as you search for digital sources.

After you have gathered your sources, skim and scan them for information that relates to your major research question. Record any relevant information that you find. **Relevant** information addresses the questions that you want to answer in your research report. CCSS W.7.8

 Planning Tip

As you learn more about your topic, you may discover a focus that looks more interesting than the one you originally chose. It's not too late to change the direction of your report.

Evaluate Sources

You should use only valid and reliable print and digital sources. **Valid sources** are relevant and accurate. **Reliable sources** are credible, objective, and current. To evaluate the quality of your sources, ask yourself the following questions:

EVALUATION TERMS	QUESTIONS
Relevant	Is the information related to your topic? Does it help answer your questions about your topic?
Accurate	Can you verify the information in another source?
Credible	Is the information written by an author or organization with a good reputation? Is the author considered an expert?
Objective	Is the information a fact or an opinion? Does the source reveal bias, or favoritism for or against something?
Current	Is the information up to date or out of date?

In your research report, you will need to demonstrate the credibility and accuracy of your sources. You will use elements such as the following:

- a current publication date
- a reference to an encyclopedia from a well-known publisher
- a quotation expressing the point of view of an expert

COMPOSITION

As you evaluate your sources, eliminate any sources that you think are not credible or accurate. When you eliminate a source, think about why you are dropping it. Then consider why a different source would be more useful.

Create Source Cards

Once you have evaluated your sources, create a source card for each source you will use. Make sure you record information about each source using a standard format. On each source card, include the following information:

- author
- title
- publication information
- access date
- location of source
- library call number or Web site URL

Give each source card a number and write it in the upper right-hand corner. These cards will help you prepare your Works Cited list. CCSS W.7.7, W.7.8

Create Note Cards

Take notes on the information you find. Write a summary, a paraphrase, or a quotation for the information that you want to use in your research report. Note whether the information is fact or opinion.

WAY OF SHARING INFORMATION	DEFINITION
A **summary** is . . .	a restatement of only the main ideas of a passage. It should be shorter than the passage.
A **paraphrase** is . . .	a restatement of the passage in your own words. It should be about the same length as the original passage.
A **quotation** is . . .	a word-for-word copy of a passage. If you think information in a source is expressed in an interesting way, you may want to reproduce the author's own words. If you quote a source directly, use quotation marks around the words.

Use note cards to record relevant facts, details, and quotations you find in your sources. Label each note card with the source number, so you can remember where you found the information. CCSS W.7.2b, W.7.7, W.7.8

Write Your Thesis Statement

The **thesis** is the main idea of an essay or a report. The thesis is usually one or two sentences. Before you write your thesis, review your major research question. Ask yourself:

- Will I have enough to write about? If not, your major research question is too narrow. Revise your research question to be broader.
- Will I have too much to write about? If so, your major research question is too broad. Revise your research question to be more specific.

Write the answer to your major research question. Your answer is your thesis statement.

Organize Information

Write the main ideas that you want to present in your research report. Remember that the main ideas must support your thesis statement.

Then take another look at the information you have gathered. **Categorize,** or arrange, information according to main ideas in order to see larger patterns. Use a logical structure to organize your ideas. You may organize ideas using the following strategies:

STRATEGY	DEFINITION
Definition	to explain technical or specialized vocabulary and terms related to specific areas of study or work
Classification	to group information by type
Comparison and contrast	to describe similarities and differences among things or ideas
Process	to explain the order of an action or an event
Cause and effect	to describe an event and what results from it
Sequence of events	to discuss events in the order that they happened

After you have categorized information, create an outline of your research report.

- Write your thesis statement at the beginning of your outline.
- List the main ideas that you want to cover.
- Add supporting details and evidence under each of your main ideas. CCSS W.7.2a, b

19.2 DRAFT

Write the Introduction

Write your introductory paragraph. Your introduction should grab your reader's attention and clearly introduce your topic. You may want to begin your introduction with

- an interesting anecdote
- a surprising fact
- a thought-provoking question

Your introduction should also preview the information in your report and present your thesis statement. CCSS W.7.2a

Write Topic Sentences

Follow your organizational plan to write the body paragraphs of your research paper. Each paragraph should contain a topic sentence that states the main idea of the paragraph. Each main idea should support your thesis statement.

Present Findings

Next develop your body paragraphs. Your paragraphs should present a summary, a paraphrase, or a quotation of the information from your sources. The facts, definitions, details, quotations, and examples you present in each paragraph should explain or develop your topic sentence. Organize the information in a meaningful format that will best develop your thesis.

Do not plagiarize. When you **plagiarize,** you take ideas from someone else and present them as your own. Plagiarizing is against the law. Always credit the source of the information.

- Write the author's last name and the page number(s) on which you found the information in parentheses. Place this information at the end of the last sentence or idea taken from the author's work.

COMPOSITION

- If the source is a Web site that does not include page numbers, do not include a page number in your citation.
- If the source does not list the author's name, use a shortened form of the title instead. If you mention the title and author in the paragraph, include only the page number in parentheses.

After you present information from your sources, draw a conclusion in your paragraph about that information. A **conclusion** is a general statement based on specific ideas. Make sure your paragraph includes relevant reasons and evidence that support your conclusion. CCSS W.7.2b, W.7.8

 Writing Tip

Don't worry about punctuation, spelling, or grammar as you draft your report. You can fix those later. The important thing is to express your ideas in a clear, organized way.

Maintain a Formal Style

Throughout your report, use precise language and vocabulary that is specific to your topic. Be sure to use and maintain a formal style. In formal writing, you usually write from the third-person point of view and avoid using slang, contractions, and conversational language. CCSS W.7.2d, e

Use Transitions

To make your writing flow smoothly, use transitions to link sentences and paragraphs. **Transitions** are words and phrases that show the relationship between ideas or events. Use some of the transitions from the chart on the next page to clarify the ideas in your report. CCSS W.7.2c

RELATIONSHIP	EXAMPLES OF TRANSITIONS
Addition	*also, and, besides, both . . . and, furthermore, in addition*
Contrast	*but, however, instead, nevertheless, on the contrary, on the other hand, still, yet*
Importance	*first, last, mainly, most important, most of all*
Cause and effect	*as a result, consequently, for, so, so that, then, therefore, thus*
Sequence	*after, as, before, next, since, then, until, when, while*

Incorporate Visual Elements

To help readers better understand the ideas in your report, you may wish to include

- graphics, such as images, maps, and charts
- formatting, such as heads and subheads
- multimedia elements, such links to video clips CCSS W.7.2a

Write the Conclusion

Finally, write the conclusion to your research report. The conclusion should restate your thesis statement. It should also follow from and support the information in your report. End your conclusion with a strong statement that leaves a lasting impression. CCSS W.7.2f

COMPOSITION

Create a Works Cited List

At the end of your report, list all the sources of information cited in your report. List your sources alphabetically by author's last name or by the first word in the title if there is no author. CCSS W.7.8

For help with citing sources and creating a Works Cited list, see pages 392–397.

19.3 REVISE

Introduction to Revision

To revise your report, you will focus on the content or the message of your writing. You will apply one or more of these four revision strategies:

- **Add** details and information to make the message clearer.
- **Delete** unnecessary words or ideas.
- **Substitute** more exact or stronger words for confusing or overused language.
- **Rearrange** phrases and sentences to be sure readers can understand the message.

The questions that follow will show you how to use these revision strategies. The questions will also help you rethink how well you've addressed purpose, audience, and genre.

- Your **purpose** is your reason for writing. Your purpose might be to describe, explain, narrate, amuse, or persuade.
- The **audience** includes the people who will read your writing.
- The **genre** is the writing mode, such as story, poem, report, or essay. CCSS W.7.4, W.7.5

Focus and Coherence

Ask yourself:

✓ Does my report have a clear thesis?

✓ Do all parts work together so that my ideas are clear to readers? CCSS W.7.2a

Organization

Ask yourself:

✓ Does the introduction include the thesis?

✓ Does the body include topic sentences that support the thesis?

✓ Does the conclusion summarize the report? CCSS W.7.2a, f

Development of Ideas

Ask yourself:

✓ Are my ideas fully developed and supported by relevant evidence? CCSS W.7.2b

Voice—Word Choice

Ask yourself:

✓ Does my report include vocabulary that is specific to my topic, as well as precise words?

✓ Does my report include effective transitions that link sentences and paragraphs? CCSS W.7.2c, d; L.7.3a

Voice—Sentence Fluency

Ask yourself:

✓ Do sentences vary in length and structure?

✓ Does the writing flow smoothly?

Revising Tip

As you revise, make sure you express ideas precisely and concisely. Use a thesaurus to find exactly the right words to communicate your ideas. Vary your words and sentences to eliminate wordiness and redundancy, or the use of too many words. CCSS L.7.3a

19.4 EDIT

Correct Errors in Grammar

Editing involves correcting errors in grammar, usage, mechanics, and spelling.

Begin the editing stage by taking a careful look at your sentences. Make sure that each sentence expresses a complete thought and is grammatically correct. Use the Sentence-Editing Checklist below to edit your sentences. CCSS W.7.5, L.7.1

Sentence-Editing Checklist

✓ Have I avoided sentence fragments?

✓ Have I avoided run-on sentences?

✓ Do verbs agree with their subjects?

✓ Have I used verb tenses and forms correctly?

✓ Have I used adverbs and adjectives correctly?

✓ Have I used pronouns correctly?

✓ Do pronouns agree with their antecedents?

✓ Are my sentences parallel?

Correct Errors in Mechanics and Spelling

Next check for and correct any errors in mechanics (punctuation and capitalization) and spelling.

Use the Proofreading Checklist below to edit your research report. Use a dictionary to check and confirm spellings. CCSS L.7.2, b

Proofreading Checklist

✓ Have I used correct punctuation?

✓ Have I written possessives correctly?

✓ Have I spelled all words correctly?

✓ Have I used capital letters as needed?

Peer and Teacher Review

In addition to revising and editing your own report, you will revise your work through peer review and teacher review. During **peer review**, you will share your writing with a partner or classmates in a writing group. You will discuss how you can each improve your writing. During **teacher review**, you will submit your report to your teacher. Your teacher will read it and make suggestions on how to improve your report.

Use the **Peer Review Guide** on page 390 to respond to your classmate's writing. CCSS W.7.5

COMPOSITION

19.5 PUBLISH

After you have written, revised, and edited your report, you will publish and present it. You may wish to consider the following publishing and presenting options. Some of these options require you to collaborate with your classmates and use technology.

- Create a class collection of research reports.
- Enter your report in a writing contest.
- Give an oral presentation of your report to classmates.
- E-mail your report to an organization associated with your topic.
- Publish a multimedia version of your report online with images and video clips. CCSS W.7.6

Reflecting on your own writing can help you improve your writing skills. Use the **Reflection Guide** on page 391 to think about the writing you did in this workshop.

COMPOSITION

Narrative

···

A **narrative** is a story or an account of a sequence of events. There are historical narratives, fictional narratives, and real-life narratives.

When you write a story, or narrative, you answer the question *What happened?* You tell events in the order that they happened, whether the events are real or made up. You also tell a story from a certain point of view. You might tell it from the outside as someone looking in, or you might tell it from a character's perspective. People write stories for a variety of reasons—sometimes to entertain, sometimes to share a lesson or message, and oftentimes for both of these reasons.

Every story needs a beginning, a middle, and an end. It also needs a setting, a conflict and resolution, characters, and dialogue. The basic elements of a narrative are defined in the chart on the next page.

ELEMENT	DEFINITION
Setting	the time and place in which the events of a narrative occur
Mood	the general feeling of a narrative
Characters	the people or animals in a literary work
Plot	the sequence of events
Conflict	a problem that the character(s) must face
Resolution	the outcome of the conflict
Theme	the overall message of the narrative

The instruction on the pages that follow will guide you through the process of writing a narrative while meeting the Common Core State Standards for narrative writing. For a list of the writing and grammar Common Core State Standards, see pages 439–447.

20.1 PLAN

Graphic Organizers

During the Plan stage, you will gather and organize writing ideas. To do this, you may wish to use graphic organizers, such as the Story Map, Character Chart, and Setting and Mood Diagram on pages 387–389.

Identify Key Elements

Write the topic of your story. The **topic** is the general subject you want to write about. Examples of story topics are climbing a mountain or going to a school dance.

Write a possible theme for your story. The **theme** is the central message that the writer expresses about a topic. For example, if your story topic is climbing a mountain, your theme might be "It takes hard work and determination to achieve your goals." You can revise your theme as you draft.

Then brainstorm the names of your main character(s) and minor characters.

Identify the setting of your story. The **setting** is the time and place in which the events of the narrative occur. The setting often helps create the **mood**, or atmosphere.

Finally, define your story's point of view. **Point of view** is the perspective, or standpoint, from which a story is told. There are two main points of view. CCSS W.7.3a

POINT OF VIEW	NARRATOR	USE
First-person	The narrator is a character in the story and refers to him- or herself as *I*.	Use first-person point of view if you want to reveal the action through the main character's eyes.
Third-person	The narrator is not a character in the story but tells the story from outside the action. The narrator refers to characters as *he* and *she*.	Use third-person point of view if you want readers to see the action from outside the story.

COMPOSITION

Develop Interesting Characters

Write the names of the main character(s) and minor characters of your story. For each character, give examples of

- the way the character looks
- what the character thinks, feels, and says
- how the character acts and interacts with others
- what the narrator or other characters think and say about the character

List precise words or phrases that describe each character. Then think of descriptive details that help develop each word or phrase. Make sure the details are related to the story. CCSS W.7.3a, b, d

Create the Main Events

To develop your **plot,** or the sequence of events in your story, identify the main conflict and resolution. The **conflict** is the central struggle or problem that the main character or characters face. The **resolution** is the outcome of the conflict.

Then write down the events of your narrative. List the events in **chronological order,** or the order in which they happen. Include well-paced action to keep readers engaged in your story. Organize an event sequence that unfolds naturally and logically.

Transitions help show the relationships between events or ideas. Some examples of transitions are *before, after, first, next, later, afterward, finally*, and *while*. Write down three transition words, phrases, and clauses that you can use to clarify the sequence of events in your narrative. Then write down three transitions that you can use to signal shifts from one time frame or setting to another. CCSS W.7.3a, c

Describe the Setting

Writers use descriptive details and sensory language to create specific, believable settings. **Sensory language** describes how people and things look, sound, feel, smell, or taste. The setting helps establish the **mood**, or atmosphere, of a story. For example, a writer might describe a dark, rainy night with loud thunder to create a frightening mood.

Write the setting and mood of your story. Then write precise words and phrases, descriptive details, and sensory language that describe the setting. Make sure that your sensory details help create the mood. CCSS W.7.3b, d

Use Literary Strategies and Narrative Techniques

Writers use a range of literary strategies and narrative techniques to develop experiences, events, characters, style, and tone. These strategies and techniques include foreshadowing, dialogue, pacing, and description.

STRATEGY OR TECHNIQUE	DEFINITION
Foreshadowing	the writer's use of clues to prepare the audience for events that will happen later in the story
Dialogue	the conversation between characters in a literary work
Pacing	the speed at which the plot events and action unfold
Description	vivid writing that helps readers **visualize**, or see in their minds, characters, settings, events, and experiences

Identify literary strategies and narrative techniques that you can use in your story. Describe how you will use them. Then explain how they will help develop the experiences, events, characters, style, and tone. CCSS W.7.3b, d

Write the Opening

Begin by writing the opening to your story. Your opening should grab your readers' attention and encourage them to keep reading. In the opening, you should

- introduce the main character
- introduce the conflict that drives the plot
- include descriptive details and sensory language that help create the setting

Include interesting details about your character from your planning notes. Choose sensory details from your planning notes that will help create the setting. CCSS W.7.3a, b, d

Writing Tip

If you can't decide how to begin your story, just get your ideas on paper. After you have written the first draft of your opening, you can revise it until you are satisfied with it.

Write Dialogue

Choose a place in your story where you can use dialogue. **Dialogue** is a conversation between characters in a literary work. Dialogue can serve many purposes. For example, it can introduce the conflict and move along the plot. It can also help develop characters and events.

Identify the purpose of the dialogue. Then think of the language you will use to show the ages, personalities, thoughts, and feelings of the characters speaking. Write dialogue that you can incorporate into the opening or the body of your narrative. CCSS W.7.3b

Writing Tip

Use tag lines so that it is clear which character is speaking. **Tag lines** are the words that identify the speaker, such as "said Charlie." However, do not use the word *said* too often in tag lines. Instead use more descriptive words, such as *questioned, cried,* or *whispered.*

Write the Body

Next, use your planning notes to write the body, or main part, of your story. Include action and details that will keep readers engaged in your story. Remember to

- follow the plot you created
- include a well-paced sequence of events related to the conflict, with events unfolding naturally and logically
- use transition words, phrases, and clauses to show sequence and to signal shifts from one time frame or setting to another
- use descriptive details to create interesting characters
- use sensory language to create a specific, believable setting and mood
- include literary strategies and narrative techniques to develop experiences, events, characters, style, and tone CCSS W.7.3a, b, c, d

Write the Ending

Finally, write the ending, or conclusion, of your story. Make sure that your ending presents the resolution to the conflict and reflects the theme of your story. The ending should also follow from and reflect on the experiences or events in your story. CCSS W.7.3e

COMPOSITION

20.3 REVISE

Introduction to Revision

To revise your narrative, you will focus on the content or the message of your writing. You will apply one or more of these four revision strategies:

- **Add** details and information to make the message clearer.
- **Delete** distracting or unnecessary words or ideas.
- **Substitute** more exact or stronger words for dull or overused language.
- **Rearrange** phrases and sentences to be sure readers can understand the message.

The questions that follow will show you how to use these revision strategies. The questions will also help you rethink how well you've addressed purpose, audience, and genre.

- Your **purpose** is your reason for writing. Your purpose might be to describe, explain, narrate, amuse, or persuade.
- The **audience** includes the people who will be reading your writing.
- The **genre** is the writing mode, such as story, poem, play, or essay. CCSS W.7.4, W.7.5

Focus and Coherence

Ask yourself:

✓ Does the story have a clear purpose and focus?

✓ Does the story maintain a consistent point of view?

✓ Does the story engage my readers? CCSS W.7.3a

Organization

Ask yourself:

✓ Does the beginning introduce the main character and conflict?

✓ Does the middle present events in chronological order, with events unfolding naturally and logically?

✓ Does my story include a variety of transition words, phrases, and clauses to clarify the sequence of events?

✓ Does the ending offer a clear resolution? CCSS W.7.3a, c, e

Development of Ideas

Ask yourself:

✓ Are the characters fully developed, interesting, and believable?

✓ Does my story include literary strategies and narrative techniques to develop experiences, events, and ideas? CCSS W.7.3a, b

Voice—Word Choice

Ask yourself:

✓ Does my writing include precise words and phrases, descriptive details, and sensory language so that readers can visualize characters, setting, and events? CCSS W.7.3d, L.7.3a

Voice—Sentence Fluency

Ask yourself:

✓ Do the sentences vary in length and structure?

COMPOSITION

20.4 EDIT

Correct Errors in Grammar

Editing involves correcting errors in grammar, usage, mechanics, and spelling.

Begin the editing stage by taking a careful look at your sentences. Make sure that each sentence expresses a complete thought and is grammatically correct. Use the checklist below to edit your sentences. CCSS W.7.5; L.7.1, c

---

Sentence-Editing Checklist

✓ Have I avoided run-on sentences?

✓ Do verbs agree with their subjects?

✓ Have I used verb tenses and forms correctly?

✓ Have I used pronouns correctly?

✓ Are my sentences parallel?

✓ Have I corrected any misplaced or dangling modifiers?

Grammar Link: Coordinate Adjectives

Sometimes you need two adjectives to describe something. Two adjectives that are not related to each other but that both describe the same subject are called **coordinate adjectives**. Coordinate adjectives should be separated by a comma.

Example: The **cute, energetic** puppy greeted each visitor at the door.

Sometimes, however, the two adjectives *do* relate to each other. These are not coordinate adjectives. When the two adjectives relate to each other, no comma is used between them.

Example: The **hot July** sun beat down on the rooftop.

You can use an easy test to figure out whether adjectives are coordinate and require a comma between them. The test has two parts:

Part 1: Can you replace the comma with *and* and have the sentence still sound correct?

Part 2: Can you reverse the order of the adjectives and have the sentence still sound correct?

If you can answer *yes* to both questions, then the adjectives are coordinate and require a comma between them.

✎ Check your narrative for coordinate adjectives. Add commas where they are needed. CCSS L.7.2a

Correct Errors in Mechanics and Spelling

Next check for and correct any errors in mechanics (punctuation and capitalization) and spelling.

Use the checklist below to edit your narrative. You should use a dictionary to check and confirm spellings. CCSS L.7.2, b

Proofreading Checklist

✓ Have I written possessives correctly?

✓ Have I spelled all words correctly?

✓ Have I used capital letters as needed?

✓ Have I used commas between coordinate adjectives?

Peer and Teacher Review

In addition to revising and editing your own story, you will revise your work through peer review and teacher review. During **peer review**, you will share your writing with a partner or classmates in a writing group. You will discuss how you can each improve your writing. During **teacher review**, you will submit your story to your teacher. Your teacher will read it and make suggestions on how to improve your story.

Use the **Peer Review Guide** on page 390 to respond to your classmate's writing.

20.5 PUBLISH

After you have written, revised, and edited your story, you will publish and present it. You may wish to consider the following publishing and presenting options. Some of these options require you to collaborate with your classmates and use technology.

- Enter your story into a writing contest.
- Create a class anthology of stories.
- Perform your story as readers' theater.
- Publish a multimedia version of your story online with images and video clips. CCSS W.7.6

Reflecting on your own writing can help you improve your writing skills. Use the **Reflection Guide** on page 391 to think about the writing you did in this workshop.

Chapter 21

Graphic Organizers

The graphic organizers on the following pages will help you plan your writing as you complete the writing workshops on pages 324–380. The chart below shows which graphic organizers go with which workshops.

WRITING WORKSHOP	GRAPHIC ORGANIZERS
Persuasive Essay	• Persuasive Essay Chart
Response Essay	• Evidence Chart
Multi-Paragraph Essay	• Evidence Chart
Research Report	• Main Idea Map • Source Card • Note Card
Narrative	• Story Map • Character Chart • Setting and Mood Diagram
All workshops	• Peer Review Guide • Reflection Guide

Copy this graphic organizer onto a separate sheet of paper and fill it out.

PERSUASIVE ESSAY CHART

Topic:

Thesis:

Evidence	How It Supports Thesis	Fact or Opinion

Other Views/Concerns/Counter-Arguments	My Response/Answer

COMPOSITION

Copy this graphic organizer onto a separate sheet of paper and fill it out.

EVIDENCE CHART

Topic or Focus:		
Controlling Idea:		
Evidence (facts, details, examples, quotations)	**How It Supports Controlling Idea**	**Source**
Related Ideas from Sources:	**Synthesized Idea:**	

Copy this graphic organizer onto a separate sheet of paper and fill it out.

MAIN IDEA MAP

Topic:	
Major Research Question:	

What Information Do I Need?	What Types of Sources Will I Use?

Thesis Statement:	

Main Ideas	Categorized Information

COMPOSITION

Copy this graphic organizer onto a separate sheet of paper and fill it out.

SOURCE CARD

Author:	**Source Number:**

Title:

City of Publication and Publisher:

Date of Publication:

Access Date:

Location of Source (e.g., name of library or Web site):

Library Call Number or Web Site URL:

Copy this graphic organizer onto a separate sheet of paper and fill it out.

NOTE CARD

Key Word or Phrase About Information: **Source Number:**

Specific Information/Details from Source:

Page Number on Which Information Was Found:

Copy this graphic organizer onto a separate sheet of paper and fill it out.

STORY MAP

Topic:	Theme:
Main Characters:	Minor Characters:
Setting (time and place):	Point of View:

Conflict:

Event 1:	Event 2:	Event 3:

Resolution:

Literary Strategies/Narrative Techniques:

Copy this graphic organizer onto a separate sheet of paper and fill it out.

CHARACTER CHART

Character's Name:	
Looks:	
Thinks:	
Feels:	
Says:	
Acts:	
Interacts:	
Narrator or Other Characters Say:	

COMPOSITION

Copy this graphic organizer onto a separate sheet of paper and fill it out.

SETTING AND MOOD DIAGRAM

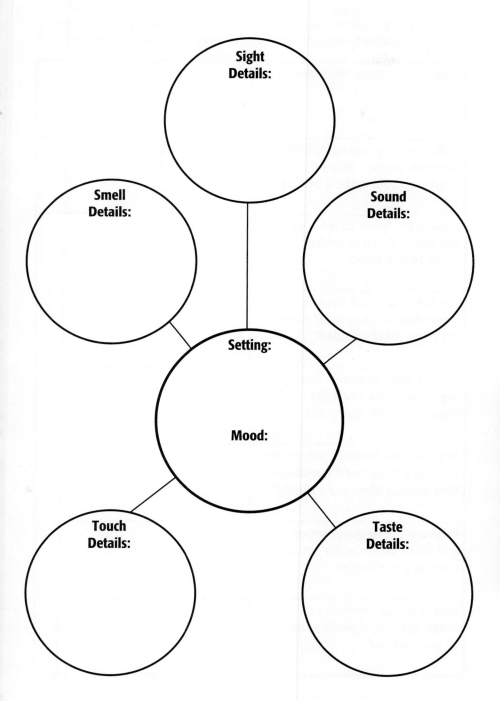

Copy this graphic organizer onto a separate sheet of paper and fill it out.

PEER REVIEW GUIDE

During peer review, you will express your opinions about a classmate's writing. You will also share your ideas about how to improve the writing. These questions can help guide you through the process of peer review.

What is best about this piece of writing?	
Is the opening interesting and attention getting? What, if anything, could make it better?	
What is the focus, or main point, of this piece? Do all of the key ideas relate to that point?	
Has the writer explained or supported each key idea? Where are more details needed?	
Are the ideas or events clearly organized? How could the organization be improved?	
Are the ideas between paragraphs related? Where could transitions help connect ideas more clearly?	
Where is the language precise and vivid? Where is the language confusing or unclear?	
Where are there errors in usage, spelling, capitalization, or punctuation?	

COMPOSITION

Copy this graphic organizer onto a separate sheet of paper and fill it out.

REFLECTION GUIDE

Reflecting on your own writing can help you improve your writing skills. You can reflect on your own writing by completing these sentence starters:

What I like best about this piece of writing is . . .	
When I look back at the project, the part I most enjoyed working on was . . .	
The most difficult part of the project was . . .	
One thing I learned from this project was . . .	
I would assess my work on this project as (outstanding, good, fair, weak) . . .	
One thing I need to improve in my next writing project is . . .	
One goal I would like to focus on in the future is . . .	

COMPOSITION

Chapter 22

MLA
Style Guide

....

CITING SOURCES

When you write an informative, explanatory, or persuasive text, you should include the sources of the information you present. You need to give credit to all ideas, statements, quotations, and facts you have taken from your sources that are not common knowledge. One reason for citing your sources is to allow your readers to check a source and judge how believable or important a piece of information is.

Another reason to cite your sources is to avoid plagiarism. **Plagiarism** is the act of taking an author's words or ideas and presenting them as your own. Plagiarism is against the law. You must credit a source not only for words you quote directly quoted but also for facts or ideas you take from it.

IN-TEXT CITATIONS

In the body of your paper, you should include citations to the sources from which you gathered information. Insert the author's last name or the title of the work (if the author's last name is not available) and a page reference in parentheses after the information. For online sources without page numbers, use the title of the Web site. Always put the period outside the parentheses.

Every in-text citation must connect to one of the entries in your Works Cited list. This connection should be by the author's last name or the title of the work—whichever is listed first in the entry.

For example, the first in-text citation below refers to the author's last name and the page number where the information was found, and the Works Cited entry for the source begins with the author's last name. The second in-text citation below refers to the title of the work (there is no author) and the page number where the information was found, and the Works Cited entry for the source begins with the title. These connections help readers easily locate sources in a Works Cited list.

In-Text Citation:
Sundiata would later be known by such titles as "Lord Lion," "Lion of Mali," and "Father of the Bright Country" (Koslow 12).

Works Cited:
Koslow, Philip. *Mali: Crossroads of Africa*. New
    York: Chelsea House, 1995. Print.

In-Text Citation:
The first transport arrived in England on December 2, 1938, carrying 200 children from Berlin ("Kindertransport, 1938–1940" 1).

Works Cited:
"Kindertransport, 1938–1940." Holocaust Encyclopedia.
    United States Holocaust Memorial Museum, 6 Jan. 2011.
    Web. 16 May 2011.

The following chart explains how to document different sources in the body of your paper, as recommended by the Modern Language Association of America (MLA). These guidelines pertain to both print and digital sources.

DOCUMENTING SOURCES WITHIN A PAPER

Kind of Source	Example
Author named in text Insert the page number in parentheses. If there is no page number (as with many Web sources), simply leave off the parenthetical citation.	According to Philip Koslow, Sundiata would be known by such titles as "Lord Lion," "Lion of Mali," and "Father of the Bright Country" (12).
Work with two (or three) authors Insert each author's last name in parentheses before the page number.	Sundiata faced a big challenge when he was a young child. He had been born with a disability. He crawled around like a baby until he was seven years old (McKissack and McKissack 49).
Work with more than three authors Give the last name of the first author listed, followed by *et al.* ("and others") and the page number.	The Gold of Africa Museum contains an important collection of gold artworks, including masks, birds, and human figures, from Mali and other African nations (Pinchuck et al. 131).
Work with no author or editor Use the title or a shortened version of the title, and give the page number. If there is no page number (as with some Web sources), include only the title of the work.	According to legend, when Sundiata learned that Dankaran Touman was to be king because Sundiata was disabled, he took an iron rod and used the rod to stand upright ("Sundiata").
More than one work by the same author Use the author's last name, the title or a shortened version of the title, and the page number.	After Sundiata's death, Mali lacked strong leadership for several decades. (McKissack, *The Royal Kingdoms* 56).
More than one source at a time Include both sources and their page numbers, separated by a semicolon.	Much of what we know about Sundiata comes from griots, the African storytellers (Koslow 12; Eisner 3).

COMPOSITION

WORKS CITED LIST

From your source cards and notes, record the publishing information about your sources in a Works Cited list. This list will appear at the end of your paper. The list should be alphabetized by the authors' last names. If a work has no author, alphabetize it by the title.

The following chart shows the proper bibliographic style for various sources, as recommended by the MLA.

Technology Tip

There are online programs that can help you build your Works Cited list. Enter "Works Cited generator" in your search engine to find such a program.

DOCUMENTING SOURCES IN A WORKS CITED LIST

Kind of Source	Example
Book with one author	Koslow, Philip. *Mali: Crossroads of Africa.* New York: Chelsea House, 1995, Print.
Book with two or three authors If a book has more than three authors, name only the first author and then write "et al."	McKissack, Pat, and Fredrick McKissack. *The Royal Kingdoms of Ghana, Mali, and Songhay: Life in Medieval Africa.* New York: H. Holt, 1994. Print.
Book with editor(s)	Lehman, David, and Heather McHugh, eds. *The Best American Poetry 2007.* New York: Scribner's, 2007. Print.
Book with an organization or a group as author or editor	Adobe Creative Team. *Adobe Photoshop CS3 Classroom in a Book.* Berkeley: Adobe, 2007. Print.

COMPOSITION

Work from an anthology	Desai, Anita. "Games at Twilight." 1978. *The Penguin Book of International Women's Stories*. Ed. Kate Figes. London: Penguin, 1996. 204-11. Print.
Introduction in a published book	Jackson, Peter. Introduction. *The Making of* Star Wars: *The Definitive Story Behind the Original Film*. By J. W. Rinzler. New York: Del Rey, 2007. iii. Print.
Encyclopedia article	"Jazz." *The New Encyclopaedia Britannica: Micropaedia*. 15th ed. 1998. Print.
Weekly magazine article	Sacks, Oliver. "A Bolt from the Blue." *New Yorker* 23 July 2007: 38–42. Print.
Monthly magazine article	Plotnikoff, David. "Hungry Man." *Saveur* July 2007: 35–36. Print.
Newspaper article If no author is named, begin the entry with the title of the article.	Long, Ray, and Jeffrey Meitrodt. "Some Budget Progress Made." *Chicago Tribune* 26 July 2007, B3 sec. Print.
Online newspaper article Include a URL only when the reader cannot locate the source without it or when your teacher requires it.	Onion, Amanda. "Americans Embracing 'Green' Cleaning." *ABC News*. ABC News Internet Ventures, 30 Jan. 2006. Web. Aug. 2007. <http://abcnews.go.com/Technology/Business/story?id=1544322>.
Online magazine article Include a URL only when the reader cannot locate the source without it or when your teacher requires it.	Parks, Bob. "Robot Buses Pull In to San Diego's Fastest Lane." *Wired Magazine*. July 2007. Web. 25 Oct. 2007. <http://www.wired.com/cars/futuretransport/magazine/15-08/st_robot>.

Web page Include a URL only when the reader cannot locate the source without it or when your teacher requires it.	Everett, Glenn. "Utilitarianism." *The Victorian Web*. Ed. George P. Landow. U Scholars Programme, Natl. U of Singapore, 11 Oct. 2002. Web. 18 May 2007.
Radio or TV program	"Jungles." *Planet Earth*. Dir. Alastair Fothergill. Discovery Channel. 19 Nov. 2006. Television.
Videotape or DVD For a videotape (VHS) version, replace "DVD" with "Videocassette."	*An Inconvenient Truth*. Dir. Davis Guggenheim. Paramount, 2006. DVD.

Part Four

Resources

Knowledge is of two kinds: we know a subject ourselves, or we know where we can find information on it.

—Samuel Johnson

Chapter 23

The Library or Media Center

Although you've probably been in a library, you might not realize how many print, digital, and media resources that the library has to offer or how to find them. This chapter will guide you through the library and help you understand how and where to find what you need.

CARD SERVICES, HELP DESKS, AND CHECK OUT

The staff of librarians and library workers can direct you to resources on any subject you're interested in. Workers at the card services desk can help you obtain or renew a library card, which you'll need in order to check out books and other materials. Librarians at the help desks can answer your questions about library resources or the research you are doing. The library also has a checkout desk or a self-checkout station at which you can use your library card to check out library books and other materials and to pay fines.

CATALOG

Catalogs tell you which books and materials are available and where to find them. A computer or card catalog will tell you about books and materials that are available in your particular library. An online catalog will tell you about books and materials that are available through a network of libraries in your city or state. You'll learn more about using catalogs in Chapter 24.

AREAS FOR ADULTS, TEENS, AND KIDS

Many libraries are divided into separate areas for adults, teens (sometimes called the "young adult area"), and kids. Although it's called the "adult area," you don't have to be an adult to use these books and materials. All three areas usually contain similar sections and materials, such as fiction and nonfiction books, DVDs and CDs, reference materials, and computers. The areas for teens and children may also include chapter books, textbooks, leveled readers for beginning readers, and picture books for very young readers.

STACKS

The stacks are rows of bookshelves in the library. The stacks are often divided into these sections:

- fiction (novels, short stories, mysteries, and science fiction)
- nonfiction (biographies and subjects such as sports, history, and science)

REFERENCE SECTION

The reference section often includes both print and digital encyclopedias, dictionaries, almanacs, atlases, and other materials. The areas for teens and children might also include textbooks for subject areas such as literature, math, science, and social studies. Books and digital materials in the reference area can be used only in the library. By not allowing people to check out these materials, the library ensures that they are always available when someone needs to consult them.

NEWSPAPERS AND MAGAZINES

In the section of newspapers and magazines (sometimes called periodicals), you can read local newspapers as well as newspapers from major cities in the United States and perhaps from other countries. You can also look through magazines and journals. You may not be able to check out the current issues, but you can usually take older issues home to read. You'll learn more about finding articles in newspapers and magazines in Chapter 24.

DVDs AND CDs

The DVDs and CDs section of the library may also be called the audio-visual section. This section may contain audiobooks, eBooks, computer games, movies, videos, and music that you can check out and enjoy at home.

COMPUTERS

The areas for adults, teens, and children may have computer sections of laptops and desktop computers with Internet access that you can use for research or to check e-mail. The computers may also contain software programs that you can use to write reports, résumés, and letters or to create spreadsheets and presentations. For a small fee per page, you can usually print the articles you've located or the papers you've written.

STUDY AREAS

Most libraries have quiet areas of desks for people who want to read or study individually. Some libraries also have group study rooms in which students and other people can gather for group study or discussions. You might need to reserve the group study rooms ahead of time.

SPECIAL COLLECTIONS AND STACKS

Some libraries have a special room or section for collections of rare books, manuscripts, and items of local interest, including works by local students and artists. Libraries may also have a "popular topics" section of stacks. These stacks are organized so readers can find books by popular topics such as cooking, finance, gardening, green living, sports, and jobs and careers.

Using Print and Digital Resources

In the course of doing research for a report, you will no doubt look at print and digital books and magazines, also known as periodicals. Books are useful sources because they give you access to information and opinions from the past. Magazines and journals are good sources of current information and opinions because they are published more often than books. In this chapter, you'll learn about some of the different kinds of print and digital resources available to you.

24.1 UNDERSTANDING CATALOGING SYSTEMS

Maybe you're looking for information on a particular subject. Maybe you want to see books by a certain author, or you want to check out a specific book. The library's catalog will help you find what you're looking for. The catalog will be either an online computer catalog or a paper card catalog. If it's an online catalog, you might be able to access it from your home computer as well as in the library.

COMPUTER CATALOGS

Each computer catalog is different. Before you use one for the first time, read the instructions. They might appear on the screen or be posted beside the computer. If you need help, ask a library worker.

Using Search Techniques

Most catalog programs allow you to search by subject using a keyword or by title or author. Computer catalogs may also allow you to do advanced keyword searches. Read the computer screen carefully to be sure the catalog is set for the type of search you want to do. For example, the screen below shows that the catalog will search for a subject by keyword. If you wanted to search this catalog by title or author or if you wanted to do an advanced keyword search, you would click on the Title, Author, or Advanced tab to change the setting.

Subject Search   For a subject search, you will type the keyword(s) for the subject. A **keyword** is a word or phrase that names or describes your topic. Whenever you search a computer database, including the Internet, the keyword you use will greatly affect the results you get.

Search Tip

Be specific. A general keyword, such as *experiments,* will get you a long list of sources, sometimes called **hits** or **matches.** Although these sources will relate in some way to your keyword, few of them are likely to focus on your specific subject. To save time, choose a keyword that better names or describes your topic, such as *cloning.* You will get a much shorter list of sources, but more of the sources will be useful to you.

Advanced Keyword Search   If the simple keyword search lists too many sources for your subject, you can narrow the list by doing an advanced keyword search. An advanced search allows you to set field limits so the computer searches for only the keywords and fields you have specified. For example, the screen on the following page shows that the user wants the computer to search for the keywords *cloning* and *animals* but not the word *dogs.* The user also wants the computer to limit the search to the following fields: sources that are "on shelf" in the library, or not checked out; sources located in any library that is listed instead of one specific library; sources in any format, such as book, CD, and DVD, instead of one specific format; sources in English instead of another language; and sources published between the years 2000 and 2011. The user chose not to limit the search to a specific publisher.

Now Searching *ALL LIBRARIES*

| Keyword | Title | Author | Advanced |

Advanced Keyword Search

Please fill in the form, select limits, and click Submit
(or choose a Simple Keyword Search)

Any Field: ⇕	cloning	And ⇕
Any Field: ⇕	animals	And not ⇕
Any Field: ⇕	dogs	And ⇕
Any Field: ⇕		

Limited to: **Sorted by:**

☑ *Limit search to on shelf*   Search and Sort: [sorted by relevance ⇕]

Location:
- ANY
- Acorn
- Acorn Juvenile
- Alsip-Merrionette Park

[Submit]

Format:
- ANY
- BOOK
- LARGE TYPE
- DVD / VIDEODISC

Language:
- Chinese
- Danish
- English
- French

Year: After [2000] and Before [2011]

Publisher: [   ]

Search Tip

Many online and computer catalogs allow you to combine keywords in various ways to broaden or narrow your search. Such searches, called Boolean searches, use a computer logic based on the work of George Boole, a 19th-century English mathematician. Some search techniques are described on the pages that follow.

Use Boolean Operators. You can combine keywords with connecting words called **operators.** The three basic Boolean operators are *and, not,* and *or.*

- *And:* Use *and* between two keywords to narrow a search to every source that contains *both* keywords. For example, *cloning and animals* directs the computer to search only for sources that contain both of the words *cloning* and *animals.*

- *Not:* Use *not* to narrow a search by excluding terms that you do not want. For example, *cloning and not dogs* directs the computer to search only for sources that contain the word *cloning* but not the word *dogs.*

- *Or:* Use *or* between two keywords to broaden, or widen, a search to every source that contains *either* keyword. For example, *cloning or twins* tells the computer to conduct two searches at once—one search for sources that contain the word *cloning* and another search for sources that contain the word *twins.*

Use Proximity Operators. You can direct the computer to search for sources that contain keywords that are near or close to each other. The main proximity operators are *near, before, after,* and *adjacent.*

- *Near:* Use *near* between two keywords to narrow a search to every source that contains *both* keywords when they are close to each other, in any order. For example, *cloning near animals* directs the computer to search only for sources that

RESOURCES

contain the words *cloning* and *animals,* in either order, when the words are near each other.

- **Before** or **After:** Use *before* or *after* between two keywords to narrow a search to every source that contains one keyword before (or after) another keyword. For example, *cloning before sheep* directs the computer to search only for sources that contain the word *cloning* when it appears before the word *sheep. Cloning after sheep* directs the computer to search only for sources that contain the word *cloning* when it appears after the word *sheep.*

- **Adj:** Use *adj* between two keywords to narrow a search to every source that contains both keywords when they are adjacent, or next to each other, in the exact order they were entered in the search box. For example, *cloning adj sheep* tells the computer to search only for sources that contain the word *cloning* when it appears before and next to the word *sheep.* **Note:** Some computer databases use adjacency as the default setting, so *cloning sheep* will produce the same search results as *cloning adj sheep.*

Use Wildcards. You can expand a search, but in a focused way, using one or more asterisks (*) to truncate, or shorten, your keyword. Then the computer will search for all words that begin with the letters before the asterisk.

- **One asterisk (*):** Type an asterisk after the first key letters of a word to direct the computer to search for sources that contain the first key letters followed by 1–5 other characters. For example, *clon** tells the computer to search for sources that contain *clon* followed by 1 to 5 other letters, such as in *clone, clones, cloned,* and *cloning.*

  You can also use this technique when you aren't sure how to spell a word. For example, you could use *Doll** if you weren't sure whether the first cloned sheep was named *Dollie* or *Dolly.*

- **Two asterisks (**):** Type two asterisks after the first key letters of a word to direct the computer to conduct an open-ended search. For example, *clon*** tells the computer to search for sources that contain *clon* followed by any number of letters and characters. The sources will include the words *clone, clones, cloned,* and *cloning,* as well as such terms as *clone wars, cloning: the science of, cloning pets, clone codes,* and *clone saga epic.*

- **Question mark (?):** Use a question mark (?) anywhere in a keyword to replace one letter or character. Using a question mark is helpful when you want to search for various spellings of a word. For example, a search for *wom?n* will produce sources that contain both *woman* and *women.*

Title Search   For a title search, you will enter the title, starting with the first two or three important words in the title. Ignore *A, An,* and *The* at the beginning of a title. For the book *The Digital Age: 1947–Present Day,* you would type the following:

Digital Age

Author Search   For an author search, you will enter the author's last name first, followed by a comma and the first name. For author Charlie Samuels, you would type the following:

Samuels, Charlie

When you enter titles and names, be sure the words you type are spelled correctly. A computer catalog can't recognize misspelled words. It will search for exactly what you type.

If you need help with the computer catalog at your library, ask a librarian for help. Many libraries also offer classes on how to use the library's computer catalog and other databases.

Understanding Search Results

After you enter the keyword(s) of a subject, the title, or the author's name, the screen will show you a list of related sources that are available at the library or libraries you selected. Let's say you're doing research on cloning and you've started a subject search by typing in the keyword *cloning*. The screen will show you a list similar to the one below.

Keywords (1-12 of 21)		
Afterschool charisma / Kumiko Suekane; [translation, Camellia Nieh]. Suekane, Kumiko. San Francisco, Calif. : Viz Media, c2009- v. : chiefly ill. (some col.) ; 21 cm	Find It Request It Add to List	c2009-
Star Wars, the Clone Wars, Clone commandos [videorecording] / Lucasfilm, Ltd. [United States] : Warner Home Video, 2009. 1 videodisc (88 min.) : sd., col. ; 4 3/4 in. DVD, widescreen.	Find It Request It Add to List	2009
Genetics in medicine / Andrew Solway. Solway, Andrew Milwaukee, WI : World Almanac Library, 2007 64 p. : col. ill. ; 27 cm. Website	Find It Request It Add to List	2007
Point blank / Anthony Horowitz Horowitz, Anthony, 1955- New York Speak, 2006. 274, 17 p. ; 20 cm.	Find It Request It Add to List	2006
Artemis Fowl. 4, The Opal deception [sound recording] / Eoin Colfer. Colfer, Eoin New York : Random House/Listening Library, p2005 6 sound discs (ca. 72 min. each) : digital; 4 3/4 in.	Find It Request It Add to List	p2005

The first row shows that the computer found 21 sources about the keyword *cloning.* The screen below that row shows entries for sources 8–12. The title in each entry appears in blue and is underlined to indicate that it is a link you can click on to see more information. If the source is in a format other than a book, the title line identifies the format in brackets. For example, the entry for source 9 above shows *[videorecording]* after the title and a DVD icon in the last column to indicate the format.

Beneath the title line in each entry is the author and/or publishing information. The entry may also include the number of pages in a book; the size of a book; whether it has illustrations, an index, a glossary, or a bibliography; the number of discs in a video or sound recording; and the number of minutes on each disc.

To find facts about cloning, you should look for nonfiction sources. Because only the title, author, format, and publishing information appears on this screen, you should click on the title link to see a more detailed description of the source. The screen on the following page shows the detailed description that appears when the link *Genetics in medicine / Andrew Solway* is clicked.

Author Solway, Andrew.

Title Genetics in medicine

Pub. Info. Milwaukee, WI: World Almanac Library, 2007.

Edition North American ed.

LIBRARY / LOCATION	CALL NUMBER	AVAILABILITY
Calumet Park Juv	616.042 SOL/Y	ON SHELF
Elmhurst Juv	J 616.042 SOL	ON SHELF
Grande Prairie Juv	J 616.042 SOL	ON SHELF
Harvey Juv	J 616.042 SOL	ON SHELF
Homewood Juv	J 576.5 SOL	ON SHELF
Justice Juv	J 616.042 SOL	ON SHELF
Lyons Juv	JUV 616.042 SOL	ON SHELF
Northlake Juv	J 616.042 SOL	ON SHELF
Orland Park Juv	J 616.042 SOL	ON SHELF
Palos Hghts Juv	J 616.042 SOL	ON SHELF

View additional copies or search for a specific volume/copy ⇕

Edition North American ed.

Phys.Desc. 64 p. : col. ill. ; 27 cm.

Series Cutting edge medicine.
Cutting edge medicine.

Note Includes bibliographical references (p. 62) and index.

Contents What is genetics? -- From genes to characteristics -- Genetic engineering -- Genetic disorders -- Cloning -- Combating aging -- The future of genetic engineering.

Subject Medical genetics -- Juvenile literature.

Standard # 9780836878653 (lib. bdg.)
0836878655 (lib. bdg.)

The detailed description may include a list of libraries that contain the source, as well as the call numbers for that source and a description of its availability. (**Call numbers** are numbers and letters used to classify books. Call numbers are explained on pages 415–419.) If the source isn't marked "fiction," then you know that it is nonfiction. Library catalogs often use the word *juvenile* to indicate books that are suitable for teens and children. If the word *juvenile* or the letters *JUV* or *J* don't appear, then you know that the source is meant for adults. For example, the screen on page 413 shows that the nonfiction book *Genetics in Medicine* is available on the shelf in juvenile literature at the 10 libraries listed.

The detailed description may also include links to other sources related to your subject or author. For example, the screen on page 413 shows that the author's name, *Solway, Andrew*, is a link. You would click on that link to see other books and materials written by Andrew Solway. The screen also shows that *Cutting edge medicine* and *Medical genetics* are links to other sources on these subjects.

Either print out or write down the call numbers for the sources you want. Then go to the location in the library, such as the teen (or young adult) nonfiction section, and find the shelf with the call numbers for the source you want. For example, for a book with call number *J 616.042 SOL,* find the shelf with call numbers between 610 and 620. Then look down the rows for the book marked *616.042 SOL.* The books are in numerical and alphabetical order, so it's easy to find the one you're looking for. Glance through the table of contents or index to be sure this book will help you learn more about cloning.

CARD CATALOGS

Some libraries have card catalogs instead of online computer catalogs. Card catalogs are stored in long, narrow drawers. The drawers hold two or more small cards for every book in the library. The cards are arranged alphabetically. Fiction books have two cards each. One lists the book by its author, and one lists the book by its title. Nonfiction books have at least three cards each. These cards list the book by its author, its title, and its subject or subjects.

The cards list the same information as the computer catalog. However, they don't tell you whether someone has checked out the book. A library may separate its card catalog into two categories: subject cards in one category and author and title cards in another. Often cards are cross-referenced, listing other available sources on the same subject or a related topic. A card catalog might also have separate cross-reference cards, filed alphabetically and listing related topics.

24.2 LOCATING BOOKS

The purpose of call numbers is to help you locate books. Most school and community libraries use call numbers based on the Dewey decimal system. Many college and university libraries use call numbers based on the Library of Congress system.

DEWEY DECIMAL SYSTEM

The Dewey decimal system was created in 1876 by a librarian named Melvil Dewey. This system divides nonfiction books into ten categories.

DEWEY CATEGORIES

NUMBERS	CATEGORY	EXAMPLES OF SUBCATEGORIES
000–099	General Works	encyclopedias, bibliographies, periodicals, journalism
100–199	Philosophy	philosophy, psychology, personality
200–299	Religion	mythology, bibles
300–399	Social Sciences	sociology, education, government, law, economics, vocations, customs
400–499	Language	dictionaries, languages, grammar
500–599	Pure Sciences	chemistry, astronomy, biology, mathematics
600–699	Technology and Applied Sciences	medicine, engineering, agriculture, home economics, business, radio, television, aviation
700–799	Arts	architecture, painting, music, photography, recreation
800–899	Literature	poetry, plays, essays, criticism
900–999	Geography and History	geography, history, travel

Let's say you want to know more about James Thurber. You'd begin by entering his last name as a keyword in a computer catalog or by looking under *T* in a card catalog.

The library might have many books by Thurber and about Thurber. One book might be *My Life and Hard Times,* a book by James Thurber. This book is placed in the 800 category, literature. Literature is broken into subcategories; for example, 810 is American literature, and 820 is English literature. James Thurber was an American author, so *My Life and Hard Times* has a call number in the 810s: 817 THU.

Some subcategories of the Dewey system contain hundreds of books. To make sure each book has its own call number, a decimal point and more numbers (and sometimes letters) are added to the number of the subcategory. For example, the book about genetics by Andrew Solway has a call number of 616.042 SOL. Many libraries also add the first three letters of the author's last name to the call number, such as THU for Thurber or SOL for Solway.

Library Tip

Two librarians may assign the same book to different Dewey categories. That's why books may have different call numbers in your library than those noted here.

Our imaginary library has another book, a biography called *Remember Laughter: A Life of James Thurber,* by Neil A. Grauer. Its call number is *B Thurber James.* The *B* (or *BIOG* or *BIOGRAPHY*) at the beginning of a Dewey decimal call number identifies the book as biography. Some libraries group their biographies together in a separate section of the library. Often there is a biography section in the adult stacks as well as in the teen (or young adult) section and the children's section. Biographies are shelved alphabetically according to the subject of the book. *Remember Laughter: A Life of James Thurber* is located in the *T* section of the biographies.

The library also has a book called *Thurber: A Biography,* by Burton Bernstein. It, too, has a call number of *B Thurber James.* Two biographies with the same call number but different authors are shelved alphabetically by the last name of the author. That puts Bernstein's book before Grauer's book in the *T* section of the biographies.

One book of short stories by James Thurber, *92 Stories,* is located in the fiction section. Most libraries using the Dewey system identify fiction with the call number *F, Fic,* or *Fiction.* The call number also includes the first three letters of the author's last name or the author's entire last name. The call number of *92 Stories* is *Fic Thurber.*

Fiction is shelved alphabetically by the authors' last names. Books by the same author are shelved by the first important word in each title, ignoring *A, An,* and *The.* (The book *92 Stories* is shelved as if the number were spelled out: *Ninety-two.*)

Reference books, such as encyclopedias, have an *R* or *Ref* before their call numbers. This means you cannot check out these sources and must use them in the library.

LIBRARY OF CONGRESS SYSTEM

The Library of Congress system divides books into twenty-one categories. Each category is represented by a letter, as shown in the chart on the following page. Like the Dewey decimal system, the Library of Congress system has subcategories identified by a second letter. For example, *N* is the category for fine arts. You would look under *NA* for books about architecture, *NB* for sculpture, *ND* for painting, and so on. Numbers added to the letter combinations identify more specific categories.

LIBRARY OF CONGRESS CATEGORIES

LETTER	CATEGORY	LETTER	CATEGORY
A	General Works	N	Fine Arts
B	Philosophy and Religion	P	Language and Literature
C–F	History	Q	Science
G	Geography and Anthropology	R	Medicine
H	Social Sciences	S	Agriculture
J	Political Science	T	Technology
K	Law	U	Military Science
L	Education	V	Naval Science
M	Music	Z	Bibliography and Library Science

In one library using the Library of Congress system, Neil A. Grauer's book, *Remember Laughter: A Life of James Thurber,* has a call number of PS 3539.H94. *P* stands for the general category of Literature, while *S* indicates a work by an American author. The next letter and numbers, *.H94,* is a code that stands for the author and the specific book.

Note that in the Library of Congress system, biographies are not filed separately but with the other books. Therefore, the call numbers of the biographies for *Thurber* begin with *PS,* indicating an American author.

FINDING INFORMATION IN NONFICTION BOOKS

Nonfiction books contain various sections that you can use to decide whether a source will be useful to you. Not every book contains all the sections described below.

Information About a Book

To find information about a book, check the following parts:

The **title page** contains the book title, the author's name, and usually the publisher.

The **copyright page** gives the publication or copyright date. This page is usually printed on the back of the title page. Check the copyright date to see how current the information in the book is.

The **table of contents** lists the main topics covered in the book. This section may help you decide whether the book has the information you're looking for.

The **foreword, introduction,** or **preface** is written by the author or an expert in the same field. This section may explain the purpose of the book or the author's outlook on the subject.

Information in a Book

To find information in a book, check the sections below:

The **index** lists alphabetically the people, places, events, and other important topics mentioned in the book. The page numbers where you can find references to these topics is also given in the index.

The **glossary** lists terms in the book alphabetically and defines them.

The **bibliography** suggests additional research sources that you might use. It may also include the sources of information found in the book itself.

The **appendix** contains additional information related to the book, such as maps, charts, illustrations, and graphs.

The **afterword** or **epilogue** is used by some authors to make a final statement about the book or offer additional findings.

24.3 LOCATING ARTICLES IN NEWSPAPERS AND MAGAZINES

You can find the latest information on a topic in newspapers, magazines, and journals. The two tools described below will make your search easier.

COMPUTER DATABASES

Many libraries have computers in a reference section that you can use for online references. These computers contain databases holding collections of magazine, journal, and newspaper articles. Most of these databases allow you to search by subject, by type of publication, or by specific publication. Some programs allow you to select the years you want to search, so you can see only the magazines or newspapers within that period of time. You usually can narrow your search to a specific magazine or newspaper, such as the *New York Times.* Some databases may allow you to review the table of contents of one issue of a magazine and read any of the articles that interest you.

To search for information in a database, begin by entering a keyword. The database will then list articles about that topic. The listing usually includes the title, the author, the publication, the date, and a sentence or two about the article. You can select any articles that seem useful. Then the database will allow you to read a brief summary or the whole article on the computer screen. For a small fee, you can print a copy of the article.

READERS' GUIDE TO PERIODICAL LITERATURE

In addition to computer databases, some libraries may have the print edition of the *Readers' Guide to Periodical Literature.* This guide includes titles of articles from nearly two hundred magazines and journals. Both subjects and authors are listed alphabetically and cross-referenced.

An update of the print edition of *Readers' Guide* is published every two weeks. Information about all the articles published that year is reprinted in a hardbound book at the end of the year. The guide is also available online so you can search using a computer.

Libraries often keep issues for the current year in their newspapers and magazines section. Issues from the previous one to five years may be stored in a different area. Older issues may be on **microfilm** (a roll or reel of film) or **microfiche** (a sheet of film). Both types of film must be inserted into special projectors that enlarge the pages so that you can read them easily. Many libraries have converted their microfilm and microfiche collections to digital microform versions that can be viewed on computers. For a small fee, you can usually print copies of articles from microfilm, microfiche, and microform to take home.

Evaluating Tip

Not every book in the library or article in library databases offers current, reliable information. The tips below will help you avoid sources that have outdated information or biased opinions.

1. **Evaluate the author of each source of information.** Look for information about the author's background. Consider whether this person is an expert or just someone with many opinions.
2. **Make sure the information is directly related to your topic.** If you try to include facts that are slightly off your topic, your report will seem unorganized.
3. **Check the publication date.** You may use older sources for information that's not likely to change, such as facts about the battles of World War II. However, your sources must be as recent as possible for topics that are in today's headlines.

4. **Evaluate the author's thinking.** Are the "facts" in a source really facts, or are they just opinions? Can they be proved or disproved? Does the author offer evidence to support his or her ideas?
5. **Gather information on the same topic from several sources.** By doing this, you'll discover different opinions on the issue or topic, but the facts should remain the same.

24.4 USING OTHER REFERENCE SOURCES

GENERAL REFERENCE SOURCES

General reference sources are easy to use and provide information on thousands of topics. Many general reference sources are available in both print and digital formats. Below are some excellent examples of general reference sources.

TYPE OF REFERENCE	EXAMPLES
General Encyclopedias General encyclopedias fill many volumes. Subjects are arranged alphabetically. An index at the end helps you find topics.	*World Book Encyclopedia* *Encyclopaedia Britannica* *Collier's Encyclopedia* *Grolier Encyclopedia*
Specialized Encyclopedias Specialized encyclopedias focus on specific topics. You might be surprised at the number of specialized encyclopedias available.	*Van Nostrand's Scientific Encyclopedia* *Encyclopedia of Opera* *Encyclopedia of Vitamins, Minerals, and Supplements* *Encyclopedia of the Geological Sciences*

TYPE OF REFERENCE	EXAMPLES
Almanacs and Yearbooks Almanacs and yearbooks are usually published annually. They provide current facts and statistics. Check the most recent issues for the latest information.	*Information Please Almanac* *World Almanac and Book of Facts* *Guinness Book of Records* *Statistical Abstract of the United States*
Atlases Atlases may contain current or historical information. They include maps and statistics about countries, climates, and other topics.	*Hammond World Atlas* *Cambridge Atlas of Astronomy* *Historical Atlas of the United States* *Goode's World Atlas* *National Geographic Atlas of the World* *Atlas of World Cultures*
Biographical References Biographical reference works include brief histories of notable people, living or dead.	*Contemporary Authors* *American Authors 1600–1900* *Cyclopedia of Literary Characters* *Webster's New Biographical Dictionary* *Biographical Dictionary of World War I* *Biographical Dictionary of World War II*
Government Publications Some large libraries have government publications on agriculture, population, economics, and other topics.	*Catalog of United States Government Publications* (Also available online.)
Books of Quotations In a book of quotations, you can find quotations by famous people or about certain subjects. The quotation from Samuel Johnson at the beginning of Part Four was taken from *The Harper Book of Quotations.*	*Bartlett's Familiar Quotations* *The Harper Book of Quotations* *The Oxford Dictionary of Quotations* *The International Thesaurus of Quotations*

PLANNING LIBRARY RESEARCH

1. Start early. If you wait, other students may have checked out the sources you want to use.

2. Begin with the general reference sources rather than those that deal with specific fields or topics. A general source will offer an overview of your topic. It may provide all the information you need, or it may guide you to additional sources.

3. List the sources you want to check and mark each one off your list after you've examined it so you won't check the same source twice.

4. Take careful notes and include the title, author, publisher, publication date, and page number of each source. (See pages 358–359 for more information about compiling note cards and source cards.)

5. Talk with a librarian about your project, its purpose, its length, and the kinds of sources you have been asked to use. Describe what you've done so far and be ready with specific questions you'd like answered. Librarians can often suggest valuable references you haven't considered and even help you locate them.

24.5 MAKING THE MOST OF WORD RESOURCES

A dictionary and a thesaurus can help you put more words on the tip of your tongue and at the tip of your pencil. Both references are essential tools for writers, and both are available in print and digital formats.

KINDS OF DICTIONARIES

You may not know that there are many kinds of dictionaries. Most of the dictionaries you've seen in school, in public libraries, and online are general dictionaries that include words from general English for a general reader. There are also specialized dictionaries that define only words used in a particular field, profession, art, or craft.

General Dictionaries

General dictionaries fall into the following categories:

School dictionaries contain fewer than 90,000 entries. They focus on common words and offer easy-to-understand definitions.

College dictionaries have about 150,000 entries. These references are used in homes, schools, and businesses. They answer most questions about spelling, and they offer a variety of definitions.

Unabridged dictionaries contain more than 250,000 entries and often fill several volumes. They are generally located in libraries and include extensive definitions and word histories.

Digital dictionaries often contain millions of definitions and meanings that you can access online at no cost. In addition to definitions, these online dictionaries often provide audio pronunciations, example sentences, and word origins.

Specialized Dictionaries

Specialized dictionaries list words used in a particular field. Following are some examples of the many kinds of specialized dictionaries.

Dictionary of Art Terms
Dictionary of Dog Terms
Dictionary of Inventions and Discoveries
Dictionary of Sports Idioms
Dictionary of Symbolism
Facts on File Dictionary of Allusions

WORD ENTRIES IN GENERAL DICTIONARIES

General print dictionaries contain entries in alphabetical order. Digital dictionaries usually present only the entry for the word you searched. An **entry** is a single word or term along with its pronunciation, definition, and other information. When you look up a word in a dictionary, you are looking for its word entry.

Finding Words in a Print Dictionary

The guide words at the top of each dictionary page can help you find words quickly. Guide words are the first word and the last word on the page. If the word you're looking for falls between these words alphabetically, it will be on that page.

For example, let's say the guide words on a page are *lintel* and *lisp.* You'll find the words *lioness, lip-synch,* and *liquid* on this page. However, *linguistic* comes before *lintel,* so it will be on an earlier page. *Lithium* comes after *lisp,* so it will be on a later page.

If you're looking for a phrase beginning with *St.,* the abbreviation will be spelled out: *Saint.* Look for *Saint Bernard,* not *St. Bernard.*

Search Tip

When you can't find the word you're looking for, consider these possibilities:

1. The word might have silent consonants, such as the *k* in *knight,* the *b* in *doubt,* or the *gh* in *blight.*

2. A consonant in the word might have an unusual spelling. For example, the *k* sound can be spelled with *k* (*kindness*), *c* (*contract, lecture*), *ck* (*mackerel*), or *ch* (*chrysanthemum, chrome*).

3. A vowel combination in the word might have an unusual spelling, such as the first vowel sound in *beautiful* and *eerie.*

4. Your dictionary might not contain enough entries. An unusual word might not be listed in a school dictionary, for example.

Understanding Dictionary Entries

Let's analyze a dictionary entry to see what kinds of information it offers.

in•fer (in fur´) *v.* in•ferred, in•fer•ring 1. to conclude by reasoning from facts known or assumed: *I infer from your frown that you're angry.* 2. to guess: *We inferred that the stranger was our new teacher.* —in•fer•able (in fur´ə bəl) *adj.* —in•fer•rer (in fur´ər) *n.* [from Middle French *inferer,* from Latin *inferre,* literally, "to carry or bring into," from *in-* + *ferre* "to carry"]

Synonyms: *Infer, deduce,* and *conclude* all mean "to arrive at a conclusion." *Infer* implies arriving at a conclusion based on specific facts. *Deduce* includes the special meaning of drawing a conclusion from a general idea. *Conclude* suggests arriving at an inference based on a chain of reasoning.

1. *The Entry Word:* The entry word itself shows the correct spelling of the word. A raised dot or a blank space within the entry word shows where the word may be divided at the end of a line of writing. The entry word will also show you when a compound word should be written as one solid word (as in **landfill**), when it should be hyphenated (as in **land-poor**), and when it should be written as two words (as in **land mine**).

2. *The Respelling:* The respelling, or pronunciation, is shown immediately after the entry word. An accent mark follows the second syllable in *infer* to show that the second syllable should be stressed in pronouncing the word. So that you can check the pronunciation of the letters and symbols in the respelling, a pronunciation key is shown on every page or every other page in most dictionaries.

3. *Part of Speech Label:* An abbreviation in italic type gives the part of speech of the entry word. The abbreviation *v.* stands for *verb; adj.* stands for *adjective;* and *n.* stands for *noun.*

4. *Inflected Forms:* Inflected forms include plurals of nouns, principal parts of verbs (past, past participle, and present participle), and comparative and superlative forms of adjectives and adverbs. These forms are included in a dictionary entry only when they have irregular spellings. When the past and the past participle of a verb are the same, only one form is shown for both. The sample entry shows that *inferred* is the past form and the past participle of *infer,* and *inferring* is the present participle. These forms are considered irregular because the final consonant is doubled when the ending is added.

   This part of a dictionary entry can help you spell irregular plural forms, such as *quizzes* for *quiz* and *rodeos* for *rodeo.* This section will also show you when to double a final consonant *(stop, stopping; sad, sadder),* when to drop a final *e (dine, dining),* and when to change a final *y* to *i (easy, easiest)* before adding an ending.

5. *Definitions:* Definitions are the heart—and the longest part—of a dictionary entry. If an entry word has more than one meaning, each definition is numbered. Example sentences are often included to make meanings clearer.

6. *Run-on Entries:* Definitions in a dictionary entry may be followed by one or more run-on entries. A run-on entry is a form of the entry word to which a suffix has been added. In the sample dictionary entry, **in•fer•able** and **in•fer•er** are run-on entries. Each run-on entry is preceded by a dash and followed by its pronunciation and its part of speech. The meanings of these words can be inferred by combining the meaning of the entry word and the meaning of the suffix. (See the list of suffixes and their meanings on pages 319–320.)

7. *Etymology:* Many dictionary entries include an etymology, which gives the origin or history of the word.

The entry for *infer* explains that this word is based on a Middle French word. The Middle French word was based on a Latin word with a literal meaning of "to carry or bring into." When you infer, you carry or bring your knowledge into a new situation. You use what you know to reach a conclusion. You can see that the Middle French and Latin versions of the word are both similar to the English spelling.

8. *Synonyms:* Some dictionary entries list synonyms, or words with the same or nearly the same meanings. Understanding small differences in meaning will help you use the right word in the right place. Some dictionaries also include antonyms, words with opposite meanings.

Some words have more than one meaning or word history; some may be used as more than one part of speech. In such cases, a dictionary may have multiple entries for a word. Let's look at three entries for the word *rest:*

> ¹**rest** (rest´) *n.* **1.** REPOSE, SLEEP **2.** freedom from activity or disturbance **3.** something that acts as a stand or a support **4.** a place for resting or lodging **5.** *Music.* a silence between musical notes **6.** a brief pause in reading [Middle English, from Old English; akin to Old High German *rasta* "rest"]
>
> ²**rest** *v.* **1.** to get rest by lying down or stopping activity **2.** to lie dead **3.** *Farming.* to remain idle or without a crop **4.** *Law.* to finish presenting evidence in a legal case: *The defense rests, Your Honor.*
>
> ³**rest** *n.* something that remains over; REMAINDER: *Jada ate the rest of the fruit salad.* [Middle English, from Middle French *reste,* from *rester* "to remain," from Latin *restare,* from *re-* + *stare* "to stand"]

Numbered Entries   Notice the small raised numeral to the left of each entry word in the preceding dictionary sample. This number indicates there is more than one entry for the word. Some dictionaries show separate entries for each part of speech. Some show separate entries for each meaning that has a different word history, or etymology.

In the first and second entries, the meanings have to do with pausing, sleeping, or remaining idle, but the entry words are different parts of speech. The third entry word is the same part of speech as the first, but the word's meaning and its etymology are different.

Cross-References   Synonyms within an entry are sometimes printed in small capital letters. In the entries for *rest,* the words *repose, sleep,* and *remainder* are synonyms for specific meanings of *rest.* You can learn more about these meanings of *rest* by looking up the words in small capital letters.

Subject Labels   Some dictionary entries include subject labels. A subject label preceding a definition indicates that the definition applies to the subject named. In the sample entries for *rest,* there are three subject labels. In ^{1}*rest* definition 5 applies to music. In ^{2}*rest* definition 3 applies to farming, and definition 4 applies to law.

The chart on the following page gives examples of other kinds of information you may find in a dictionary entry.

TYPE OF INFORMATION	DESCRIPTION	EXAMPLE FROM AN ENTRY
Capitalization	Indicates that certain uses of a word should be capitalized	**earth** ... *Often capitalized.* the planet that is third in order from the sun
Out-of-date label	Identifies meanings that are no longer used or used only in special contexts	**anon** ... *Archaic.* at once; immediately
Style label	Indicates a meaning that is appropriate only in a very informal context	**cool** ... *Slang.* very good; EXCELLENT
Regional label	Indicates a meaning used in a certain geographical area	**bon•net** ... *British.* an automobile hood
Usage note	Offers guidelines for using—or not using— a word	**ain't** ... Although inappropriate in formal speech or writing, *ain't* is sometimes used to attract attention or add humorous emphasis.

OTHER KINDS OF INFORMATION IN GENERAL DICTIONARIES

You can find other kinds of information in the back of some dictionaries. Here is a list of some of the kinds of information you may find in a dictionary.

Biographical Names

Do you remember James Thurber? Who was he? When was he born? When did he die? A section of biographical names gives the spelling and pronunciation of thousands of people's names, from Berenice Abbott (an American photographer who lived from 1898 to 1991) to Stefan Zweig (an Austrian writer who was born in 1881 and died in 1942).

Geographical Names

How do you pronounce *Kilimanjaro*? What is it, and where is it? In a section of geographical names, you can find the correct spelling, pronunciation, and location of countries, cities, mountains, lakes, rivers, and other geographical features. Entries range from Lake Abitibi, in Ontario, Canada, to Zimbabwe, a country in southern Africa.

Abbreviations, Signs, and Symbols

Is the postal abbreviation for Maine MA, MN, or ME? A dictionary may include lists of abbreviations, signs, and symbols. Check this section if you can't remember, for example, what *NOAA* stands for (National Oceanic and Atmospheric Administration) or what the symbol & means *(and)*.

Style Handbook

Some dictionaries include a style guide. This section may include rules for spelling, punctuation, and capitalization. It may also include other matters of writing style. Investigate your dictionary to find out what it has to offer.

THESAURUSES

A thesaurus lists **synonyms,** or words with the same or nearly the same meaning. Thesauruses are available in both print and digital formats. A print thesaurus may be organized in dictionary style or traditional style. A digital thesaurus may present entries in alphabetical order.

Print Format

A thesaurus in print, or book, format will be organized in either dictionary style or traditional style.

Traditional Style   Let's say you've used the word *continue* several times in a report, and you want to find a synonym. To use a traditional thesaurus, begin by looking in the index. There you might find these choices:

> **continue** endure 110.6
>> protract 110.9
>> go on 143.3
>> extend 201.9
>> persevere 623.2

Let's say that *extend* seems like a good word to replace *continue* in your report. You could use *extend,* or you could look in the front of the book under 201.9 for more choices. Guide numbers at the top of each page help you find the number you want quickly. They're similar to a dictionary's guide words.

On the page with the guide numbers 201.3–203.7, you find paragraph 201.9, a group of synonyms for *extend.* The most commonly used words are printed in bold type.

> VERBS **9. lengthen, prolong,** prolongate, **elongate, extend,** produce [geom.], **protract,** continue, lengthen out, let out, **draw out,** drag out, string out [coll., U.S.], spin out; **stretch,** draw; tense, strain.

A page in the back of the thesaurus explains that *geom.* stands for *geometry* and *coll.* stands for *colloquial,* or *informal.*

Dictionary Style   A dictionary-style thesaurus is organized much like a dictionary. Using the guide words at the top of the page, locate the word *continue.* Checking the front of the book, you learn that an asterisk (*) indicates that a term is colloquial or slang.

CONTINUE

> *Verb.* **1.** [To persist] persevere, carry forward, maintain, carry *or* roll *or* keep *or* go *or* run *or* live on, never stop, sustain, remain, press onward, make headway, move ahead, *leave no stone unturned; see also ADVANCE.

> *Antonyms:* cease, end, give up

2. [To resume] begin again, renew, begin *or* carry over, return to, take up again, begin where one left off, be reinstated *or* restored; see also RESUME.

Antonyms: discontinue, halt, postpone

Digital Format

A digital thesaurus requires you to type into a search box the word for which you want a synonym. Although each thesaurus program may present synonym entries differently, most will display entries by definition and synonyms alphabetically. Each entry identifies the part of speech, one or more definitions, and a list of synonyms with similar meanings. Some or all of the synonyms may link to other words. Linked words may be underlined or a different color. You can click on linked words to see additional entries for the word you clicked.

Let's say you've typed *continue* into the thesaurus search box. You might see the following entries:

Entry:	**continue**
Part of speech:	*verb*
Definition:	to extend
Synonyms:	drag out, draw out, elongate, <u>extend</u>, <u>lengthen</u>, lengthen out, let out, <u>produce</u>, <u>prolong</u>, prolongate, <u>protract</u>, spin out, <u>stretch</u>, string out

Entry:	**continue**
Part of speech:	*verb*
Definition:	to resume
Synonyms:	<u>begin</u>, begin again, begin over, begin where one left off, carry on, carry over, <u>reinstate</u>, <u>renew</u>, <u>restart</u>, <u>resume</u>, return to, take up again

Chapter 25

Accessing Digital Resources

When you're looking for up-to-date information, electronic resources can provide an excellent starting point. The Internet is an increasingly important source of information for people of all ages around the world. CD-ROMs and other digital resources that are not connected to the Internet also offer vast amounts of information.

The Internet is a computer-based, worldwide information network. The World Wide Web, or WWW, is software that determines what is displayed on the Internet. Working together, the Internet and the World Wide Web allow you to gather information without leaving your home, school, or library.

UNDERSTANDING ADDRESSES

The information on the Internet is organized by locations, or sites. Each site has its own address. An address is also called a Uniform Resource Locator, or URL.

Most addresses begin with *http://*, which stands for "hypertext transfer protocol." The *http* identifies a way in which information is exchanged among computers connected by the Internet. The last part of an address, or its suffix, indicates the type of site it is. The chart on the following page lists some of the suffixes in use.

SUFFIX	TYPE OF SITE
.com	commercial
.edu	educational
.gov	government
.mil	military
.net	network organization or Internet service provider
.org	organization

ACCESSING WEB SITES

Let's say you're connected to the Internet, and you want to view the information at a certain site or address. You can enter the address on the computer screen and be connected to the site.

You can also access specific reference sources, such as the *New York Times* or *Encyclopædia Britannica,* in this way. Some of these sources are free. For others you must subscribe and perhaps pay a fee. A screen will explain any extra charges that are required. Then you can choose whether to continue.

Evaluating Tip

No one oversees Web sites to make sure they offer accurate information. You must evaluate each site yourself. First, review the "Evaluating Tip" on pages 422–423. The tips listed there also apply to Internet sources. The following tips will also help you evaluate Internet sources.

1. Determine whether a Web site actually relates to your topic. A search engine will use every possible meaning of your keyword to produce its list of sites.

2. Check the source of the information at a Web site. (You may have to press the "back" key several times to identify a source.) Many Web sites are personal pages. Just because you find information on the Web doesn't mean it's true or accurate.

3. Evaluate the accuracy and fairness of the information on a Web site. Is it based on more than one source? Are differing opinions included? After doing some of your own research elsewhere, are you aware of important information that was omitted from the site? Does the site include a bibliography and links to other sites? The answers to these questions can help you decide whether to use that source.

COMMON CORE STATE STANDARDS CORRELATION

Writing	
Text Types and Purposes	
1. Write arguments to support claims with clear reasons and relevant evidence.	Persuasive Essay, pp. 324–333
a. Introduce claim(s), acknowledge alternate or opposing claims, and organize the reasons and evidence logically.	Persuasive Essay, pp. 324–333
b. Support claim(s) with logical reasoning and relevant evidence, using accurate, credible sources and demonstrating an understanding of the topic or text.	Persuasive Essay, pp. 324–333
c. Use words, phrases, and clauses to create cohesion and clarify the relationships among claim(s), reasons, and evidence.	Persuasive Essay, pp. 324–333
d. Establish and maintain a formal style.	Persuasive Essay, pp. 324–333
e. Provide a concluding statement or section that follows from and supports the argument presented.	Persuasive Essay, pp. 324–333
2. Write informative/explanatory texts to examine a topic and convey ideas, concepts, and information through the selection, organization, and analysis of relevant content.	Response Essay, pp. 334–343 Multi-Paragraph Essay, pp. 344–353 Research Report, pp. 354–368

a. Introduce a topic clearly, previewing what is to follow; organize ideas, concepts, and information, using strategies such as definition, classification, comparison/contrast, and cause/effect; include formatting (e.g., headings), graphics (e.g., charts, tables), and multimedia when useful to aiding comprehension.	Response Essay, pp. 334–343 Multi-Paragraph Essay, pp. 344–353 Research Report, pp. 354–368
b. Develop the topic with relevant facts, definitions, concrete details, quotations, or other information and examples.	Response Essay, pp. 334–343 Multi-Paragraph Essay, pp. 344–353 Research Report, pp. 354–368
c. Use appropriate transitions to create cohesion and clarify the relationships among ideas and concepts.	Response Essay, pp. 334–343 Multi-Paragraph Essay, pp. 344–353 Research Report, pp. 354–368
d. Use precise language and domain-specific vocabulary to inform about or explain the topic.	Response Essay, pp. 334–343 Multi-Paragraph Essay, pp. 344–353 Research Report, pp. 354–368
e. Establish and maintain a formal style.	Response Essay, pp. 334–343 Multi-Paragraph Essay, pp. 344–353 Research Report, pp. 354–368
f. Provide a concluding statement or section that follows from and supports the information or explanation presented.	Response Essay, pp. 334–343 Multi-Paragraph Essay, pp. 344–353 Research Report, pp. 354–368
3. Write narratives to develop real or imagined experiences or events using effective technique, relevant descriptive details, and well-structured event sequences.	Narrative, pp. 369–380

a. Engage and orient the reader by establishing a context and point of view and introducing a narrator and/or characters; organize an event sequence that unfolds naturally and logically.	Narrative, pp. 369–380
b. Use narrative techniques, such as dialogue, pacing, and description, to develop experiences, events, and/or characters.	Narrative, pp. 369–380
c. Use a variety of transition words, phrases, and clauses to convey sequence and signal shifts from one time frame or setting to another.	Narrative, pp. 369–380
d. Use precise words and phrases, relevant descriptive details, and sensory language to capture the action and convey experiences and events.	Narrative, pp. 369–380
e. Provide a conclusion that follows from and reflects on the narrated experiences or events.	Narrative, pp. 369–380

Production and Distribution of Writing

4. Produce clear and coherent writing in which the development, organization, and style are appropriate to task, purpose, and audience. (Grade-specific expectations for writing types are defined in standards 1–3 above.)	Persuasive Essay, pp. 324–333 Response Essay, pp. 334–343 Multi-Paragraph Essay, pp. 344–353 Research Report, pp. 354–368 Narrative, pp. 369–380
5. With some guidance and support from peers and adults, develop and strengthen writing as needed by planning, revising, editing, rewriting, or trying a new approach, focusing on how well purpose and audience have been addressed.	Persuasive Essay, pp. 324–333 Response Essay, pp. 334–343 Multi-Paragraph Essay, pp. 344–353 Research Report, pp. 354–368 Narrative, pp. 369–380

6. Use technology, including the Internet, to produce and publish writing and link to and cite sources as well as to interact and collaborate with others, including linking to and citing sources.	Persuasive Essay, pp. 324–333 Response Essay, pp. 334–343 Multi-Paragraph Essay, pp. 344–353 Research Report, pp. 354–368 Narrative, pp. 369–380
7. Conduct short research projects to answer a question, drawing on several sources and generating additional related, focused questions for further research and investigation.	Research Report, pp. 354–368
8. Gather relevant information from multiple print and digital sources, using search terms effectively; assess the credibility and accuracy of each source; and quote or paraphrase the data and conclusions of others while avoiding plagiarism and following a standard format for citation.	Research Report, pp. 354–368 Multi-Paragraph Essay, pp. 344–353
9. Draw evidence from literary or informational texts to support analysis, reflection, and research.	Response Essay, pp. 334–343 Research Report, pp. 354–368
a. Apply *grade 7 Reading standards* to literature (e.g., "Compare and contrast a fictional portrayal of a time, place, or character and a historical account of the same period as a means of understanding how authors of fiction use or alter history").	Response Essay, pp. 334–343
b. Apply *grade 7 Reading standards* to literary nonfiction (e.g. "Trace and evaluate the argument and specific claims in a text, assessing whether the reasoning is sound and the evidence is relevant and sufficient to support the claims").	Response Essay, pp. 334–343

Range of Writing	
10. Write routinely over extended time frames (time for research, reflection, and revision) and shorter time frames (a single sitting or a day or two) for a range of discipline-specific tasks, purposes, and audiences.	Persuasive Essay, pp. 324–333 Response Essay, pp. 334–343 Multi-Paragraph Essay, pp. 344–353 Research Report, pp. 354–368 Narrative, pp. 369–380

Language

Conventions of Standard English

1. Demonstrate command of the conventions of standard English grammar and usage when writing or speaking.	This standard is met throughout the book.
a. Explain the function of phrases and clauses in general and their function in specific sentences.	Appositives, pp. 89–90 Sentences and Clauses, pp. 192–193 Complex Sentences, pp. 193–195 Adjective Clauses, pp. 195–196 Essential and Nonessential Clauses, pp. 197–198 Adverb Clauses, pp. 198–200 Noun Clauses, pp. 200–201 Participles and Participial Phrases, pp. 206–208 Gerunds and Gerund Phrases, pp. 208–210 Infinitives and Infinitive Phrases, pp. 210–212 Diagraming Adjectives, Adverbs, and Prepositional Phrases, pp. 232–233

<table>
<tr>
<td></td>
<td>
</td>
</tr>
<tr>
<td>
b. Choose among simple, compound, complex, and compound-complex sentences to signal differing relationships among ideas.
</td>
<td>
</td>
</tr>
</table>

	Diagraming Complex Sentences with Adjective and Adverb Clauses, pp. 238–239 Compound Sentences, pp. 287–288 Compound Elements, pp. 288–289
c. Place phrases and clauses within a sentence, recognizing and correcting misplaced and dangling modifiers.	Appositives, pp. 89–90 Sentences and Clauses, pp. 192–193 Complex Sentences, pp. 193–195 Adjective Clauses, pp. 195–196 Essential and Nonessential Clauses, pp. 197–198 Adverb Clauses, pp. 198–200 Noun Clauses, pp. 200–201 Participles and Participial Phrases,pp. 206–208 Gerunds and Gerund Phrases, pp. 208–210 Infinitives and Infinitive Phrases, pp. 210–212 Diagraming Adjectives, Adverbs, and Prepositional Phrases, pp. 232–233 Diagraming Complex Sentences with Adjective and Adverb Clauses, pp. 238–239 Diagraming Noun Clauses, pp. 240–242 Diagraming Verbals, pp. 242–244 Prepositional Phrases, pp. 289–291 Appositives, pp. 291–292 Adjective and Adverb Clauses, pp. 292–294 Persuasive Essay, pp. 324–333

2. Demonstrate command of the conventions of standard English capitalization, punctuation, and spelling when writing.	Capitalizing Sentences, Quotations, and Letter Parts, pp. 248–249 Capitalizing Names and Titles of People, pp. 250–251 Capitalizing Names of Places, pp. 251–253 Capitalizing Other Proper Nouns and Adjectives, pp. 253–255 Using End Punctuation, pp. 261–262 Using Commas I, pp. 262–265 Using Commas II, pp. 265–266 Using Commas III, pp. 266–268 Using Semicolons and Colons, pp. 268–270 Using Quotation Marks and Italics, pp. 270–273 Using Apostrophes, pp. 273–274 Using Hyphens, Dashes, and Parentheses, pp. 275–276 Using Abbreviations, pp. 276–278 Writing Numbers, pp. 278–280 Persuasive Essay, pp. 324–333 Response Essay, pp. 334–343 Multi-Paragraph Essay, pp. 344–353 Research Report, pp. 354–368 Narrative, pp. 369–380
a. Use a comma to separate coordinate adjectives (e.g., *It was a fascinating, enjoyable movie* but not *He wore an old[,] green shirt*).	Narrative, pp. 369–380

b. Spell correctly.	Spelling Rules, pp. 299–307
	Improving Your Spelling,
	    pp. 307–310
	Persuasive Essay, pp. 324–333
	Response Essay, pp. 334–343
	Multi-Paragraph Essay,
	    pp. 344–353
	Research Report, pp. 354–368
	Narrative, pp. 369–380

Knowledge of Language	
3. Use knowledge of language and its conventions when writing, speaking, reading, or listening.	Persuasive Essay, pp. 324–333 Response Essay, pp. 334–343 Multi-Paragraph Essay, pp. 344–353 Research Report, pp. 354–368 Narrative, pp. 369–380
a. Choose language that expresses ideas precisely and concisely, recognizing and eliminating wordiness and redundancy.	Persuasive Essay, pp. 324–333 Response Essay, pp. 334–343 Multi-Paragraph Essay, pp. 344–353 Research Report, pp. 354–368 Narrative, pp. 369–380

INDEX

Entries with bold page numbers represent terms and definitions in the Glossary of Terms, pages 4–28.

in forming possessive pronouns, 274
Appendix, in nonfiction books, 420
Appositive phrases, **7,** 89–90
    commas with, 90, 264
    in sentence combining, 291
Appositives, **6,** 89–90
    commas with, 90, 264
    in sentence combining, 291
Articles, definite and indefinite, 7, 147
    capitalizing, in titles of works, 254
Articles, newspaper and magazine
    locating, 421–423
    quotation marks for titles of, 271
As, as if, as though, like, 43
Atlases, 401, 424
Audience, in persuasive essay, 325
Auxiliary verbs. *See* Helping verbs
A while, awhile, 31

B

Bad, badly, 32, 165
Bare, bear, 32
Base, bass, 32
Base form, **7**
    of adjectives, 149, 151
    of adverbs, 163
    of verbs, 104, 110, 113–116
Bass, base, 32

Bear, bare, 32
Beside, besides, 32
Between, among, 31
Bibliography, in nonfiction books, 420
Biographical names in dictionaries, 432–433
Biographical references, 424
Blew, blue, 32
Blue, blew, 32
Boar, bore, 32–33
Body
    in multi-paragraph essay, 348
    in narrative, 375
    in persuasive essay, 327–329
    in research report, 361–363
    in response essay, 338–339
Books
    capitalizing titles of, 254
    italics for titles of, 272
    locating, in library, 404–420
    quotation marks for titles of chapters in, 271
    source cards for, 358
Boolean operators, 408
Bore, boar, 32–33
Bow, 33
Brake, break, 33
Brand names, capitalizing, 253
Break, brake, 33
Bridges, capitalizing names of, 252
Bring, take, 33
Buildings, capitalizing names of, 252

Description
  in narrative, 373, 375
  in response essay, 337
Desert, dessert, 37
Details, in multi-paragraph
  essay, 345
Dewey Decimal System of
  Classification, 415–418
Diagraming sentences, 227–245
Dialogue, in narrative, 373, 374
Dictionaries, 425–433
  abbreviations in, 56, 428,
    433
  biographical names in,
    432–433
  cross-references in, 431
  entries in, 428–431
  finding words in, 427
  geographical names in, 433
  numbered entries in,
    430–431
  signs in, 433
  style handbook in, 433
  subject labels in, 431
  symbols in, 433
Diner, dinner, 37
Direct address, **12,** 263
Direction words
  abbreviations for, 57
  capitalizing, 252
Direct objects, **12,** 98–99, 100
  compound, 99
  diagraming, 231, 240
  gerunds as, 209
Direct quotations, **12,** 248
  capitalizing first word of,
    248

  punctuating, 267, 270–271
Documents, capitalizing
  names of, 253
Doe, dough, 37
Doesn't, don't, 38
Double comparison, 150
Double negatives, **12,**
  166–167
Dough, doe, 37
Draft, 327, 336, 346, 361, 374
DVDs, 402

E

Eager, anxious, 31
Edit, 331, 341, 352, 366, 378
Effect, affect, 29–30
Ei, spelling, 300
Encyclopedias, 423, 401
End marks, **13,** 66–67, 261
Ending, in narrative, 375
Essays
  capitalizing titles of, 254
  quotation marks for titles
    of, 271
Essential clauses, **13,** 197, 293
Essential phrases, **13,** 207, 291
Ethnic groups, capitalizing
  names of, 254
Everywheres, 31
Evidence
  in multi-paragraph essay,
    345
  in persuasive essay, 325–
    326, 327
  in response essay, 335
Except, accept, 29

Government publications as resources, 424
Graphic organizers, 381–391
Grate, great, 39

H

Hadn't ought, shouldn't ought, had ought, 39–40
Had of, 39
Had ought, hadn't ought, shouldn't ought, 39–40
Hardly, scarcely, 40
He, she, it, they, 40
Hear, here, 40
Help desks, in libraries, 400
Helping verbs, **14**, 104–106
    with perfect tenses, 108–109, 110
    with progressive forms, 107
Here, hear, 40
Highways, capitalizing names of, 252
Historical events, capitalizing names of, 253
Holidays, capitalizing names of, 253
How come, 40
Hyphens, **15**
    in compound modifiers, 275
    in compound nouns, 82, 275
    in compound numbers, 275
    to divide word at end of line, 275

in fractions, 275
after prefixes, 275

I

I, capitalizing, 251
I, eye, 38
Ie, spelling, 300
Imperative sentences, **15**, 66
    diagraming, 229–230
    punctuating, 66, 261
    subject in, 72
In, into, in to, 40
Incomplete comparisons, 127
Indefinite articles, **7**, 147
Indefinite pronouns, **15**, 132–133
    possessive, 274
    subject-verb agreement with, 222
Index, in nonfiction books, 420
Indirect objects, **15**, 100
    compound, 100
    diagraming, 231, 241
Indirect quotations, **15**, 248
Infinitives and infinitive phrases, **16**
    definition, **16**, 210–211
    diagraming, 243
    distinguished from prepositional phrases, 211
Informative writing. *See* Multi-paragraph essay, Research report, Response essay
Initials, capitalizing, 250

M

Magazines
    capitalizing titles of, 254
    italics for titles of, 272
    locating articles in,
        421–423
    source cards for, 358
Mail, male, 43
Main, mane, 43–44
Main clauses, **17,** 192, 193
Main verbs, **18,** 104–105
Major research question, in
    research report, 355, 359
Male, mail, 43
Mane, main, 43–44
Many, much, 44
May, can, 34
Measurements, abbreviations
    for, 57–59, 277
Meat, meet, 44
Media center. *See* Library
Microfiche, 422
Microfilm, 422
Might of, 36
Minute, 44
Misplaced modifiers, 332
Misreading, comma to prevent,
    267
MLA Style Guide, 392–397
Months
    abbreviations of, 56
    capitalizing names of,
        253
Monuments, capitalizing
    names of, 252
Mood, in narrative, 370, 371,
    373

Most, almost, 30, 165
Movies, italics for titles of,
    272
Much, many, 44
Multi-paragraph essay,
    344–353
    analogy in, 347
    anecdote in, 347
    body in, 348
    cause and effect in, 348
    classification in, 348
    comparison and contrast
        in, 348
    conclusion in, 350
    controlling idea in, 345,
        346
    definition in, 348
    details in, 345
    facts in, 345
    formal style in, 348
    introduction in, 346–347
    parallelism in, 347
    process in, 348
    quotation in, 347
    repetition in, 347
    rhetorical question in, 347
    sequence of events in, 348
    synthesizing ideas in, 346
    thesis in, 345
    topic in, 345
    transitions in, 349
    visual elements in, 349
Music albums, italics for
    titles of, 272
Musical compositions, italics
    for titles of, 272
Must of, 36